REPORTING NEWS ABOUT RELIGION

Reporting News about Religion

AN INTRODUCTION FOR JOURNALISTS

Judith M. Buddenbaum

IOWA STATE UNIVERSITY PRESS / Ames

JUDITH M. BUDDENBAUM is a professor in the Department of Journalism and Technical Communication at Colorado State University, where she teaches courses in reporting, communication law and media research, as well as seminars on religion and mass media. She also has taught journalism at St. Mary-of-the-Woods College in Indiana and has been a newspaper religion reporter, a freelance magazine reporter specializing in religion, and a communication researcher for Lutheran World Federation, Geneva, Switzerland. Her research on religion and mass media has been published in the *Journalism Quarterly* and *Newspaper Research Journal,* and as book chapters. Buddenbaum is coeditor of *Religion and Mass Media: Audiences and Adaptations.*

IOWA STATE UNIVERSITY PRESS
2121 South State Avenue, Ames, Iowa 50014

Orders: 1-800-862-6657
Office: 1-515-292-0140
Fax: 1-515-292-3348
Web site: www.isupress.edu

♾ Printed on acid-free paper in the United States of America

First edition, 1998

International Standard Book Number: 0-8138-2977-1

Library of Congress Cataloging-in-Publication Data

Buddenbaum, Judith Mitchell
    Reporting news about religion: an introduction for journalists /
Judith M. Buddenbaum.—1st ed.
        p.   cm.
    Includes bibliographical references and index.
    ISBN 0-8138-2977-1
    1. Journalism, religious—United States.   2. Religion and the press—
United States.   I. Title.
    PN4888.R44B83   1998
    070.4'492—dc21   98–3005

The last digit is the print number: 9 8 7 6 5 4 3 2 1

Contents

Preface, ix

Introduction, xiii

PART I
UNDERSTANDING RELIGION, 1

1. Religion in America, 3
    American Religiosity: The Puritan Legacy, 4
    American Religiosity: The Spirit of Revivalism and Reform, 7
    American Religiosity: From Particularism to Pluralism, 9
    American Religiosity: The Current Climate, 13

2. The Role of the First Amendment, 19
    Understanding Original Intent, 22
    Applying the Religion Clauses, 26
    Court Interpretations, 27
    Recurring Problems, 29
    Reporting with Understanding, 33

3. The Varieties of American Religions, 37
    General Classification Schemes, 38
    Using Classification Schemes, 43
    Classifying Christian Religions, 43
    Other World Religions in America, 51
    Other Religions in America, 53
    Other Considerations, 54

4. Beliefs and Behaviors, 59
Internal Behaviors: Worship Practices and Rituals, 61
External Behaviors, 64
Other Considerations, 69

5. Organization and Leadership, 73
The Church-Sect Typology, 74
Church Polity: The Structure of Religious Organizations, 77
Leadership in Voluntary Organizations, 81
Special Purpose Organizations, 84

PART II
UNDERSTANDING RELIGION NEWS, 89

6. Trends in Religion News, 91
The Birth of Modern Religion Reporting, 92
Newspaper Coverage of Religion, 94
Magazine Coverage of Religion, 96
Radio Coverage of Religion, 97
Television Coverage of Religion, 98
Content and Meaning, 100

7. The Audiences for Religion News, 105
Journalists' Perceptions of the Audience, 106
Audience Demographics, 107
News Preferences, 108
Religious Criticisms of Religion News Coverage, 109
The Problem of Mismatches, 112
Content and Consequences, 112

8. Responses and Responsibility, 119
Rethinking Religion News, 120
Allocation of Space, 123
Staffing Arrangements, 124
The Religion Journalist, 128
Points to Consider, 131

PART III
REPORTING RELIGION NEWS, 135

9. Recognizing and Reporting Religion News, 137
    News Values, 138
    Finding Story Ideas, 140
    Stories for Dedicated Space, 144
    Religion Stories for Other Beats, 148
    Building Bridges, 150

10. Choosing and Using Sources, 155
    Facts, Opinions and Religious Truth, 158
    Primary and Secondary Evidence, 159
    People as Sources, 160
    Dealing with People, 163
    Documentary Sources, 165
    The Internet, 169

11. Writing Stories, 171
    Framing Stories, 172
    Organizing Stories, 178
    Choosing and Using Words, 181
    Telling Stories, 184

12. Improving Religion Reporting, 189

Appendix A. Reference Materials, 197
Appendix B. Important Meetings, 205
Appendix C. Professional Support Groups, 207
Appendix D. Contests, 209
Appendix E. Educational Opportunities, 211

Glossary, 215

Index, 223

Preface

RELIGION. It's the greatest story never told—or at least, the greatest story that's rarely told very well.

To some, religion news is only bingo and bean suppers at the local church. To others, religion is news only when the news is bad: David Koresh at Waco, priests and pedophilia, Islam and the World Trade Center bombing. But religion news shouldn't be just routine announcements, and it can be—and should be—more than just bad news, as important as bad news is to those who take the watchdog role of the press seriously.

Religion motivates people to act, and it shapes cultures. It has a way of connecting itself to everything. For journalists who are trained to look for the 5Ws and the H, finding, exploring and explaining those connections are crucial. The who, what, where and when are usually clear-cut, but the answers to how and why often depend on who is asked and what they are asked. Failing to consult religious sources or ask religious questions can, at best, result in an incomplete story. At worst, it can miss the story entirely.

As the Hutchinson Commission on Freedom of the Press said in 1947, stenographic journalism that simply provides an accurate account of what someone or some group said or did is not enough. Serving the public requires telling the truth about the fact in a context that provides meaning. That context can be a religious one. Understanding events in the Middle East and Bosnia, for example, is impossible without also understanding the religious roots of the conflicts.

At a more local level, controversies over education, environmentalism, entertainment and euthanasia are usually also debates about values. When those values stem from different religious understandings, ignoring the "religion factor" will miss the point of the debate from the standpoint of those most fervently engaged in it.

Asking "why" questions about the beliefs and values gives people a chance to speak in their own voice and tell their own stories. Finding room for those voices and airing those stories is necessary if, as the Hutchinson Commission suggested, the media are to serve as a forum through which the public can debate and clarify goals and values. That purpose fits nicely with the current emphasis on civic or public journalism.

Because so many people are religious and take their faith seriously, good reporting about religion is one answer to the questions many journalists are asking themselves about how they can reconnect with people who have come to distrust the media, each other, their government and, indeed, most everyone and everything else. But good reporting about religion is not easy, especially for journalists who have had little encouragement or training for the task.

The few journalism students who know they want to cover religion may pursue a minor or double major in philosophy and religion or religious studies, but few of their classmates take even one course in religion, the history of religion or the sociology of religion to fulfill their degree requirements. However, even those who study religion seldom receive much help when it comes to actually reporting about religion. Few journalism programs offer even an occasional course in religion reporting. Most textbooks, including those organized to provide instruction in beat reporting, do not mention religion or the religion beat.

As a result, most students enter the profession woefully unprepared to recognize and report on the religious dimensions of news. Yet some will seek careers as religion reporters; others will find themselves assigned to the religion beat in the course of their careers. Almost all, regardless of beat, will report on stories involving religion more often than they imagine.

Many of the problems with religion coverage could be avoided if journalists from all beats knew more about religion and if they considered carefully the implications of the way they report stories that involve religion. Therefore, this book includes substantive information about religion and the religion beat as well as practical advice. It is intended as a supplement to standard reporting texts, not a replacement for them. Its purpose is to provide the kind of information about religion and guidance for finding and covering religion news stories that all journalists can use, regardless of the medium they work for or the beat to which they are assigned.

Like other reporting texts, this one draws heavily on the experiences and advice of professional journalists. However, the advice it offers is also informed by a study of history, law and social science research.

Part I is designed to provide the background information about religion that journalists need to know in order to understand religion in all its infinite varieties and the role of religion in American culture. Part II takes up the place of religion news in the mass media, changes in news coverage over time, the audience for religion news and media responses to public interest and concerns. Part III addresses reporting and writing practices such as sourcing, story framing and language use that can be especially problematic in religion reporting because of the ideological and value-laden nature of the subject matter. Each chapter concludes with an annotated list of works that can be consulted for more detailed information. Appendices at the end of the book provide additional help.

Many journalists and professors whose concern for religion, for religion reporting or for the First Amendment, which protects both religion and journalism, mirrors my own interests contributed to this book. I learned from their work and I thank them. Above all, I thank Debra Mason, for her help and encouragement.

Introduction

AT A JUNE 1995 symposium in Santa Monica on religion and prime-time television, the tension between religious leaders and media professionals was sometimes palpable. People from the entertainment industry professed their own religiosity; they also tried valiantly to explain their commitment to the First Amendment and to democratic values. But it was clear from their comments that many religious spokespersons saw such statements as hypocritical. The entertainment industry, they said, promotes immorality by emphasizing sex and violence while willfully and systematically misrepresenting, denigrating or ignoring religion.

That opinion of media performance is not limited to entertainment. Those attending a conference on religion and the news at Columbia University made similar complaints about the press. In response to a 1993 survey, top leaders from Christian churches listed in the *Yearbook of American and Canadian Churches* gave the media only a D+ for news coverage. For coverage of religion, the average grade was even lower—a D.

Research conducted over the past 20 years consistently shows that many journalists seriously underestimate both audience interest in news about religion and their dissatisfaction with what passes for coverage in many newspapers and on television. Respondents to a 1989 nationwide survey ranked religion news second only to news of education in importance. By way of contrast, sports ranked as the least important of nine kinds of specialty news. In terms of audience satisfaction, however, sports coverage moved to the top of the list. Religion news fell from second in importance to last in public satisfaction with the coverage.

Certainly complaints about coverage are sometimes overblown, especially when they come from people who believe journalists should support, defend and even promote their kind of religion at the expense of others. But the complaints come from all quarters. They come from people who are religious but who are members of very different religions and also from those who, having no religion, have little personal stake in how any particular religion is portrayed.

Therefore, the criticism cannot easily be dismissed. Dissatisfaction is so widespread and the complaints are repeated so regularly that they affect public perceptions and understanding of the press and its role. They feed public distrust of the media and foster a kind of cynicism and suspicion that affects people's relationships with each other and their opinions about public institutions.

The media do miss, misinterpret, sensationalize or otherwise bungle stories about religion in ways that fail to convey both the reality and the power of religion for individual believers and for society. Initially most media missed the political significance of the electronic church; more recently they overlooked the role churches played in the crumbling of communism throughout eastern Europe. Journalists misinterpreted and overplayed Jimmy Carter's *Playboy* interview with its reference to "lusting" in his heart; they are even more prone to misconstrue and sensationalize less conventional beliefs. The *New York Times* once published a series of stories misidentifying the Unification Church as the "Reunification Church." The *Washington Post* assigned a science writer to cover a court case challenging, on religious grounds, the teaching of evolution in public schools; the paper published stories replete with stereotypical references to "fundamentalists" wearing "polyester suits."

Inaccurate stories make journalists look dumb; they also invite the public to dismiss even those stories or parts of stories journalists get right. Missing a religion story or missing the religious dimension of one deprives the public of information they may want or need. Inadequate coverage presents a misleading picture of the world; it affects public understanding of people, events and issues in ways that can perpetuate stereotypical thinking, fuel tensions and thwart problem solving.

Because people care so deeply about religion, poor reporting also causes them to cancel newspaper and magazine subscriptions, switch channels, or turn off their television sets entirely.

One reason that missed stories and ones that are overplayed, sensationalized or full of errors and misinterpretations abound is that journalism and religion often seem to belong to two different worlds. Journalists work in a world of facts. Truth means accuracy, but also empirical evidence. Religion, however, rests on a faith that is largely impervious to the kind of proofs that will satisfy those who do not already believe. Its truths must be accepted because they are from god.

Those differences invite misunderstandings and suspicions. Journalists, for their part, too readily dismiss religious people as charlatans or fools because their truths cannot always be proved. In the process, journalists forget how often they report the claims of politicians, business leaders or scientists without insisting on proof or checking the evidence those sources offer.

At the same time, religious leaders too often distrust reporters' motives when journalists insist that a story conform to traditional news values or that balanced reporting requires giving space to countervailing claims. To them, both the standards that journalists see as reasonable and fair and the cases of overblown coverage and missed or misinterpreted stories are evidence of bias against religion in general and their religion in particular.

But the problem is not so much that journalists are a-religious or anti-religion, as many critics contend. Contrary to popular opinion, surveys conducted over the past 20 years repeatedly show that journalists are as likely to have a religion, to be active in it and to take it as seriously as anyone else. Even at the elite media, where journalists are less likely than the population as a whole to be religious, there are highly religious reporters and others who simply have a soft spot for religion.

Nor is the problem that there is something about religion that inherently turns a reporter's brain to mush. Much of the problem lies with the very complexity of the subject.

In politics there are two major political parties and a few minor ones. Sports reporters must know the rules of a dozen or so sports, most of which they have played and all of which can be observed in person or on television with little expenditure of time and effort. But those who would cover religion must deal with countless different faiths.

Directories list well over 200 Christian denominations and at least 100 non-Christian ones representing various strains within Judaism, Islam, Buddhism and Hinduism. In addition to those major religions, some experts put the number of cults, sects and miscellaneous new religions as high as 2500. Add to those the countless number of ecumenical, parachurch, special purpose and religion-related organizations and lobbying groups as well as the innumerable people who consider themselves religious but who are not members of any organized religious group and the task of making sense of religion can be daunting at best.

Each religion has its own beliefs; those beliefs vary both across religions and within them. To compound the problem, people from different religions may use very similar language to describe their beliefs, but the meanings they attach to those words are not always the same. People from the same religion sometimes use different words to describe their faith. But even if journalists can understand the beliefs and get beyond the language problems, efforts to represent religious people's activities and actions, their motives and goals as they appear to members of a religion and as they may be for nonmembers produce a whole new level of problems about meaning and truth.

As Hiley Ward, a veteran religion reporter who recently retired from teaching journalism at Temple University, accurately points out, good religion reporting, like good reporting in general, depends on knowing the field, cultivating good sources, asking good questions, and then carefully crafting the story. But knowing the field, finding and then selecting appropriate sources, asking the "what ifs" and "whys" and finally understanding and explaining the answers has always been a difficult task for journalists.

Part of the mystique of journalism is the belief that a good reporter can cover anything. Certainly, a "good" reporter can cover almost anything better than a "poor" reporter can. Still, "No paper would ever send someone who didn't know what a quarterback is to cover a football game. But they routinely send reporters who are clueless about the role and authority of bishops to cover the Catholic Church; they assign people who don't know the difference between a Mormon and a Baptist to cover evangelism," says *Pittsburgh Post-Gazette* religion reporter Ann Rodgers-Melnick.

Even journalists who are personally religious may know little about the history of their own religion or be unaware of the nuances of its theology. While it's hardly reasonable to expect journalists to be knowledgable about all the infinite varieties of religions in the United States and the world, that is precisely what the audience demands.

Lack of knowledge about religion can render even "some of the glibbest persons in the nation ... oddly tongue-tied when the Bible [is] brought up," as Garry Wills said in his 1990 book *Under God: Reli-*

gion and American Politics. The standard assumptions and methodologies of journalism, the complexity of the subject and lack of in-depth knowledge of their own faiths and of other religions conspire to create what John Dart and Jimmy Allen describe in their report on the state of religion reporting as "blind spots" and "tone deafness."

Fortunately, neither "blind spots" nor "tone deafness" need be permanent conditions.

Religion reporting can be excellent. In 1996 Pulitzer Prizes went to David Rohde of the *Christian Science Monitor* for his coverage of the massacre of thousands of Bosnian Muslims in Srebrenica and to Bob Keeler of *Newsday* for his series reporting a year in the life of a Roman Catholic parish on Long Island. Other prize-winning examples of religion reporting show up almost every time national and local press associations sponsor a contest. In recent years, Laurie Goodstein's work for the *Washington Post* and the weekly religion sections of the *Dallas Morning News* were repeat winners in contests sponsored by the Religion Newswriters Association.

Prize winners illustrate the kind of variety, depth and overall excellence that is possible. However, commitment to religion journalism varies markedly from newspaper to newspaper and magazine to magazine, between the print and the broadcast media, and also among television and radio stations. Many journalists still see religion news as little more than endless announcements of bingo games and bean suppers sponsored by local churches. At other papers and in most television newscasts, religion is news only when it "enters the world of party politics, pageantry or pedophilia," as Brian Healy, the senior political producer for CBS News, so aptly put it.

Little stories about local congregational events and the "politics, pageantry and pedophilia" are part of religion reporting, but focussing on one or the other, or even both together, is to be blind and tone deaf to the presence and prevalence of religion and to the distinctions among and within religions and between religious peoples.

Not everyone will make a career of covering religion, but all journalists will cover stories that involve religion or that have—or should have—a religion angle more often than they imagine. Religion has a way of connecting itself to everything. It gives purpose and meaning to the lives of many people. It affects opinions and motivates people to action. It also shapes societies. Historically, religion has been considered the "glue" that holds society together, but it also has the potential to tear societies apart.

Religion is part of the events that transpire in international trouble spots such as the Middle East, Northern Ireland and Bosnia. It also pops up in national and local stories about politics, law, education, science and medicine, crime and the courts. Often it's a part of stories that traditionally, and properly, belong on the business and financial pages, in arts and entertainment columns and in sports sections. Therefore, good religion reporting is not just the province of the religion reporter. Religion news occurs on every beat; often it transcends them.

But good religion reporting, especially outside the religion beat, is still too rare. Alleviating the problems about which so many people so rightly complain means eliminating the blind spots and conquering tone deafness. But that requires effort.

"The best advice," says *New York Times* religion writer Gustav Niebuhr, "is to set aside all your preconceptions and give it a try. Religion will take you into every other aspect of culture. Religion is more complex and more interesting than you can imagine."

The learning curve can be steep, says Barbara Falconer Newhall who covers religion for the *Contra Costa Times* in Walnut Creek, California. Covering religion well requires life-long learning, enterprise, experience and dedication. It also requires integrity, professionalism and, above all, an open mind.

No book can provide all the information about religion or about religion reporting that a journalist may need, but this one can help you get started.

For Further Reading

Dart, John and Jimmy Allen. *Bridging the Gap: Religion and the News Media.* Nashville, Tenn.: The Freedom Forum First Amendment Center, 1993.

   This report is a thorough analysis of problems associated with religion reporting by print and broadcast media. It also contains recommendations for improving coverage.

Hubbard, Benjamin J. *Reporting Religion: Facts and Faith.* Sonoma, Calif.: Polebridge Press, 1990.

   Much of this book is really about religious media, but the first three chapters provide thoughtful discussions of religion reporting in the mass media. There are also chapters on evangelical Christian opinions about mass media coverage of religion.

Rockefeller Foundation. *The Religion Beat: The Reporting of Religion in the*

Media. New York: Rockefeller Foundation Conference Report, 1981.
    Some of the information about the status of the religion beat is a bit dated, but this early report is still a good source for background information.

Suman, Michael. (ed.). *Religion and Prime-time Television.* Westport, Conn.: Greenwood Press 1997.
    This book focuses on the treatment of religion by entertainment media, but many of the points made by religious leaders, media professionals and academics are applicable to news coverage.

PART I
UNDERSTANDING RELIGION

CHAPTER 1

RELIGION IN AMERICA

Nine out of 10 Americans believe in God. About six in 10 say religion is "very important" and that it "can answer every question." As George Cornell, former religion writer for the Associated Press, was fond of telling anyone who would listen, more Americans worship each weekend than attend all the sporting events held in the United States in an entire week.

The actual numbers and percents vary somewhat from year to year and from survey to survey, but from all evidence Americans are a very religious people—at least in comparison to those who live in other Western nations.

In 1981 more than half of all Americans told Gallup pollsters they were affiliated with a church or religious organization. But only 4 percent of the French respondents, 5 percent of the Italians, 13 percent of West Germans, 15 percent of the Spaniards and 22 percent of the British answered "yes" to the same question. Similar Gallup polls conducted in 1979 and again in 1989 also affirm American religiosity. Even among young adults, who surveys and church membership data show to be the least religious segment of the population, Americans ranked first among their peers from other nations in religious commitment.

Contrary to the conventional wisdom, there is little evidence that religiosity is on the decline. While there are no public opinion polls from 200 years ago, careful analysis of church membership data indicate that Americans today are at least as likely to believe in a god as were their colonial forebears. They are also more than twice as likely to be members of a church or religious organization and to worship rather regularly. In fact, according to data compiled by sociologists of religion Roger Finke and Rodney Stark for their 1992 book, *The Churching of America 1776-1990,* a young woman living in the American colonies was more likely to have been sexually active before marriage than to have been a member of a church.

Even if many baby boomers stay away from church and membership in some churches is declining, overall membership and monetary contributions to churches are up. The index of religious commitment, as measured by the Gallup-based Princeton Religion Research Center, hit a 10-year high in 1996. In fact, the "religious commitment" of the American people is what "sets the United States apart from other modern democracies," the *Economist* reported in an August 1992 article.

How can that be when everyone knows that America is fast becoming, if it has not already become, secular? Part of the answer lies in what one means by "religious" and by "secular." But the answer is also rooted in history.

The coexistence in America of a people and a culture that are highly religious and yet are perceived as, and in many ways are, secular is the paradoxical byproduct of the circumstances surrounding American colonization by England and America's own unique religious history. That history has been one of a progression from limited diversity within a rather narrow band of Protestant Christianity to a situation today that can more accurately be described as true religious pluralism.

American Religiosity: The Puritan Legacy

Jamestown, established in Virginia by good Anglicans, was the first English colony in North America. The Pilgrims came a decade later, but it was the Puritans who left their imprint on American culture.

Most of those who settled in Virginia were members of the Church of England and satisfied with that church and its teachings and practices. Like them, the Pilgrims and Puritans were Protestant Christians; however, their religious understanding was based on the teachings of John Calvin. As dissenters to the established religion, the Pilgrims and Puritans came to America seeking the freedom to practice their beliefs and to create a society informed by those beliefs.

Both Pilgrims and Puritans believed the Church of England needed to be "purified" of its "popish" tendencies as well as its rather lax en-

forcement of moral standards. As Calvinists, they believed that everyone is born sinful, but they also believed that some people are foreor-
dained by God to be his elect or chosen people. Others are not. Those
who are predestined for salvation and eternal life with God have the
duty to be an example to the world.

As heirs to Reformation theology, Pilgrims and Puritans rejected the
idea that people need a mediator or priest to communicate with God.
They also rejected the divine right of kings. Instead of being governed
by a hereditary monarchy, they believed those who are God's elect
should rule.

Upon arriving in Massachusetts in 1620, the Pilgrims signed the
Mayflower Compact. In it they "covenanted together," binding themselves to each other and to God. Through their Compact, they created
a community organized on the congregational model, with each parish
autonomous and self-governing. But the Pilgrim's Plymouth Colony
was absorbed into the Massachusetts Bay Colony founded by the Puritans. And it was that Puritan colony that came to dominate New England life and culture.

As Calvinists, Puritans shared with the Pilgrims the belief in original sin and also in predestination. Like them, their society was organized on the congregational model, with only the elect entitled to
membership. But for the Puritans, America was not just a place where
they could exercise their religious beliefs free of persecution. For
them, it was the "New Israel," a "New Jerusalem." Their "errand in the
wilderness" was to build a "shining city on the hill" as an example for
the world. Their model for that "shining city" was John Calvin's
Geneva.

Freedom meant freedom to do what is good and right because even
the elect could be lost if they did not obey God's word. Where the Pilgrims had separated church and state and given ministers little say outside church affairs, the Puritan colony was to be ruled by God through
his church. In Puritan society there was no division between church
and state. Both were ruled by the elect as God's agents in this world.

To curb sinful impulses and to preserve their community as an example to the world, the Puritans accepted laws that today would be
seen as intrusive and suffocating. Worship and work were acceptable;
recreation was not. In Massachusetts, as in John Calvin's Geneva,
there was to be no drinking, gambling, theaters, dancing, music or
books other than religious ones.

In spite of the fact the Congregational Church never accounted for more than 20 percent of the total population in the colonies and was losing its pre-eminent place in Massachusetts by the eve of the Revolutionary War, Puritanism shaped American culture. The Puritan religio-political system required an educated clergy and a literate membership. To meet that requirement, the Puritans established schools to teach children to read and Harvard University to train clergy leaders. Harvard's press printed books and tracts; clergy, faculty and students also contributed to Boston's newspapers. From Boston, printed materials could easily be shipped to other colonies.

The Congregational Church had at its disposal effective communicators and the infrastructure necessary to spread its vision throughout the colonies. That vision struck a responsive chord because so many of its basic assumptions were compatible with other Christian theologies. The Quaker William Penn, for example, described Pennsylvania as a "holy experiment" that was to be "an example to the nations."

Even those who came to America for reasons other than religious freedom easily adopted the idea that their willingness to embark on a difficult journey made them special people who were going to a special land. That view was encouraged by an England intent on establishing permanent, stable colonies in the New World. Finding primarily religious dissenters and misfits willing to go to the New World, England used biblical and messianic language similar to that of the Puritans to encourage emigration by citizens loyal to church and crown. That language was written into colonial charters from Georgia to Connecticut.

If the assumption that America was a special place and they were special people was widely shared, so, too, was the corollary: prospering in the new land was a sign of God's favor. When prosperity came from hard work and individual effort, it seemed to validate the idea of America as a special place and the people who prospered in America as special people.

Because almost all of the early immigrants to America were Christian, they also shared with the Puritans the basic Christian tenet that people are born sinful and that even those who are saved can be lost. Therefore, even if they could not accept the Calvinist belief in predestination, they agreed with the Puritans that proper behavior is necessary both as an appropriate response to being saved and as a protection against losing that salvation. They differed primarily on which pleasurable things beyond work and worship are sinful and which are not.

American Religiosity: The Spirit of Revivalism and Reform

Although the Puritans came to America for religious freedom, they had no intention of extending that freedom to those who did not accept their Calvinist form of Protestantism. To good Puritans like the clergyman and civic leader Cotton Mather, religious diversity would be the downfall of civilized society. But in spite of their best efforts, the Puritans quickly found themselves sharing their New Israel with other Christians and even with nonbelievers.

Travel was difficult, but not impossible. People from the religiously more tolerant New York and Pennsylvania colonies drifted into Massachusetts; immigration from England continued and many of the newcomers were Anglicans. Every boat from England and stage coach from another colony brought letters, pamphlets and books bearing new ideas. Protestant theology that freed religion from ecclesiastical control fueled Enlightenment thought. The political philosophies of John Locke and Jean-Jacques Rousseau re-enforced citizen participation even as they challenged religion's role in civic affairs. Deism took root in the southern colonies and also in Boston.

The major challenge to Puritan hegemony, however, began in 1720 when the first of many recurrent waves of religious revivalism began to sweep through the land. With its call for people to turn away from "licentiousness" and toward true religion, initially revivalism delighted the clergy. However, the message preached first by Jonathan Edwards and then by the Methodist George Whitefield threatened the established Congregational Church even as it undergirded Puritan morality.

In place of the doctrine of predestination, the message of The Great Awakening, as this period of religious fervor came to be called, was one of free will. The same God who gives people the reason and ability to read and understand the Bible gives them the freedom to choose whether or not they will believe and be saved.

Whitefield, in particular, also taught that Jesus would return to earth very soon. That message gave new meaning and urgency to the American "errand in the wilderness." Whitefield's "conversionist theology," which emphasized saving souls before it is too late, introduced evangelistic and millenarian strains. It also infused a sense of optimism. That initial optimism was captured by Ezra Stiles in his 1783 Connecticut election sermon, "The United States Elevated to Glory and Honor":

> This will be a great, a very great nation, nearly equal to half [of] Europe.
> ... Before the millennium the English settlements in America may become
> more numerous millions than that greatest domain on earth, the Chinese
> Empire. Should this prove to be a future fact, how applicable would be ...
> [our] text [Deut. 26:19] when the Lord shall have made his American Is-
> rael high above all nations which he has made—in numbers, and in praise,
> and in name, and in honor.

And at first such sentiments seemed justified. The new nation quickly found itself able to compete with Europe in both trade and manufacturing. Agriculture flourished. With the Louisiana Purchase, land, resources and opportunity seemed limitless.

But both territorial expansion and industrialization produced changes in the social fabric. The seemingly endless frontier attracted adventurers. To those who remained in the East, frontier life appeared increasingly lawless and licentious. Industrialization led to urbanization as people from rural areas of America and from Europe moved to the cities. Some of those had no religion; others were Catholics from Ireland and from continental Europe who brought with them strange languages and strange customs.

To these changes, religion could not remain indifferent. Although there were varying responses, the dominant reaction to problems posed by an expanding frontier and increasing industrialization and urbanization was to call for people to turn to God. As in the Great Awakening, this Second Awakening emphasized saving souls. Revivals, tent meetings and chautauquas were organized with the sole aim of getting people to accept Jesus as their savior. Those who turned to Christ would naturally give up their sinful lifestyles and thus make the nation the shining city on a hill it was meant to be.

While all Protestant churches participated to some extent in this kind of evangelistic crusade, the Methodists' beliefs, worship style and openness to a lay ministry put them in the forefront of this revival movement. Methodist circuit-riding lay preachers blanketed the western regions from the Ohio Valley through the Great Plains.

Like other Protestant denominations, Methodists generally accepted the doctrine of original sin. But to Methodists, sinful people can be made better if they can be persuaded to accept God's gift of salvation and follow appropriate "methods" to live a God-pleasing life in response to that gift. This belief that people can be "perfected" opened up the possibility that society itself can be made more God-pleasing.

In a little over a century Methodism had been transformed from a small movement made up of a handful of members of associations located primarily in the New York area into a dominant force in American culture. Its perfectionist teachings fostered and perpetuated revivalism. They also encouraged and legitimated religiously inspired social reform.

The reformist strain within Methodism gathered strength in the mid-1800s when the question of slavery divided the nation, but its underlying message that sin manifests itself in structural arrangements as well as in individual behavior took on new importance at the turn of the century. Inspired by the Baptist Walter Rauschenbusch who joined the faculty of Rochester Theological Seminar in 1897 and published his seminal *Christianity and the Social Crisis* in 1907, Methodists embraced the social gospel.

The reform efforts spawned by the social gospel movement were both cause and effect of a greater acceptance of science and the scientific method. Those who accepted the social gospel did not see science as a threat to religion. As "modernists," they believed God the Creator had made the world and given people the gift of reason that let them recognize patterns in His creation and discern cause and effect relations. To them, science was simply a tool God had given them to use in order to reform society and make it more pleasing to God.

But coexisting with this reform spirit was the spirit of traditionalism and revivalism. At the beginning of the 20th century, Billy Sunday and Dwight Moody drew crowds with their revival message: turn to God, give up your sinful ways and be saved. Reformers worked to establish programs that would alleviate suffering, poverty and injustice.

American Religiosity: From Particularism to Pluralism

In 1776 in Puritan New England, almost two-thirds of those who were members of any church were still Congregationalists; Baptists, mostly in Rhode Island, made up 15 percent of the church members and Episcopalians accounted for 8 percent. The rest found a home in other Christian religions.[1]

In the southern colonies, Baptists slightly outnumbered Episcopalians; there were almost as many Presbyterians. Together, those three churches accounted for 80 percent of the churched population.

In Maryland, the only officially Roman Catholic colony, Catholics were only about 10 percent of the total population. As in other Middle Colonies, diversity reigned. In Pennsylvania, the Quaker State, Quakers made up just under 10 percent of the population—less than half the number of Baptists, Episcopalians or Presbyterians.

Even in New England, the most religiously homogeneous region, diversity was becoming the norm as it had been in New York and Pennsylvania. But with only 56 Roman Catholic churches and six Jewish synagogues, religious options in America were still limited primarily to a rather narrow range of Protestant churches. At the beginning of the 19th century most Americans and most outside observers agreed that America was united by its Protestant faith. But the same revivalism that initially supported the Puritan vision introduced an entrepreneurial element that paved the way for religious diversification.

The first wave of revivalism produced divisions in the Congregational and Presbyterian churches as some people and some local congregations accepted the new emphasis on conversion and a more enthusiastic and experiential approach to religiosity while others did not. It also led to a proliferation of Baptist congregations and opened the door to Methodism. The second wave of revivalism produced what theologian and historian Martin Marty describes as a "sectarian heyday."

As in the First Awakening, again churches split. In a climate of religious fervor, new churches, some of them Protestant but emphasizing different strains within Christianity and others of them quasi-Christian at best, emerged. Utopian communities sprang up: Amana, Oneida, Brook Farm, New Harmony. Transcendentalism, Millerism, mesmerism and phrenology attracted attention. New denominations and new religions took shape. Seventh-Day Adventists, Disciples of Christ, Christian Scientists, Unitarian-Universalists and Mormons trace their origins to the Second Great Awakening.

Baptists and Methodists emerged as the dominant strains within Protestantism, but answers to the question of whether the priority should be placed directly on saving souls through evangelism or less directly by first perfecting society led to divisions within Methodism. The same questions also divided Baptists and other Protestant denominations. Initially those splits occurred primarily along geographic lines. Most churches in rural areas and the South emphasized saving souls; many churches in larger cities and in the North preferred to address social problems. In the South, the revivalist spirit led to justifications for slavery, partly on the grounds that the slave trade brought Africans to America where they would benefit from exposure to Christianity. In the North, the reform spirit fed the call for abolition.

In the years after the Civil War both revivalists and reformists worked together briefly to pass the Comstock laws that restricted American access to art and literature that circulated freely in Europe. In the 20th century, they again cooperated in support of prohibition, but divisions between them remained deep. The divisions lost their geographic character as those who embraced the social gospel began using science and other modern forms of scholarship to understand the Bible instead of merely as a tool to identify and solve social problems.

Different understandings of the Bible and biblical authority divided churches and split towns into traditionalist and modernist camps. Traditionalists fought to keep the teaching of evolution, and indeed much of science, out of public schools. Modernists argued for a freedom of inquiry that would allow for new understandings. For much of the 20th century, the modernist, reforming spirit prevailed.

Roman Catholics and Jews shared the modernist interest in identifying and rectifying social problems in the cities. Like the Protestant churches allied with the reform tradition, they accepted government programs meant to alleviate problems caused by the depression more readily than did many of the more revivalist-oriented Protestant churches. After World War II, their mutual interest in peace and justice led to a brief period of church mergers and ecumenical activity among Protestant churches and to further cooperation among reform-minded Protestants, Roman Catholics and Jews such that it became fashionable to believe that sectarian differences were giving way to a tripartite faith that would ultimately become a single "American religion."[2]

At midcentury, America was a land of boundless optimism and enthusiasm, but Americans also longed for peace and security. With their inclination to identify and rectify problems and a shared concern for peace and justice, the "three great faiths" supported American efforts to rebuild and remake Europe in its own image. Catholics, Jews and Protestants affiliated with the reformist tradition also supported and promoted efforts to create democracies and promote economic development in the former European colonies.

On the domestic front, they worked to reduce prejudice and foster understanding through education, economic development, and social reforms. Their joint efforts on behalf of civil rights presented a model of cooperation for society; the programs themselves were designed to promote peace and justice by creating a more inclusive society.

But peace and stability proved to be an illusion. Calls for civil rights blended and merged with other forms of activism that ushered in an era of rapid social change. As in the early 1800s, again there was a religious response. But where earlier changes led to a denominational society, in this case reform movements intended initially to create a more inclusive and just society paved the way for true religious pluralism.

Liberation theology developed within Catholicism as an effort to empower the poor and chasten the wealthy landowners, clergy and political leaders who presided over near-feudal lands throughout South America, but its image of Jesus as a radical social activist divided churches and paved the way for new strains of religiosity. Most Christians rejected liberation theology as un-Christian and Marxist and Pope John Paul II subsequently denounced it. Others, however, accepted it, sometimes changing it in the process into "black theology" or "feminist theology."

While most Americans remained at least nominally Christian, others took the idea of liberation even further. Some African Americans sought "liberation" from Christianity, which they rejected as the white man's religion. Some of those became Muslims or joined the Nation of Islam. Others, seeking a more indigenous sense of spirituality, adopted native African religions or quasi-African ones brought to the United States by 20th-century immigrants from the Carribean.

For similar reasons, some women sought a distinctly female form of spirituality outside what they considered a male-dominated Christian church with its impossibly patriarchal God. Wiccans and goddess worship entered the picture. If Native Americans who had joined Christian churches either out of coercion or conviction never adopted a liberation theology of their own, many of them also sought a return to their traditional religions.

Just as African Americans, women, and Native Americans were openly practicing a variety of faiths free of persecution in the climate of protection for individual rights and freedom ushered in by the civil rights protests, so too were members of immigrant communities. Although many of the Chinese who came to America in the mid-1800s to work on the railroad had never adopted Christianity, the number of people practicing Buddhism and Confucianism greatly increased with the influx of war brides and exchange students after World War II and of spouses, students, refugees and immigrants after the Vietnam War. Through trade, travel, student exchange programs and immigration,

Islam, Hinduism and Baha'i also gained toeholds.

The changes sweeping the United States were not lost on white youth. Products of a midcentury religiosity that preached peace and justice through understanding and brotherhood, they also had learned to question authority. Many concluded their churches and synagogues were hypocritical places, preaching brotherhood and inclusivity while remaining in practice the most segregated sector of society. Christian exclusivity, in particular, seemed incompatible with the goal of inclusiveness.

Among the first wave of baby boomers, unprecedented numbers dropped out of the churches in which they had been raised for the same reason African Americans, Native Americans and white women did, becoming in the process a "generation of seekers."[3] Some found what they were looking for in Eastern and Native American religions with their underlying themes of unity across time and with nature or in Americanized versions of them. Others found it in the religious or quasi-religious communes that flourished for a time as other utopian communities had a century earlier.

The religious buffet had become a smorgasbord of seemingly endless choices. Zen and transcendental meditation, Krishna Consciousness, Tao, reincarnation, Eastern mysticism, ashrams, base communities and covens were now part of religion in America. And if the choices didn't satisfy, the way was open to create new dishes by combining bits from those religions already on the table.

American Religiosity: The Current Climate

In less than half a century Americans who had been taught to think of their nation as a Protestant New Israel saw it redefined briefly as embracing a tripartite faith and then as a truly pluralistic one. For most Americans the implications of such change seemed to shake the very foundation of society.

In leading challenges to the status quo on the political and social front, religious leaders also had taught the public to challenge the authority of religious institutions and of religion itself. By pushing for inclusion and tolerance for those who historically had been excluded from positions of power, they encouraged religious minorities to become more visible and more outspoken in their demands for inclusion and acceptance.

With religious options to choose from, the traditional religious institutions lost much of their authority over members. Instead of staying with the religion they were born into, people began behaving more as religious consumers, picking and choosing from among the many available religions. When none suited, they abandoned religion or created their own.

Taking what they had learned from the civil rights movement to heart, they demanded their own rights: the right to practice their own religion or to eschew all religions free from official or quasi-official pressures to conform to conventional notions of American religiosity. They also demanded acceptance of the practices and lifestyle choices that flowed naturally from their beliefs.

Although those who had no religion or chose to practice "unconventional" ones remained a tiny minority, survival of conventional American religiosity could no longer be assumed.

But for many, its survival was worth fighting for. The result has been what sociologists such as James Davison Hunter refer to as a "culture war." At stake were

competing non-negotiable claims about how public life ought to be ordered: these claims emerge out of our ultimate beliefs and commitments, our most cherished sense of what is right, true, and good. ...[4]

Those ultimate beliefs and commitments are, at core, religious. Religion is, says *Toledo Blade* religion editor Rebekah Scott, "a thread woven through all discourse and motivation of action, public and private." It is, adds *New York Times* religion writer Gustav Niebuhr, "an enduring force." Religion shapes people, and through them, their culture.

Widely shared beliefs created what Sydney Mead has called the "religion of the republic" and made of America "the nation with the soul of a church."[5] But just beyond and below the tenets of the "religion of the republic" that most Americans have always held in common are the particular beliefs that divide churches, separate peoples, fuel tensions and create conflict within a society.

Assumptions rooted in Puritanism and revivalism fueled anti-Catholic riots, shaped immigration policy, and gave rise to the Know Nothing Party in the 1840s. Religious beliefs and religiously inspired visions of how people should behave and how society should be ordered justified and motivated both sides in the Civil War, the period of reconstruction, and during the civil rights movement. They were behind America's Indian policy for nearly 300 years and they inspired Native American resistance. They separated hawks from doves during the Vietnam War. They have been and still can be found on both sides in debates over immigration, civil rights, equal rights and affirmative action, school curriculum, television and the movies, welfare, contraception and abortion, environmental protection, homosexuality, and school prayer.

Those are the issues of the culture war. The war itself is often presented as one being fought between religion and secularism. If secularism is taken to mean a decline in religious authority, then America is becoming increasingly secular. The presence of so many competing religions makes it impossible for any religion to command allegiance and provide the explanations that create shared meanings and a sense of direction the way the Roman Catholic Church could before the Reformation or Puritans could for a brief time in colonial New England. Because there are now so many religions and so many religious understandings, each officially equal, it also becomes easier than it once was for people to disregard the authoritativeness of the religion they claim as their own.

But even if religion is no longer the authoritative force it once was, the nation is not secular in the sense of being indifferent to religion. People care passionately about religion, and especially about their own. The answer to the paradox of a nation whose people are highly religious and yet one that is widely perceived to be secular lies in religious diversity. Because religions by their very nature tend to be exclusive, each one sees the other as false. Therefore, it becomes very easy to see in the existence of different beliefs and lifestyles evidence of a decline in true religiosity and to dismiss those other beliefs and behaviors as secular.

Because different religions carry with them different beliefs about how people should live their lives and how society should be ordered, the culture war is more often between those with different religious visions than between those who are religious and those who are not. In many cases, the "struggle to define America" is led by traditionalist heirs to the revivalist spirit who believe America was meant to be a Christian nation. Their opponents more often are modernist heirs to the reform spirit who believe the nation was founded to provide religious freedom for all. But people shift sides depending on the issue. Muslims, Jews, Buddhists, Baha'is, Hindus and members of alternative religions also have a stake in the outcome and join in, sometimes on one side, sometimes on the other. In the process, coalitions are formed; religio-political realignments occur.

Religion may not be the sole cause or even the primary or proximate cause for every instance of conflict. Self-interest, including economic self-interest, culture and class, race and ethnicity, personal experience and education can all be part of the explanation for conflict. But wherever fights are protracted and bitter and compromise seems impossible, deeply held beliefs and values are probably lurking in the background. Finding them can be difficult, but finding and explaining the connections is an important part of the job for journalists.

"The enduring question for the nation and the one religion journalists must tackle," says Laurie Goodstein, who covered religion for the *Washington Post* before moving to the *New York Times* in 1997, "is how we will manage our religious diversity—how a predominately Christian nation assimilates religious minorities and how they cope with a predominately Christian society."

Notes

1 All figures are from Roger Finke and Rodney Stark, *The Churching of America 1776-1990: Winners and Losers in Our Religious Economy* (Brunswick, N.J.: Rutgers University Press, 1992); and Barry A. Kosmin and Seymour P. Lachman, *One Nation Under God: Religion in Contemporary American Society* (New York: Harmony Books, 1993).

2 The idea comes from Will Herberg, *Protestant, Catholic, Jew* (New York: Doubleday, 1955).

3 The phrase is from Wade Clark Roof, *A Generation of Seekers: The Spiritual Journey of the Baby Boom Generation* (San Francisco: Harper SanFrancisco, 1995).

4 James Davison Hunter, "Before the Shooting Begins," *Columbia Journalism Review* July/August 1993:30. For a more thorough discussion of the idea of culture wars, see Hunter, *Culture Wars: The Struggle to Define America* (New York: BasicBooks, 1990). For a discussion of religious realignment in a culture war context, see Robert Wuthnow, *The Restructuring of American Religion* (Princeton, N.J.: Princeton University Press, 1989).

5 See Sydney E. Mead, *The Nation with the Soul of a Church* (New York: Harper & Row, 1975).

For Further Reading

Finke, Roger, and Rodney Stark. *The Churching of America 1776-1990: Winners and Losers in Our Religious Economy.* New Brunswick, N.J.: Rutgers University Press, 1992.

The authors apply economic theory and models drawn from consumer behavior to data from church membership figures, census data and public opinion polls in an effort to explain the shifting fortunes of various Christian churches. The many figures and tables provide much useful data.

Herberg, Will. *Protestant, Catholic, Jew.* New York: Doubleday, 1955.

Although the conclusion that America's "three great faiths" are coming together in harmony to produce a "religion of the American way" seems dated today, this classic work was highly influential at a time when most people agreed with the metaphor of America as a melting pot. It still is worth reading for the insight it provides on religion in America in the years between World War II and the birth of the civil rights movement.

Hunter, James Davison. *Culture Wars: The Struggle to Define America.* New York: BasicBooks, 1990.

This examination of the beliefs, values and styles of moral reasoning that fuel conflicts in contemporary American society made the term "culture war" a part of public discourse.

Kosmin, Barry A., and Seymour P. Lachman. *One Nation Under God: Religion in Contemporary American Society.* New York: Harmony Books, 1993.

The authors use data from the National Survey of Religious Identification to examine links between religious identification and standard demographics, geographic region and issue positions. Reporters will find the appendix of religious statistics helpful.

Marty, Martin E. *Pilgrims in Their Own Land: 500 Years of Religion in America.* New York: Penguin Books, 1984.

Almost any book by the noted historian and theologian is worth reading. This chronological history also devotes some attention to the impact of religion on social issues and provides brief sketches of religious "pathfinders."

Mead, Sydney E. *The Nation with the Soul of a Church.* New York: Harper & Row, 1975.

This influential work examines the shared beliefs that unite Americans and the particularistic ones that lie just below the surface. A shorter version can be found in *Church History* 36(1967):262-283.

Roof, Wade Clark. *A Generation of Seekers: The Spiritual Journeys of the Baby Boom Generation.* San Francisco; Harper SanFrancisco, 1994.

This work examines the life experiences that shaped the baby boomers' approach to religion, their beliefs and practices, the impact of their spiritual quest in their own lives and its effect on the nation's religious climate.

Yarnold, Barbara M. (ed.). *The Role of Religious Organizations in Social Movements*. New York: Praeger, 1991.

The chapters in this edited collection discuss sanctuary, peace, gay and lesbian, and Christian Right organizations and their significance.

CHAPTER 2

THE ROLE OF THE FIRST AMENDMENT

The first 16 words of the First Amendment to the United States Constitution promise:

Congress shall make no law regarding an establishment of religion or prohibiting the free exercise thereof ...

Those words acknowledge more clearly than the prohibition on religious tests for public office embedded within the Constitution itself that the government has no authority over what people choose to believe. They also signal that in the United States there will be, and must be, room for religious diversity and that religious discourse, like political speech, is an appropriate part of the marketplace of ideas.

In place of a government legitimized by religion and religion supported and promoted by its ties to government, the First Amendment decreed separation, and perhaps even a divorce. Whether such an arrangement would work was unknown. Like so much else about the new system created by the Constitution and its Bill of Rights, the separation of church and state was unprecedented.

Both fear of a powerful, central government and pragmatic recognition of religious differences among the colonies and within them led the majority of political leaders, clergy and average citizens to place their trust in the people instead of in powerful elites. That trust was born of enlightenment philosophies. But the writings of John Milton, John Locke and Jean-Jacques Rousseau, in turn, have their roots in

Reformation Protestant theology that placed individual conscience above ecclesiastical or temporal authority.

Instead of trusting an elite to decide for the people what information they need and what opinions are good and true in matters of politics or religion, the founding fathers believed it was prudent, proper and safe for people to have the rights enshrined in the First Amendment. Although they recognized that ideas and opinions are, to some degree at least, a matter of faith or personal preference, they assumed truth is recognizable and that people are rational and will search for truth, recognize it and act accordingly.

But others remained unconvinced. On the question of providing for religious freedom, some Americans and most outside observers accepted the conventional wisdom. To them, a single established church seemed the best way to assure political stability and personal morality. Like the Puritan clergyman Cotton Mather, they believed religious diversity would inevitably divide society and lead to interminable religious wars like those that had occurred throughout Europe as Catholics and Protestants fought for dominance, or else it would spell the decline of religion with an attendant increase in licentiousness and lawlessness.

But instead of the endless religious wars or, alternatively, the decline in religion that some predicted, the reality has been quite different. On his visit to the United States in 1831, the French Catholic historian Alexis de Tocqueville observed that, instead of destroying religion, the separation of church and state had produced a kind of religious vitality and sense of purpose unknown in Europe.[1]

In a society where no religion has an automatic claim to legitimacy, Tocqueville concluded that all had become voluntary associations—interest groups—competing with each other and with other interest groups for members and for money. According to Tocqueville, competition produced the commitment, activism, tolerance and cooperation necessary for democracy to flourish. Although deprived of a direct role in government and politics, religion nevertheless shaped the manners and mores of the people and thus influenced American culture.

A part of that influence rested on the natural alliance between voluntary organizations and the press. Newspapers carried information about what people were doing and what they cared about. By reading the papers, people could identify problems. Through them, people could find other like-minded people with whom they could build coalitions to address those problems. Moreover, churches could use the media to their own advantage. Because only the press has the ability to plant the same idea simultaneously in thousands of minds, religions could spread their message by making news.

If Tocqueville overlooked the fact that, even as he traveled through the United States, religious riots between Protestants and Catholics were occurring in New York and Philadelphia, he may also have been a bit naive in his conclusion that an alliance between voluntary associations and the press created a climate of tolerance by fostering democratic principles and civic virtues. However, his observation that only the press can plant the same notion simultaneously in a thousand minds presaged by more than 200 years media research that documents the cultivation and agenda-setting effects of media coverage.

For religions, that power to plant ideas makes the media both friend and foe. Each religion, believing it has the truth, wants coverage because attention is necessary to attract members, find allies and further its interests. But believing it has the truth, it fears coverage for other religions which it considers dangerous and wrong lest they be the ones to gain influence.

By scheduling events, uttering pronouncements, supporting causes or withholding support from them, religions can get news coverage which attracts widespread attention. Coverage, and especially favorable or neutral coverage by an outside entity such as the press, creates an illusion of legitimacy. Being ignored or receiving unfavorable coverage has the opposite effect. Therefore, each religion has a vested interest in how it and its causes are covered.

While all journalists must deal with people and organizations with vested interests, the protection provided by the First Amendment combined with the difficulty, if not the impossibility, of verifying the truth underlying religious beliefs that lead to those different interests produce additional problems for those who cover religion. Strictly speaking, only government can establish a religion or limit the free exercise of religion. But as a practical matter, public opinion, shaped by media coverage, can both limit the free exercise of religion and create a *de facto* establishment.

Covering primarily those religions that are dominant in a region or those that are most outspoken in their demands can have the effect of legitimizing them and their claims at the expense of smaller or less intrusive religions. Conversely, coverage of minority faiths gives them the legitimacy that comes with being noticed by an independent, outside observer. That, in turn, can increase their power and influence.

As James Davison Hunter points out, the current culture war to define America is being fought in courts of law and in the court of public opinion. Because the sides are rooted in different strains of religiosity and different forms of moral reasoning, people on all sides frequently look to the religion clauses for protection. They are quick to claim their freedom of religion is being abridged whenever their individual behaviors or their collective activities are held up to public scrutiny. When their preferences do not prevail, they quickly claim someone else's religion is becoming the *de facto* established religion. They are very serious about their claims. They want desperately to have their views reported as if they are the correct ones.

"The First Amendment is the basis for our existence," says Rebekah Scott, religion editor for the *Toledo Blade*. It provides for an open forum and drives beliefs into public discourse. Many who say their freedom of religion has been violated are both correct and knowledgeable about the law. But journalists cannot assume that is true.

As Ann Rodgers-Melnick, religion writer for the *Pittsburgh Post-Gazette* points out, misinterpretations and distortions abound. Some simply do not know the law; others knowingly misinterpret it to their own advantage. Those making claims that are fully justified and those making claims that are not justified can sound equally plausible and persuasive. They can also seem equally absurd.

Unless journalists have some independent understanding of the origin and meaning of the religion clauses, they are at the mercy of their sources. By accepting at face value what others tell them, they risk spreading misinformation. Information that is wrong or that lacks necessary backgrounding and perspective can inflame public opinion or shut off reasonable discourse. As the Rev. Jesse Jackson told those attending the 1997 convention of the Association for Education in Journalism and Mass Communication, "A text out of context is a pretext."

Understanding Original Intent

In cases raising constitutional issues, judges look to the precedents set by previously decided cases. However, they also must look to those who were most intimately involved in writing the Constitution or its amendments as well as to the political debates that surrounded their creation and adoption and to the practices of that era for clues about how the Constitution and its amendments should be interpreted. But in the case of the religion clauses, those clues lead in different directions.

When the First Amendment was adopted in 1791, all of the states except Rhode Island, Delaware and Pennsylvania had established religions. Some had multiple establishments. In the southern colonies, the Episcopal Church was the established church. In New England, where the Congregational Church was originally the single established church, inroads by Baptists and others led to multiple established churches. People living in a community selected their church by popular vote and that church, whether Congregational or of some other Protestant faith, became the official church for the parish. Essentially the same model prevailed in New York.

However, sentiment in favor of establishment was diminishing. Changes in English law had made some measure of religious toleration the official, if not universally accepted, law in colonial America. Religious diversity increased. Members of minority religions chafed under state-sanctioned restrictions.

Pennsylvania never had an established religion, but Jews could not hold public office. For a time, atheists and deists were banned from even living in Pennsylvania. In the southern colonies, where the Episcopal Church was the established church, Baptists and other "dissenters" were tolerated, especially when their growing numbers made it impossible to do otherwise. But that tolerance guaranteed them primarily the right to worship in their own churches. In Virginia, only clergy from the Episcopal Church could perform marriages; only Episcopalians were eligible for public office.

As early as 1708 Massachusetts had its own "religious toleration" statutes that provided some protection for those who were not members of Puritan Congregational churches, but those "others" remained at a disadvantage just as they did in the southern colonies. Whether there was a single established church or multiple established ones, governments collected taxes from everyone and then distributed the money to the established church or churches. In most cases, "dissenters" could be excused from paying the tax, but only if they could prove their status. Those who lived too far from a church of their choice to attend regularly and those who chose not to belong to any church were not eligible for exemption. Those who were eligible had to file documents supporting their claim. In New England, the cost for the required paperwork was 4 pence. The English tax on tea, which led to the Boston Tea Party, was 3 pence.

In the anti-tax climate that contributed to the Revolutionary War, such arrangements became increasingly intolerable. With suspicion of centralized government widespread, especially among the anti-Federalists who were the leading proponents for a Bill of Rights, there was general agreement there should be no established national church or churches. But beyond that there was little consensus on what should or should not be permitted.

Thomas Jefferson, who along with James Madison was most instrumental in crafting the First Amendment, was one of the most outspoken proponents of a complete separation, if not a divorce, between church and state. But he was not alone in his opinion. Before sending his letter with the famous "wall of separation" reference to the Danbury Baptist Association in Rhode Island, Jefferson consulted the attorney general who concurred the First Amendment meant such a wall should exist. As president, Madison vetoed a bill that would have given a church free land in settlement of a surveying error because it "compromises a principle and precedent for the appropriation of funds ... for the use and support of religious societies, contrary to the [establishment clause]."[2]

But whatever Jefferson and Madison might have intended or thought the law to be, the wall of separation Jefferson described never was an impermeable barrier. Just as Congress ignored the speech and press clauses when it passed the Alien and Sedition Act of 1798 which made seditious libel a punishable offense and also prohibited foreigners from operating newspapers, it ignored the religion clauses in order to pass a law authorizing the use of tax money to establish a chaplaincy for the Congress.

Only Jefferson steadfastly maintained that the First Amendment prohibited all official or quasi-official support or encouragement for religion. Where Jefferson refused to call for or endorse a day of national thanksgiving and prayer, other presidents from George Washington through Bill Clinton have used their position to encourage religiosity.

Therefore, for many it was obviously enough that there be no national church and that people be allowed to worship in the church of their choice. Assuming America was and was forever meant to be a Protestant Christian nation, some had no problem with laws that would merely tolerate people who were not Christian, or even those who were Catholics or members of minority Protestant religions.

However, in supporting changes in Virginia's statutes regarding religion, James Madison argued that toleration and freedom of conscience are not synonymous. To him, "toleration" implied that there is a "tolerator" and a merely "tolerated" whose freedoms would forever be at the mercy of the majority.

As finally adopted, the Virginia Declaration of Rights described religion as "the duty which we owe to our Creator, and the manner of discharging it." George Washington and Patrick Henry, among others, clearly believed religion requires a belief in a Supreme Creator. They probably equated that Creator with the Christian God. In arguing for the Bill for Establishing Religious Freedom in Virginia, however, Thomas Jefferson said religious freedom was

> meant to comprehend, within the mantle of its protection, the Jew and the Gentile, the Christian and Mahometan, the Hindoo, and infidel of every denomination.

In his public comments concerning religious freedom, the Baptist Roger Williams went even further. He would also have protected the rights of pagans and those who are avowedly anti-Christian.

Although the founding fathers differed in their understanding of the free exercise clause and also disagreed among themselves on how complete the separation of church and state should be, all seem to have agreed that the religion clauses were meant only as a safeguard against actions by the federal government. The First Amendment placed no limitation on state or local government.

When the Bill of Rights was adopted, most states did have an establishment of religion. They enforced religious tests for public office and punished blasphemy. But today, states rights are an oxymoron where the rights protected from federal intrusion by the Bill of Rights are concerned. The change came after the Civil War when Congress passed and the states ratified the 14th Amendment. Therefore, the intent of those who framed and adopted that Amendment must also be taken into account.

The climate in which the 14th Amendment became part of the Constitution clearly indicates it was intended to prevent the southern states from denying the privileges of citizenship to the newly freed slaves. However, the amendment never mentions race or previous condition of servitude. Instead, Section One states:

> No State shall make or enforce any law which shall abridge the privileges or immunities of citizens of the United States; nor shall any State deprive

any person of life, liberty, or property, without due process of law; nor deny to any person within its jurisdiction the equal protection of the law.

Both the language of the 14th Amendment and the debate surrounding its adoption make it clear that the intent was to prevent states or local governments from placing limitations on the rights and freedoms guaranteed by the Bill of Rights. Although the Supreme Court rarely enforced its provisions until the 20th century, today the 14th Amendment provides the Constitutional justification for civil rights and equal opportunity laws that prevent discrimination on the basis of gender, race, ethnicity, religion, and probably also on the basis of any other identifiable characteristic.

Together the First Amendment and the 14th Amendment protect against the establishment of religion and also against abridgements of the free exercise of religion by any level of government. As a corollary, they also prevent behaviors by public and private entities that discriminate against individuals or identifiable groups.

Applying the Religion Clauses

From efforts to apply the religion clauses to cases that arise under them, two principles have emerged. To guard against the establishment of a religion, the principle of neutrality prevents favoring one religion over another. To prevent abridgements of the free exercise of religion, the principle of accommodation requires protecting behaviors that flow from belief as much as possible without infringing on other rights.

However, determining how those principles should apply in any particular case is often a judgment call. Those who agree with the principle of neutrality and/or the principle of accommodation quickly divide into **preferentialists** and **nonpreferentialists**. Those who accept and those who reject either or both of those basic principles, as well as the preferentialists and nonpreferentialists within each camp, can find legal and historical precedents for their positions.

Preferentialists understand the religion clauses to protect only those who subscribe to a belief system that qualifies as a religion. Based on language in the Virginia statutes and the reality that the nation was undeniably a Protestant one when the First Amendment was adopted and that many people believed it should always be Protestant or at least

Christian, some go so far as to argue that the religion clauses were meant to protect only Christians and Christianity. *Nonpreferentialists* favor the positions of Jefferson and Williams. To them it seems inappropriate to protect Christianity over other religions. It seems equally inappropriate to protect religion and religious people at the expense of those who choose not to subscribe to any religion.

Court Interpretations

Just as there are and always have been deep divisions in public understanding of what the religion clauses were meant to protect and protect against and in how the religion clauses should be applied to particular situations, courts have been and still are divided. The depth of that division can be seen in the many 5-4 rulings in Supreme Court cases involving the religion clauses. Over time, however, the direction of court decisions has shifted.

Initially most courts accepted the preferentialist position. However, as historical research uncovered more information about the diversity of views that existed when the First Amendment was adopted and as the country became religiously more pluralistic, nonpreferentialist views have become more common. But even as courts have moved toward neutrality among all religions and between religion and nonreligion, they have increasingly supported accommodation in so far as accommodating religious practices does not present a threat to public safety or interfere with other important rights and freedoms.

Until well into the 20th century, courts assumed the United States is and should remain a Christian nation. In the 1811 case of *Ruggles v. Williams,* for example, a New York court ruled that blasphemy against the Christian God, but not against other gods, is a punishable offense because

we are a Christian people and the morality of the country is deeply ingrafted upon Christianity, and not upon the doctrines or worship of the imposters.

But eventually the Supreme Court concluded that it is both impossible and inappropriate to make legal distinctions between true religion and "imposters." In a 1939 decision involving the I Am movement, Justice William Douglas wrote for the court:

Religious experiences which are as real as life to some may be incomprehensible to others. Yet the fact that they may be beyond the ken of mortals does not mean that they can be made suspect before the law.

Interpreted strictly, Justice Douglas' opinion could imply that a person must believe in some god in order to be protected under the religion clauses, but courts no longer consider that necessary. In the 1982 case of *Africa v. Commonwealth of Pennsylvania,* the Court of Appeals for the Third Circuit listed three indicators of a religion:

First, a religion addresses fundamental and ultimate questions having to do with deep and imponderable matters. Second, a religion is comprehensive in nature; it consists of a belief-system as opposed to an isolated teaching. Third, a religion often can be recognized by the presence of certain formal and external signs.

Although the Supreme Court denied certiorari in that case, it frequently uses variants of the Third Circuit's indicators. In deciding Vietnam-era cases involving conscientious objectors, for example, the Supreme Court insisted only that beliefs be sincerely held and that violating those beliefs would cause the person deep pain. Those sincerely held beliefs no longer have to be connected to any recognized religion or to belief in a god.

Just as courts now generally accept the nonpreferentialist views of Roger Williams and Thomas Jefferson, they explicitly or tacitly accept Jefferson's belief that there should be a "wall of separation" between church and state. They differ primarily on when that wall has been breached.

The most commonly used test for determining when government has breached that wall comes from the Supreme Court decision in the 1971 case of *Lemon v. Kurtzman,* which prohibited financial help from the government for teaching nonreligious subjects in church-related schools. According to the Lemon Test, in establishment cases arising from legislative action, statutes must have a "secular purpose." Furthermore, their "principal or primary effect must be one that neither advances nor inhibits religion." Finally, there can be no "excessive government entanglement with religion."

Similar reasoning also informs many decisions arising under the free exercise clause. Where once only Christians were firmly protected, courts now generally protect all religious expression and religiously inspired behaviors so long as those behaviors are not a threat to public safety or to the rights of others.

In the 1879 case of *Reynolds v. United States,* the Supreme Court ruled that prohibitions on the practice of polygamy by members of the Church of Jesus Christ of Latter-day Saints were constitutional even though at that time polygamy was an integral part of Mormon doctrine. To rule otherwise, it said, would undermine the government interest in promoting public order and morality and "make each man a law unto himself."

Since then, there have been other decisions that went against the interests of religious minorities, but as a general rule courts have become more inclined to protect unconventional religiously inspired activities. In perhaps the high point of sensitivity, the Supreme Court used both the principle of neutrality and the accommodation principle to reach its decision in the 1993 case of *Church of Leucoma v. Hialeah.* In that case, the court ruled that ordinances prohibiting the slaughtering of animals within city limits cannot be enforced against the kind of ritual slaughter practiced by members of the Santeria religion because the practice is integral to that religion and because the prohibition was never enforced against kosher slaughterhouses or against those who trap rodents or hunt other animals within the city limits of Hialeah, Florida.

Recurring Problems

On balance, court decisions generally give great protection for conventional and unconventional religious practices and do not seriously disadvantage either religion or ir-religion. Protection for both belief and unbelief provides freedom of conscience.

People may hold whatever religious opinions or opinions about religion they wish. But the behaviors that follow from those opinions are a different matter. Just as courts make distinctions between expression and action in deciding cases arising under the speech and press clauses, they sometimes make similar distinctions under the free exercise clause. As is also true in cases arising under the speech and press clauses, rulings can sometimes be difficult to reconcile with well-established legal principles.

During prohibition, for example, alcohol laws were never applied to Christian churches that use wine for communion, but in the 1990 case of *Employment Division v. Smith* the U.S. Supreme Court upheld the firing of drug counselors who, as members of the Native American Church, used peyote. Under the Lemon Test, employment rules and statutory laws banning use of hallucinogens certainly serve a serious government interest but extending them to the ceremonial use of peyote seriously threatens the free exercise of religion. As numerous *amicus curiae* briefs filed by Christian churches pointed out, a finding for the Employment Division would appear to allow similar retribution against devout Christian adults who take communion. It would also allow punishing them for letting their children receive the sacrament.

As the *Employment Division v. Smith* case suggests, public interest in health and safety currently appears to offset claims to religious freedom. While courts have usually sided with adults who shun conventional medical care or refuse to have a particular medical procedure such as a blood transfusion, they have been more inclined to allow state intervention when parents withhold medical care from their children or when their religiously motivated concept of child rearing differs substantially from current societal norms. Courts have, for example, upheld criminal sanctions against Christian Science parents who did not seek conventional medical care for their children.

Although that kind of case is becoming more common, the number of those cases remains small. In the past decade, workplace rules have been a more common battleground as religious people have been more vocal in claiming a right to practice their religion wherever they please and in demanding special accommodations because of their religion. In spite of relative consistency in court rulings, complaints by religious people that their interests are being ignored became so common that Congress passed and President Bill Clinton signed into law the Religious Freedom Restoration Act.

But even without that law, in most cases the First and 14th Amendments work together to protect religion. With the exception of churches and religious organizations, neither the government nor private organizations may make hiring or firing decisions on the basis of religion. With the exception of the military, they must accommodate religious practices—dress, time off for religious observance—and allow employees to speak about their religion as long as the behaviors do not place an undue burden on the employer, harm the business or intimidate or harass others.

But extending the rights guaranteed in those situations to other settings that are more directly under the control of the government or its agencies is more difficult because in those settings the free exercise and establishment clauses become intimately intertwined. In public schools, for example, teachers may not be hired or fired because of their religion, but in the classroom they must forego some of their right to exercise their beliefs because their actions can easily be perceived as an establishment of religion.

Schools have lost their ability to require or encourage prayers, to teach that one religion is true or tailor lessons to promote a faith, and to make curricular decisions on the basis of religion. Contrary to popular opinion, however, Supreme Court rulings never banished religion from the public schools. Teaching about religion has always been permitted. Courts have simply ruled unconstitutional those practices that create the appearance of an establishment of religion.

Under the free exercise clause students have the right to engage in private prayer, dress in accordance with the demands of their faith or wear symbols of it, and read and exchange religious literature. Courts generally require reasonable accommodations without retaliation for students demanding on religious grounds to be exempt from a particular course or lesson or to miss school for religious observances. Students cannot legally be punished for those activities unless their behavior is disruptive of the education process or threatens or harasses other students.

Although educators often misunderstand or ignore Supreme Court rulings, they cannot totally prevent students from distributing religious literature to their classmates, but neither can they ban distribution of underground student newspapers. If they allow some kinds of student interest groups to meet or provide subsidies to some student publications, they must also make facilities and support available for religious organizations and religious publications. Schools today may prohibit speech that may be perceived as having the imprimatur of the school, such as that in a school newspaper or in an assembly. They may impose reasonable regulations, but they cannot ban individual expression that merely takes place in a public school.

Similar balancing of interests occurs in cases that arise from people's claims to exercise their religious freedom in other public settings. Outside of public schools, some of the messiest cases arising from the religion clauses also involve political speech. In those cases, the speech, press and assembly clauses also apply.

Time, place and manner restrictions may be imposed, but those restrictions must be content neutral. Religion cannot be singled out for restriction. The general principles of First Amendment law have led the court to uphold some limitations on religiously inspired anti-abortion protests at clinics, but they have also upheld some restrictions on anti-war protestors and environmentalists whose concerns are often only tenuously related to religious beliefs. The same body of law that gave Jehovah's Witnesses the right to engage in street-corner preaching and demonstrations subsequently protected a Neo-Nazi parade in heavily Jewish Skokie, Illinois. It also protects Promise Keepers rallies and the Million Man March.

Government can neither ban a parade, protest, rally or soapbox oration because of its content nor compel its organizers to open up their event to speakers or groups with whom they disagree. But where the government appears to be the organizer or the funding organization, the establishment clause again comes into play. The government cannot easily discriminate among speakers or participants.

For displays on public property, courts are usually guided by the principle of neutrality. The Supreme Court has, for example, allowed public displays of religious symbols from various faiths and also religious symbols mixed with secular ones. It has also ruled against nativity scenes standing alone on public property during the Christmas season on the grounds that they tend to support Christianity. However, in the 1995 case of *Capitol Square and Advisory Board v. Pinette* the Court upheld the right of the Klan to place a cross on public property, reasoning that the Klan's symbol was primarily political and political displays on public property are common.

When government funding is the issue, courts usually follow the Lemon Test, albeit with difficulty. Historically, the federal government subsidized missionary endeavors to "Christianize and civilize Indians," but as early as 1804 Congress refused to pass a law providing funding for religious instruction in schools believing such use of government money to be a violation of the establishment clause. Today, governments pay for transportation of students to parochial schools, but direct aid for religious instruction in parochial schools is still considered unconstitutional. School vouchers and student-led prayers at school-sponsored events remain unsettled areas. Some courts interpret them as violating the establishment clause. Others approve of them, believing they fall within the principle of strict neutrality so long as vouchers can also be used for schools that are not affiliated with religion and students remain equally free to offer thoughts that are unrelated to religion or give readings from secular sources.

Reporting with Understanding

Individual cases sometimes produce court opinions that seem to flout long-standing traditions as well as the basic principles that have evolved from almost a century of church-state decisions. Like Justice Antonin Scalia, almost everyone at least occasionally bemoans the "strange ... geometry of crooked lines and wavering shapes" that has emerged from attempts to apply the religion clauses to the novel situation raised by each case.[3]

There simply is no easy way to reconcile the religion clauses with each other or to balance protection for religion with other important interests. Differences over what the religion clauses were meant to protect and protect against and how they should be applied persist. The depth of the feeling on each side can be seen in the reaction to almost every court decision. When the preferentialist position prevails, nonpreferentialists feel threatened. When nonpreferentialists win, preferentialists complain. Accommodation leads to cries of "establishment." Neutrality leads to claims that "free exercise" is under siege.

"Why," some ask, "does the establishment clause seem to trump freedom of speech and the free exercise of religion?" But others would reverse the question: "Why should someone's freedom of speech or right to the free exercise of religion be allowed to create an establishment of religion, or even the appearance of one?" Both are serious questions that deserve careful consideration.

There is widespread ignorance about the law. There are also those who take advantage of that ignorance to misinterpret it for their own purposes. "The First Amendment is," says Marcia Z. Nelson of the *Aurora (Ill.) Beacon-News*, "frequently taken in vain." Therefore, it is incumbent upon religion reporters to take the time to explain the law carefully and accurately in order to answer people's questions and address their concerns.

Thorough reporting requires sensitivity to the claims from all sides. In most cases, it is not a simple matter of one side being the religious side and the other side being anti-religion. Careful reporting requires being able to distinguish true threats to First Amendment freedoms from problems that arise when individuals misinterpret or misapply the law. Explaining the issues requires putting them into a broader context that includes both the origin of protections for religion and the overall thrust of court decisions. Eradicating differences of opinion about the religion clauses may be impossible, but thorough reporting can reduce misunderstandings and help defuse tensions.

Notes

1 For Tocqueville's comments on religion, voluntary associations, the press, and the relationships among them, see Alexis de Tocqueville, *Democracy in America,* Vol. 1 (New York: Longmans, Green & Co., 1889), 93-114, 180-197, 307-319.

2 For supporting evidence, see Leonard W. Levy, *The Establishment Clause: Religion and the First Amendment,* 2nd ed. (Chapel Hill, N.C.: The University of North Carolina Press, 1994), 119, 246-249.

3 The quote is from Justice Antonin Scalia's opinion in the 1993 case of *Lamb's Chapel v. Center Moriches Union Free School District.*

For Further Reading

Flowers, Ronald B. *That Godless Court? Supreme Court Decisions on Church-State Relationships.* Louisville, Ky.: John Knox Press, 1994.
  This book is both a careful examination of what the Supreme Court has and has not said and an argument for nurturing religious freedom. Among the volatile religion-related topics discussed are prayer in public schools, religion in the workplace, and taxation.

Frankel, Marvin E. *Faith and Freedom: Religious Liberty in America.* New York: Hill and Wang, 1994.
  Argued from the nonpreferentialist position of Roger Williams and Thomas Jefferson, this short and highly readable book is a powerful plea for protecting both belief and unbelief. Frankel is a former law professor, assistant solicitor general, and U.S. district judge for the Southern District of New York.

Levy, Leonard W. *The Establishment Clause: Religion and the First Amendment,* 2nd ed. Chapel Hill, N.C.: The University of North Carolina Press, 1994.
  In this classic work based on a careful examination of historical documents and of the climate of public opinion in colonial America, Levy develops the argument that the founding fathers meant to prohibit all aid to religion, even on an impartial or informal basis.

Whitehead, John W. *The Rights of Religious Persons in Public Education,* Rev. ed. Wheaton, Ill.: Crossways Books, 1994.
  This book is valuable for its careful critical analysis of Supreme Court decisions from the preferentialist and accommodationist point of view. The author is the founder of the Rutherford Institute which is committed to supporting the First Amendment rights of religious people.

Wood, James E. Jr. (ed.). *The First Freedom: Religion and the Bill of Rights*. Waco, Texas: J.M. Dawson Institute of Church-State Studies, Baylor University, 1990.

    This edited collection contains examinations of the original and current meaning of the religion clauses written by noted historians and legal scholars. The chapter by Henry J. Abraham is a clear explanation of the purpose of the 14th Amendment and its current importance in protecting religious freedom against the authority of state and local governments and the tyranny of the majority.

CHAPTER 3

THE VARIETIES OF AMERICAN RELIGIONS

Because the establishment clause makes all religions officially equal and legitimate in the eyes of the law and the free exercise clause guarantees people the right to believe and to worship as they please, the First Amendment created a climate in which religiosity flourished but religions proliferated.

J. Gordon Melton, editor of *The Encyclopedia of American Religion,* has identified more than 1200 religions in the United States that have one congregation with at least 2000 members, several smaller congregations, or that draw members from more than one state. By counting religions with a single small congregation, mail-order religions and even a single person with a mimeograph machine and a few names on a mailing list, others find at least twice as many.

Not all of those religions will be found in each city, state or region. However, entries under "churches" and "religious organizations" in the phone book for even fairly small cities will often list 50 or so religious options, each with one or more congregations. Larger cities have even more.

Ideally, of course, nonspecialists should know everything about the ones they are most likely to encounter in their work; journalists who specialize in religion reporting should know everything about every religion. However, achieving that ideal is hardly realistic, especially because new religions and new variants of old ones continually appear. More achievable as a goal, and equally useful for journalists, is to learn about types of religions.

For that, social scientists who study religion have come up with classification schemes. While each scheme has its own shortcomings and none can provide all the details for individual religions one might want, each has its use. Together, they can help journalists make sense of the bewildering array of religions and serve as a guide in the reporting process.

General Classification Schemes

For understanding religions, the theological and geographic schemes discussed in this chapter are most important. Structural schemes that classify religions according to their internal organization can also be useful. They will be discussed in Chapter 5.

Theological Schemes

Theological schemes focus on what religions actually teach and what their adherents actually believe. The most basic ones classify religions according to the number and nature of their gods or other supernatural or sacred beings. Other classifications are, in effect, corollaries of what religious people believe those beings are like and what those beings demand.

Religions are commonly categorized as **pantheistic, polytheistic** or **monotheistic.** *Pantheistic religions* do not make sharp distinctions between the everyday world and the realm of the sacred. In these religions virtually everything in the real world is imbued with something of the sacred and has its own spirit or supernatural element worthy of respect, if not reverence and worship. *Polytheistic religions* have more than one god whose locus is outside the everyday world, although the gods may also take the form of elements of that world: the sun, an animal, a mountain, or a person with extraordinary power. *Monotheistic religions* teach that there is only one god and that god is totally or mostly other than anything in the real world. Therefore, they usually make the sharpest distinction between the sacred and the profane or everyday world.

Monotheistic religions teach that their god demands faithfulness and is, in all aspects, worthy of total allegiance. Most also see that god as the creator and judge of the world. As a corollary, monotheistic religions see the world, time, and life as finite. Religions with multiple gods and those that find the sacred in all things may teach that some sacred beings are more powerful than others, but they rarely teach that any sacred being demands total allegiance. Even those that ascribe a divine origin to the world rarely think of the world as ending through divine intervention. Therefore, to think of the beginning or end of the world or even of the beginning and end of a human's existence makes sense primarily in monotheistic belief systems.

On the basis of the number and nature of their gods, most monotheistic religions might be called "one chance" religions; most others might better be characterized by the axiom "practice makes perfect." That is, most monotheistic religions teach that each person exists only once and that person's ultimate fate after death depends on how the person relates to the supernatural before death. Therefore, "one chance" religions might also be characterized as "one way" religions. That is, they usually teach there is only one correct understanding of god and god's commands. "Practice makes perfect" religions more commonly allow people to pick from among multiple paths to escape from evil, suffering and death. In them, ultimate escape may come only after many lifetimes.

As those basic differences suggest, some religions are more comfortable with the world than others. Therefore, most religions can also be classified according to whether they **accept the world and accommodate to it, try to change it** or **counsel withdrawing from it.**

Those that *accept the world* believe either that the world is basically good or that it cannot be changed. Those that *attempt to change the world* may try to do so directly or indirectly. They may try to reform or change the basic institutions and structures of the society to make it more god-pleasing and, therefore, more conducive to true religiosity or they may try to redeem the world by converting people and through that conversion create behavioral changes that will make society more pleasing to god. Those that *reject the world* may live in it but try very hard to avoid as much contact with those outside the faith as possible. They may also retreat into separate communities as a shield against worldly influences or set up utopian communities in the hopes their way of life will become a model for others.

Because pantheistic religions see an essential unity between the sacred and the profane world, they are most likely to be world-accepting. However, all religions tend to have strains within them that fall into each of the categories. Within some of the indigenous religions, shamans, for example, may live apart from the community. Monotheistic religions, especially Christianity and Islam, are less likely to accept the world than are polytheistic or nontheistic religions. But here it is worth noting that accepting or accommodating to the world may be viewed more as being realistic than as an agreement that the world is as it ought to be.

Geographic Schemes

Geographic schemes classify religions according to the region of the world where they originated or where they have their greatest strength. There are also regional differences in the distribution of religions as well as regional variations in their teachings. Geographic schemes can best be considered as an overlay on theological ones.

Two overlapping geographic schemes are common because they are useful for mapping similarities and differences among religions. The first geographic scheme separates religions into **Eastern** or **Western,** or to be more precise, **Eastern** and **Western/Middle Eastern**. The second classifies them as **world religions, regional religions, national religions** or **local religions**. While categories in both schemes are based on location of origin and greatest strength, the one classifying religions as **Eastern** or **Western/Middle Eastern** also has a theological basis.

World religions began in a specific country and then spread so that today they have members in many countries. Those members make up a significant portion of the world's population. *Regional religions* have spread throughout one area of the world but have not gained many adherents in cultures that differ markedly from that of the place of origin. *National religions* have members and some influence within a single nation. Truly *local religions* have an even more limited sphere of influence.

Of all the thousands of religions in the world, only five are commonly classified as world religions. They are Judaism, Christianity, Islam, Buddhism and Hinduism (Table 3.1). A sixth religion, Baha'i, has spread far beyond its place of origin in the Middle East, but in terms of membership and influence it is a minor world religion. Important regional religions include Zoroastrianism and Jainism, which like Hinduism and Buddhism, have their origins on the Indian subcontinent but have not really gained a hold in other areas of the world. Religions that

TABLE 3.1. WORLD RELIGIONS

Western/Middle Eastern: Religions of the Book

RELIGION	JUDAISM	CHRISTIANITY	ISLAM
The Divine	Monotheistic God (sometimes called by the Hebrew name Yahweh)	Monotheistic God (triune, three persons: Father, Son, Holy Spirit. The Son is Jesus, the Christ, Savior/Redeemer)	Monotheistic God (sometimes called by the Arabic name Allah)
Scripture	Hebrew Bible (the Christian Old Testament including the Apocrypha; the Torah is the divine law found in the first five books of the Bible; the Talmud is a collection of interpretive rabbinical writings)	Bible (All consider the Old Testament and New Testament authoritative; some add extra books, the Apocrypha, at the end of the Old Testament; others do not)	Koran (Qu'ran) (The Hebrew Bible is instructive; New Testament tells about Jesus, whom Muslims consider a relatively minor historical figure)
Main Branches	Orthodox Conservative Reform Reconstructionist	Catholic Protestant	Sunni Shi'ite

Eastern Religions

RELIGION	HINDUISM	BUDDHISM
The Divine	Polytheistic (Multiple gods generally considered different manifestations of the Ultimate; Brahma, the creator, Vishnu, the preserver, and Shiva, a destroying god, are most important; these male gods also assume female forms)	Nontheistic (Siddhartha Gautama, the Buddha, is an enlightened one whose teachings provide guidance)
Scripture	Veda; Bhagavad Gita (The Veda is a collection of Indian sacred literature; the Bhagavad Gita, or "Song of the Blessed Lord," is part of a longer epic poem that conveys classic religious beliefs)	Sermons and writings by the Buddha (The first sermon contains the Four Noble Truths of Buddhism)
Main Branches	Nonsectarian Bhakti or devotional Neo-Hinduism	Mahayana Theravada

began in one nation and remain important primarily in that nation include Shintoism in Japan, Confucianism and Taoism in China, and The Nation of Islam in the United States. The Unification Church began in South Korea but now is more important in the United States than in its place of origin.

Regardless of whether a religion is a world, regional, national or local one, most can be typed as Eastern or Western. Of the world religions, two are Eastern. Three began in the Middle East. Eastern world religions are Hinduism and Buddhism. Judaism, Christianity and Islam began in the part of the Middle East that is now the nation of Israel. Judaism and Christianity are usually classified as Western religions because they spread first into Europe and then throughout the world. Because of its theological affinity to both Judaism and Christianity, Islam is best classified as a Western religion, although it is strongest in the Middle East, northern Africa and Indonesia.

Theologically, the Western religions are monotheistic. Judaism, Christianity and Islam are all "religions of the Book." That is, their basic beliefs are found in written scriptures, parts of which they share. All trace their origins to one God and to the covenant between that God and Abraham. Their understanding of that God and of the covenant relationship makes them essentially "one chance" and "one way" religions.

With the exception of Zoroastrianism, Eastern religions are not monotheistic. Hinduism is polytheistic; Buddhism is essentially non-theistic, leading some scholars and some Buddhists to consider it more a philosophy than a true religion. Although the indigenous religions of Africa, Australia, and North and South America do not fit well into this classification scheme, as pantheistic religions they have more in common with Eastern religions than with Western ones.

In truly Eastern religions, time is endless. People pass through cycles of life, death and rebirth. What one does in one's lifetime affects one's position in the next. Ultimate liberation from evil and suffering may happen in one lifetime or over the course of many. Both Hinduism and Buddhism make room for multiple paths that lead to that ultimate liberation. Therefore, Eastern religions more readily accommodate new gods and new forms of religiosity borrowed from other religions and other cultures than do the monotheistic Western/Middle Eastern religions.

Using Classification Schemes

For making sense of the varieties of religions in America, the general classification schemes serve as a useful guide. Because Christianity is the dominant religion, categorizing religions as Christian, another world religion, or some other alternative is the first step for journalists working in the United States. However, it is also necessary to categorize strains within each religion according to variations in the basic theology and orientation to the world in order to truly make sense of them. Because there are so many religious options, application of the schemes to Christian, other world religions and alternative religions in America are treated in subsequent sections.

For journalists, the schemes that classify religions according to variations in basic theology and orientation to the world are useful for identifying similarities and differences. Further divisions according to the area of the country where they are strongest can provide further refinements. Noting similarities can help make unfamiliar religions seem less strange. The differences are useful for identifying those features of a religion that distinguish it from others and that can fuel tensions among religions or between religion and the culture.

These classification schemes can also help journalists increase their odds of finding sources with different viewpoints. They can also be useful for checking stories to make sure they include representative viewpoints and that they reflect both the range of religious options and the relative influence of individual religions.

Because religion shapes society and is also shaped by it, adding the geographic schemes can help journalists understand a local community as well as regional differences. For reporters who cover international news or foreign relations, understanding the religions practiced in the countries they cover as well as the basic differences among them can be the key to explaining events and issue positions.

Classifying Christian Religions

Christianity may be a monotheistic "one way" religion, but the belief that each person has only one life in which to achieve salvation makes it incumbent that the "one way" be the "correct way." While all Christians believe there is one God and all consider the Bible an authoritative source for understanding God and His commands, disagreements among them over God's nature, the extent and meaning of biblical authority, and the proper way to relate to God and to each other have led to divisions and subdivisions within the religion.

The Catholic-Protestant Divide

For almost 500 years disagreements over doctrine and practice have been at the heart of the division between Catholics and Protestants. However, differences over ecclesiastical versus lay responsibility, the role of the Bible and the proper way to understand it have also caused splits within both Catholicism and Protestantism. Today, they are also producing something of a religious realignment such that some Protestants and some Catholics have more in common with each other than some Protestants do with other Protestants and some Catholics do with others who ostensibly share their faith.

Catholicism is the oldest strain within Christianity. Theologically its most distinguishing feature is insistence there is no salvation outside the church. That church is perpetuated and its teachings are preserved through an apostolic succession of church leaders who trace their authority back through their predecessors to Peter, whom Jesus called "the rock" on which He would build His church. In Roman Catholicism, the pope is considered the successor to Peter. Because of his position in what Catholics consider an unbroken chain of apostolic succession, the pope is the final authority on matters of faith and doctrine.

Protestantism began in 1517 when Martin Luther nailed 95 theses for debate to the church door in Wittenberg, Germany. Theologically its main feature is the insistence that there is no need for a pope or for other religious authority figures to act as intermediaries between people and God or to tell them what they must believe. People can understand and interpret the Bible for themselves. They can also go directly to God with their prayers and receive forgiveness directly from God.

Faith Families

Because divisions within Christianity are primarily the result of different beliefs about the role of the Bible and the proper interpretation of it, schemes that categorize strains within Christianity into theological groupings or faith families have historically been most common and most useful. That kind of grouping is appropriate both within Catholicism and within Protestantism.

By the time of the Reformation, Christianity had already been divided into **eastern-rite** and **western-rite Catholic** churches for more than 500 years. Today, the eastern-rite churches are known collectively as the *Eastern Orthodox Church.* For all practical purposes, the western-rite branch is the *Roman Catholic Church.*

Divisions within eastern-rite Catholicism are primarily along national or ethnic lines. The Eastern Orthodox Church is virtually the same as the Greek Orthodox Church, but there are many other national churches that are part of Eastern Orthodoxy. In America there are at least a dozen such churches whose names reflect the country or region of origin.

For the most part, the Roman Catholic Church has avoided division through the strategy of creating orders or organizations within the church that allow for variations in emphasis, but some groups have broken away. Those western-rite churches disagree with the Roman Catholic Church over matters of doctrine or practice such as the use of the vernacular language instead of Latin in worship services and the role of women and of the laity.

Both eastern- and western-rite churches have as their head a spiritual leader—the Patriarch of Constantinople in eastern-rite Catholicism, the Pope in Roman Catholicism—who, they believe, stands in a direct line of authority that can be traced back to Peter. However, the Roman Catholic Church teaches that papal pronouncements, when made *ex cathedra,* are infallible and stand on an equal footing with the Bible as a source of church doctrine. Neither eastern-rite Catholics nor mainstream Protestants make such a claim for their spiritual leaders. Neither do they accept the distinctly Roman Catholic teaching that Mary, the mother of Jesus in his human form, was the product of an immaculate conception and was assumed bodily into heaven when she died.

Luther's rejection of papal authority and his insistence that people are competent to interpret the Bible for themselves vested greater power in the laity than they have in the Catholic churches. However, that authority to interpret the Bible for themselves led inevitably to further splits.

Like Catholicism, Protestant religions can be classified into faith families on the basis of their beliefs and practices. Over the years **Protestant** has become something of a default option for any Christian religion that rejects key elements of Catholic doctrine, including some whose beliefs differ from those that most Christians hold in common. Because some insist that only those who trace their heritage to the Reformation era are truly "Protestant," the term needs to be used with care.

There are seven major faith families or denominations in the United States that are usually classified as Protestant. Each includes several related churches that share the basic theology, but differ in emphasis. The *Lutheran, Reformed (Calvinist)* and *Presbyterian* faith families trace their origins to the Protestant Reformation that swept Europe in the 16th century. *Methodism* and the *Baptist* movement arose as reactions to the established Anglican Church in England. The *Adventist* and *Pentecostal* families represent newer strains of Christianity that trace their origins to religious revivals in the United States.

However, Protestantism also includes many other individual churches and some smaller faith families such as the *Mennonites, Churches of Christ/Disciples of Christ* and *Churches of God.* Some others are often classified as Protestant simply because they clearly are not Catholic. Even though they base their understanding of God on the Bible, some of them reject or are indifferent to such common Christian beliefs as the triune nature of God or the divinity of Jesus. Others have their own unique understandings of the Bible, add their own scriptures to it, or allow for continuing revelations from God. These include the *Jehovah's Witnesses, Quaker (Friends), Unitarian-Universalist, Mormon (Latter-day Saints)* and *Christian Science* religions.

Although differences among Protestant faith families are to some extent cultural and may also involve matters of church organization and practice, there are doctrinal differences among them. Most of those differences center on their answers to the same kinds of questions that gave rise to the Reformation: who is competent to interpret the Bible, how it should be understood, how a person comes to be saved, and as a corollary, the meaning and proper administration of baptism.

Those faiths, such as Lutheranism and Presbyterianism, that predate the Great Awakening or that embody the reformist tradition tend to be **credal**. Those, such as the Baptists, that emerged from waves of revivalism are usually **noncredal**.

In general, most credal churches baptize infants. Most teach that the Bible is God's word and that its message is true. Although most do not believe Bible passages can be understood literally, they expect adult members to accept or acquiesce to specific teachings drawn from the Bible.

Noncredal churches place greater emphasis on an experiential relationship with God than on specific teachings embodied in formal creeds or statements of belief even though many noncredal churches teach that every word in the Bible is literally true. In noncredal churches, membership is the result of an adult, conversion or "born-again" experience through which one accepts Jesus as Savior and then continues to experience His presence in everyday life through everyday behaviors that are in accord with biblical injunctions.

Orientations to the World

As a general rule credal faith families tend to be world-accepting and/or world-reforming. Noncredal ones tend to be world-redeeming and/or world-rejecting. At the same time, credal churches are more likely to be world-redeeming than noncredal ones are to be world-reforming. If at first that seems paradoxical, it is really the logical byproduct of basic beliefs.

Most Protestants who emphasize a continuing experiential relationship with God and who consider the Bible to be literally true also have millennial beliefs. Because they believe the world will end very soon, they are more likely than other Christians to try to redeem the world by saving others before it is too late. Therefore, they are more inclined to counsel people to shun anything that could tempt them away from a continuing relationship with God than to try to lessen temptations by working for social change.

Most members of credal churches agree that it is important to try to save souls because people are lost without a faith in the one true God. While they would also agree that the world will end with the second coming of Jesus, their less literal interpretation of the Bible leads them to see sin in social conditions as well as in individual behaviors. Therefore, they are more likely than members of noncredal faiths to try to eliminate social and structural arrangements that perpetuate sinful tendencies and make it more difficult to reach and convert others. Although their emphasis is often on reforming the world, for them accepting or accommodating the world can also be a pragmatic response to uncertainty. Because they also believe people are inherently sinful and remain sinful even if they have been saved, they find it difficult to believe that imperfect people can understand God and His commands perfectly.

The Conservative-Liberal Continuum

Until rather recently, categorizing Christians as Catholic or Protestant or placing them within a particular faith family pointed to meaningful differences among Christians. However, that is no longer as true as it once was.

At the institutional level, doctrinal differences have broken down or become blurred as the result of ecumenical relationships among churches belonging to different faith families, church mergers, patterns in clergy training and the proliferation of nondenominational churches. At the individual level, greater church tolerance for intermarriage plus a generally more mobile population mean that many people were raised in one church and maintain much of its teachings as part of their belief system even though they now are members of a church whose teachings are quite different.

Therefore, placing churches and church members on a *conservative-liberal continuum* is becoming increasingly common. Where classifications according to denomination focus on what churches teach, the strength of this scheme is that it can be used with faith families, congregations and individuals. It accommodates equally well individuals and institutions who fit comfortably within a faith family, those whose teachings or beliefs have more in common with other strains of Christianity than with the faith family to which they ostensibly belong, and those that are not part of any larger group.

In one version of this classification system, **conservative** denotes little more than a preference for "tried and true" ways of doing things. **Liberal** means primarily openness to change. However, neither preference may have much to do with accepting or rejecting official teachings of any particular faith family. Within Roman Catholicism, for example, conservatives generally accept papal and ecclesiastical authority; liberals are more attracted to the Protestant belief that people should test church teachings against their own understanding of the Bible. However, many conservative Catholics are uncomfortable with the changes in doctrine and practice that were brought about by Vatican II; liberals are more likely to accept changes such as the use of English in worship services and a greater role for the laity.

In the other version, the endpoints on the conservative-liberal continuum roughly reflect the distinction between credal and noncredal or revival and reform strains within Protestantism. Typically, Christian denominations and individuals are placed into categories according to their agreement/disagreement with items asking about belief that the Bible is inerrant and literally true, the imminent return of Jesus to earth, and the importance of being born again. Those that disagree with the doctrinal statements go into the liberal category. Those that agree with them are classified as conservative, but the conservative category is usually further subdivided. Those who strongly agree with the born-again question but agree less strongly with the other statements may be placed in an **intermediate, moderate** or **evangelical** category. At the individual level, people from any denomination or church may fit into any camp, although the proportions usually reflect the institutional position (Table 3.2).

In spite of its general utility, the definition of the categories and the labels given to the endpoints on the continuum can easily be misinterpreted. The doctrinal statements that make up the measure of conservatism/fundamentalism are the "fundamentals" as outlined in a tract written in protest against the teachings of most credal churches. Because the belief in an inerrant and literally true Bible and the importance of the born-again experience are not part of Catholic or classic Reformation Protestant teachings, there is nothing inherently fundamental or conservative about believing them. Neither is there anything inherently liberal or un-Christian about rejecting them. Yet it is very easy to assume that those who agree with the doctrinal statements are truly Christian and truly religious, while those labeled "liberal" merely claim to be Christian but really are secular. Substituting the term *mainline* for those churches that were the dominant form of Protestantism for more than 400 years suggests they have the correct understanding of God's Word. Using *old-line* instead of *mainline* can be equally offensive to "conservative" Christians, just as describing beliefs they do not share as "conservative" or "fundamental" can offend those in the liberal or mainline category.

In some cases journalists can avoid giving offense to one group or the other by using a more precise term for a more general label— *Southern Baptist* for *conservative Christian* or *evangelical; United Church of Christ* for *mainline* or *liberal*. In other cases, they may be able to insert enough information about what churches teach or people believe to let audience members draw their own conclusions about where subjects fit on the continuum. However, those strategies will not always work. Terms drawn from the conservative-liberal classifications are so commonly used that eliminating them is almost impossible. Coining new terms would be counterproductive. Therefore, the

TABLE 3.2. PLACEMENT OF SELECTED DENOMINATIONS ON THE
CONSERVATIVE-LIBERAL CONTINUUM

Fundamentalist (Orthodox)	Conservative/Moderate (Evangelical)	Liberal (Mainline)
ADVENTIST FAITH FAMILY		
Adventist (most) Seventh-Day Adventist		
BAPTIST FAITH FAMILY		
Baptist (most)	Southern Baptist Convention	American Baptist Churches in the USA
LUTHERAN FAITH FAMILY		
	Lutheran Church–Missouri Synod Lutheran Church–Wisconsin Synod	Evangelical Lutheran Church of America
METHODIST FAITH FAMILY		
Free Methodist Primitive Methodist Wesleyan Church	Evangelical Methodist Church Southern Methodist Church	United Methodist Church African Methodist Episcopal Church African Methodist Episcopal Church Zion
PENTECOSTAL FAITH FAMILY		
Pentecostal (all) Assemblies of God Churches of God Full Gospel Church of the Foursquare Gospel		
PRESBYTERIAN FAITH FAMILY		
	Presbyterian Church in America	Presbyterian Church USA
REFORMED (CALVINIST) FAITH FAMILY		
	Christian Reformed Church in North America Reformed Church in America Reformed Church in the United States	United Church of Christ
OTHER DENOMINATIONS		
Amish Brethren Church of the Nazarene Jehovah's Witnesses Mennonite	Church of Jesus Christ of Latter-day Saints Evangelical Free Church of America Friends (some)	Church of Christ, Scientist Churches of Christ/Disciples of Christ Episcopal Church Friends (most) Unitarian-Universalist

best journalists can do is to let people use the labels they prefer to describe themselves and their organizations, resolve not to let people label each other without checking to see if the label is appropriate and acceptable, and then define the term carefully so people can understand the way the label is being used within the context of a particular story.

Other World Religions in America

All of the other world religions are also present in America and, like Christianity, all were brought here by immigrants. Over time, the number of adherents to these world religions has grown, but their members still make up less than 10 percent of the population. In the United States today, less than 3 percent of the total population is Jewish. Although Islam appears to be growing rather rapidly, most surveys put the number of Muslims in the United States at under 3 percent of the total population. Together, Hinduism and Buddhism account for another 1 or 2 percent.

Like Christianity, none of these world religions is monolithic. Each has diverse strains that can be classified according to their doctrine and orientation to the world or placed on a conservative-liberal continuum. Some strains can also be classified along ethnic lines.

In the United States, as throughout the world, there are four or five main branches of **Judaism.** World-shunning strains include *Orthodox Judaism* and *Hasidic Judaism.* The *Conservative, Reform,* and *Reconstructionist* branches are, in order, increasingly more liberal in their interpretations of scripture and rabbinical teachings.

Most Jews can also be classified as *Ashkenazim* or *Sephardim.* The Ashkenazim, who once lived in Europe and especially eastern Europe, are the largest group in the United States. A smaller number of Sephardim came from Asia Minor where they had taken refuge after being driven from Spain or Portugal. Although those geographic distinctions do little to explain doctrinal divisions within Judaism, they are commonly used in writings about Jews and Judaism and have some value in explaining cultural differences.

Some Muslims have been in the United States for at least a century, but most have arrived since the end of World War II. In the United States, most Muslims belong to the *Sunni* branch of **Islam,** which on a worldwide basis accounts for 85 percent of all Muslims, but some belong to the *Shi'ism* branch.

Sunnis attempt to follow their religion exactly as it was established by the Prophet Muhammad and the four caliphs who succeeded him, although there are several schools of thought about how those teachings should apply to current conditions. Shi'ites believe in the possibility of continuing revelations from God, but those revelations combined with the circumstances surrounding the split between Sunnis and Shi'ites over lines of ecclesiastical authority lead the Shi'ites to see themselves as the true defenders of the faith. Therefore, Shi'ism is generally considered the conservative/fundamentalist branch of Islam. It is the branch that gave rise to the Islamic revolution that replaced the secular government of Iran under the shah with a government under the religious leadership of an ayatollah.

In the United States, **Hinduism** is also primarily a religion of recent immigrants. There are four main religious strains, each with multiple variations. Most immigrants from India and their descendants belong to the *nonsectarian, Bhakti* or *devotional* strains. Others belong to the *Neo-Hindu reformist-nationalist* strain or are part of the *guru-internationalist-missionizing* strains. The Self-Realization Fellowship of Los Angeles, the Spiritual Regeneration Movement (Transcendental Meditation), the Siddha Yoga Movement and the International Society for Krishna Consciousness are the Neo-Hindu variants most popular with Americans who are not of Indian descent.

Unlike Islam and Hinduism which are rather recent imports, **Buddhism** has been a part of the American religion scene for well over 100 years. In the 1840s and 1850s intellectuals such as Henry David Thoreau and Ralph Waldo Emerson picked up and incorporated Buddhist beliefs into their own philosophies; Asian immigrants brought it with them when they came to work on the railroads. At the end of the 19th century, Asians also sent Buddhist missionaries to the United States.

Although there are many kinds of Buddhism in the United States today, there are two main branches: the *Mahayana,* widely practiced in China, Japan and Korea; and the *Therada,* originally practiced in South and Southeast Asia. Of the two, the Mahayana is the more liberal version. While the *Jodu Shinshu* strain, represented by the Buddhist Church of America, and the *Pure Land* strain are popular with Asian Americans, those who are not of Asian descent have found the intuitive *Zen* strain most attractive. Because Zen, in particular, is a godless religion, many engage in its meditational practices while maintaining ties to Christianity.

Other Religions in America

Regardless of whether there are 1000 religions in the United States or 4000, at least three-fourths of them are generally classified as *alternative religions* or *new religious movements*. Theologically they might be classified according to the number and nature of the gods. They might also be classified as primarily Eastern or Western, a new creation, an import or a revival of some religion currently practiced or formerly practiced somewhere else, or as occult. However, those categories are not mutually exclusive, nor are they exhaustive. An import of a national religion, for example, might be Eastern, it might be more Western, or it might not fit well into either category. Some of these alternative religions are also complex blends of two or more strains within a single religion or a blend of strains from different religions.

Therefore, it is somewhat simpler and at least as useful to classify them according to their place of origin and, within those categories, by their roots. According to such a scheme, religions may be classified as **imported religions** and **indigenous religions.** Those two categories can, in turn, be subdivided into religions that are currently *practiced elsewhere, revivals of older religions, blends of several religions or religious strains,* and *new creations.*

While it is impossible to list all the religions that might fall into each category and subcategory, some are clearly more noteworthy than others. Imports that have relatively large followings or that have made some impact and that are currently practiced elsewhere include Tao, Confucianism, the Baha'i faith, the Unification Church, voodoo and santeria. Imported blends include Sufi, Rastafarian, and New Age religions. Revivals include theosophy, Druidism, goddess worship, neopaganism and witchcraft.

Although they are similar to pantheistic religions practiced in other areas, the Native American religions certainly qualify as important and entirely indigenous. The quite different Church of Scientology, founded by the science fiction writer L. Ron Hubbard, qualifies as an important indigenous new creation. The Nation of Islam is an indigenous new creation that borrows from Islam but also contains some features of Christianity.

Other Considerations

Journalists who write about religion quickly discover there are regional and demographic differences among religions, among faith families within them and among those institutions and people who are religious conservatives and those who are classified as being more liberal. Although it is impossible to avoid classifying religion and then using those classifications to explain differences, classifying them needs to be done carefully.

Geographic differences can be quite useful for explaining local cultures and for noting regional similarities and differences, but relying too much on them or on demographic distinctions can easily lead journalists to attribute to religion behaviors and opinions whose roots lie elsewhere. Both regional differences and demography may result more from individual choice, missionary activity, residential patterns or history than from anything inherent in particular religions.

In general, rural areas of the United States are more Protestant than are urban areas. The East and West coasts and large cities are religiously more diverse than the rest of the country.

Judaism is strongest in the Northeast; Hinduism and Islam are more common in large eastern cities and university towns than elsewhere. Buddhism and other Asian religions are most common on the West Coast and in university towns. Alternative religions can be found anywhere, but they are more numerous in large cities, the Northeast and on the West Coast.

Roman Catholicism has a strong presence in major East Coast and Midwestern cities and in the Southwest. Eastern-rite Catholic churches are most numerous in large cities of the East and Midwest. Protestantism is everywhere, but conservative Protestant churches are dominant in the South; other Protestant churches are generally stronger in other areas of the country. Historically, the South is "Baptist country"; the Midwest and Great Plains are "Methodist." There is a strong Lutheran presence in the Dakotas and Minnesota. Utah and its neighboring states make up the "Mormon empire."

There is a Korean Presbyterian Church in America, but Catholicism and Lutheranism are the most divided along ethnic lines of all major Christian faith families. Although theological differences among them are minor, there are at least a dozen eastern-rite Orthodox Churches, each with its own ethnic identity. Similarly, Roman Catholic parishes in large Eastern or Midwestern cities may have a strong Irish, Italian, or Polish identity and those in the Southwest may be heavily Hispanic, but their ethnic identity shows up primarily in church names, the saints' days they choose to celebrate and in church festivals. In both membership and emphasis Lutheran churches often retain elements of their German or Scandinavian heritage. Some local churches still conduct services in languages other than English, at least on an occasional basis.

Doctrinal differences, to the extent they divide the more conservative German Lutheran churches from the more liberal Scandinavian ones, can be traced to Old World conditions that influenced decisions to emigrate. Similarly history, and particularly slavery and the ensuing segregation, explains the existence of predominantly African American Protestant churches.

Major black churches within the Methodist faith family include the African Methodist Episcopal Church, the African Methodist Episcopal Church Zion, and the Christian Episcopal Church; within the Baptist faith family, the National Baptist Convention, USA and the National Baptist Convention of America are African American. The Church of God in Christ is an African American Pentecostal church.

Although they are rarely a product of religious beliefs, both religions and local congregations exhibit stratification by race, ethnicity, education and income. However, almost every religion and almost every congregation has some members who have little education and are quite poor and others who are highly educated and affluent. Therefore, generalizations can be misleading and offensive. In any case, demographics change over time.

Schemes that attempt to categorize religions by geographic area, race or ethnicity, or social class are, like all classification schemes, an attempt to impose order on chaos. They highlight some features while ignoring others. At best, they can help journalists recognize theological similarities and differences as well as similarities and differences in lifestyles, interests and goals. Used carefully, they can serve as a guide for finding relevant sources and for checking to make sure stories are thorough and comprehensive. But they are just a guide. Used carelessly, they can lead reporters to overlook essential elements of a faith or cause them to spread offensive stereotypes.

For Further Reading

Ahlstrom, Sydney. *A Religious History of the American People*. New Haven, Conn.: Yale University Press, 1972.

Chapters in this standard history provide detailed information about Catholicism, Judaism and most forms of Protestantism in America. There is also some limited discussion of non-Christian religions.

Haddad, Yvonne Yazbeck, and Jane Idleman Smith. *Muslim Communities in North America.* Albany: State University of New York Press, 1994.

This book provides information on Muslim and Muslim-related communities in major cities. Among the major groups discussed are Shi'ism, Nation of Islam, Dar-ul-Islam Movement, Bawa Muhaiyaddeen Fellowship, and the Five Percenters.

Hopfe, Lewis M. *Religions of the World,* 6th ed. New York: Macmillan, 1994.

This introductory textbook focuses on the history and development of eight major world or regional religions as well as Native American and African religions. Introductory chapters define religion. Excerpts from sacred texts, illustrations and a glossary are helpful features.

Kurtz, Lester. *Gods in the Global Village: The World's Religions in Sociological Perspective.* Thousand Oaks, Calif.: Pine Forge Press, 1995.

The primary value of this textbook lies in its use of themes borrowed from the sociology of religion to examine the nature of religion and of religious responses to problems such as modernity and multiculturalism. However, Chapter 2 is a nice overview of the five major world religions. Other information about them can be found by referring to the excellent index.

Miller, Timothy. (ed.). *America's Alternative Religions.* Albany, N.Y.: State University of New York Press, 1995.

Chapters written by academics and other outside experts treat 43 religions or types of religions currently practiced in the United States. These range from "established" Christian alternative (Quaker, Mormon, Christian Science) to UFO cults and satanism. Appendix I gives a thumbnail sketch of over 100 alternative religions.

Neusner, Jacob. (ed.). *World Religions in America: An Introduction.* Louisville, Ky.: Westminster/John Knox Press, 1994.

This basic textbook provides background information on the five major world religions, a clear description of the variants practiced in the United States and a helpful listing of major festivals. There are also separate chapters on other Asian religions, Eastern Orthodoxy, Roman Catholicism and Protestantism and Native American religions, as well as discussions of Hispanics and their religions, the place of women in various religions and the relationship between religion and politics and culture.

Smith, Tom W. "Classifying Protestant Denominations," *Review of Religious Research* 31(1990):225-245.

This article examines and then uses various criteria to locate well over 100 Protestant denominations on the conservative-liberal continuum.

Williams, Raymond Brady. *Religions of Immigrants from India and Pakistan: New Threads in the American Tapestry.* New York: Cambridge University Press, 1988.
This book provides information on beliefs, demographic characteristics and adaptive strategies of the Hindu, Jain, Sikh, Muslim, and Zoroastrian religions as well as of Judaism and some alternative Christian religions.

CHAPTER 4

BELIEFS AND BEHAVIORS

The interconnected beliefs that make up a religion form what the sociologist Peter Berger calls a "sacred canopy."[1] Under that canopy, the beliefs work together forming a plausibility structure built of answers to ultimate questions about the meaning and purpose of life.

The beliefs from which the canopy is woven help those who are born under it or choose the canopy as their own to make sense of their life and fit themselves into a cosmic scheme. Where there is only one religion, the canopy it provides extends to the entire society so that there is no threat to the plausibility structure. But where multiple religions coexist within the same society, there are multiple sacred canopies such that their very existence raises questions about the credibility of each plausibility structure.

Evidence that one god or set of gods is the true one and one explication of what any god requires is correct may come from observing the consequences of accepting or rejecting a particular religion, but people live happily and well under very different sacred canopies. Therefore, ultimately choosing to remain a part of the religious plausibility structure into which one was born or to locate oneself under a different canopy requires making a leap of faith. Because final outcomes cannot be proven, one must simply believe that one religion is correct and others are not.

But beliefs do not exist in a vacuum. They carry with them behavioral implications. Just as the beliefs vary, so do the behaviors which follow from them. Long before the idea of culture wars became firmly embedded in popular discourse, theologian-historian Martin Marty noted that religion in the United States has long been "balkanized" in "territories and denominations" that are as much behavioral as theological.[2] That is, people are more likely to choose a religion, define themselves as religious and judge other people and other people's religions on the basis of behaviors than on the basis of what people believe or why they believe it.

Where people can freely choose their own religion, balkanization can occur both among religious options and within each one. As Marty points out, the existence of multiple religious traditions produces a kind of tribalization within a society, but the tribes are usually made up of clans each with its own identity. In American religions, the tradition or faith family is the tribe and congregations are clans. Differences among clans that belong to the same religious tribe can sometimes be as great or greater than differences among tribes. Behaviorally, one Presbyterian clan, for example, may have more in common with a certain kind of Roman Catholic, Pentecostal or Hindu clan than with another Presbyterian one.

At the level of the religious tribe, for clan leaders, and sometimes for clan members, beliefs and behaviors are often intimately connected. Those behaviors can be divided into private ones that are internal to a religion and those that are external. Internal behaviors are those practices and rituals that usually occur in sacred spaces as part of corporate worship. External ones can be further subdivided into those personal expressions intended primarily to support and protect the faithful and other more public expressions intended to promote and extend the faith and its accompanying worldview. Both internal behaviors and the more external ones have implications for the broader culture, but the public expressions are the kind that move religion into truly public affairs.[3]

For generations Americans were taught that religion and politics don't mix, but today the two are so intimately connected that it is almost impossible to report on religion and public affairs in isolation from each other. Religious beliefs motivate civic involvement but different beliefs lead people to become active on behalf of different causes and in different ways. They also place people on multiple sides of many issues.

Knowledge of patterns of civic involvement, issue concern, issue positions and voting behavior can help journalists determine whether any particular instance is likely to be representative or an anomaly. Understanding how, when and why people may express their beliefs at home, among friends, in other relatively private places or in public can also help journalists report accurately and sensitively on the place of religion in people's private lives.

Although journalists are usually most concerned with religion when it becomes public, those expressions are nurtured outside the public arena. Knowing how and why people worship the way they do is key to understanding how religious people conceptualize the sacred and their place in the world and to explaining many disputes within a religion or among them. That kind of knowledge will also help journalists feel more comfortable when they talk to religious people or visit a place of worship.

Internal Behaviors: Worship Practices and Rituals

In dedicated places such as a church, a shrine or other sacred place, there is a direct connection between beliefs and behaviors. In those places, people engage in corporate worship consisting of rituals. Those regularly repeated, carefully prescribed observances or sets of behaviors symbolize values or beliefs. They give character and structure to worship services and other religious observances. Depending on their form, rituals also transmit the faith, facilitate communication with the god or gods, organize life by marking seasons and major transition points such as birth and death, and sustain the faithful as they go about their everyday lives.

In Judaism, collective worship occurs on Saturday, the Sabbath, to underscore belief about God's creation of the universe. Holy days throughout the year serve as remembrances of God's interventions on behalf of his people. Membership in the faith community is by birth, but it is noted with circumcision for male babies and later by a ceremony, the bar mitzvah for boys and bat mitzvah for girls, marking their full participation in it. When men wear a skull cap, or yarmulke, for worship it serves as a reminder of their community, their traditions and their position as God's chosen people.

Although some Christians, such as the Seventh-Day Adventists, retain Sabbath worship as a reminder of God's creation, most Christians worship on Sunday in remembrance of the resurrection of Jesus following his death on the cross. The two major holy days, Christmas and Easter, mark Jesus' birth and resurrection. Other minor holy days serve as reminders of God's intervention in history, important occasions in the earthly ministry of Jesus or in the life of the church.

Catholicism and those credal strains of Protestantism that emphasize God's power and majesty and strive to maintain doctrinal purity
and authority most often have highly stylized, liturgical forms of worship. Because the worship services are always essentially the same,
they create a sense of unity with God and with all believers that transcends time and space. People learn core teachings by reciting creeds
and listening to passages from scripture and to sermons. When clergy
face the congregation, they are teaching; when they face the altar, they
are talking to God. Kneeling or genuflecting at the beginning of the
service or for prayer underscores submission to God and humility in
his presence.

Other strains of Christianity have less formal worship services to
emphasize the immanence of God, the role of Jesus as savior and
friend, and the ability of people to understand God's message without
interpretation or mediation by religious leaders. Instead of kneeling for
prayer, people may sit or stand, sometimes with arms outstretched as a
symbol that they are inviting God into their lives. In some churches,
leaders and members engage in a kind of dialogue as worshippers
spontaneously call out their reactions to the leader's words. In charismatic churches, such as those belonging to the Pentecostal faith family, worshippers may begin dancing, singing, shouting or "speaking in
tongues" as they are moved by God.

For most Christians, the two central rituals are baptism and the eucharist, or communion. In Catholicism and in some strains of Protestantism, both are considered sacraments. That is, they are rituals that
were ordained by God as ways for people to appropriate the gift of salvation.

Baptism marks entry into the community of the faithful. Its placement soon after birth or later in life following a "born again" or adult
conversion experience depends on beliefs about what it means to be
saved and how one appropriates the gift of salvation. In faith families
where infant baptism is practiced, a later confirmation ceremony, considered a sacrament among Catholics and a rite of passage by most
Protestants, is the gateway to full adult participation in the religious
community.

In Catholicism and in most credal forms of Protestantism, commu-
nion is a sacrament through which God continues His gift of salvation.
Catholics believe the bread and wine become the body and blood of
Jesus freely given on the cross as the priest or minister reads the

"words of institution" from scripture. Lutherans also believe the bread and wine become the body and blood of Christ, but they do not believe the elements lose their everyday nature. In most other Protestant churches communion is simply a remembrance of the "Last Supper" Jesus had with his disciples before his crucifixion, rather than a sacrament. They do not believe the bread and wine become body and blood. In fact, many Protestant churches use grape juice instead of wine. Those that emphasize God's continuing presence or ongoing revelations rarely if ever include communion among their ritual practices.

As a way of life embedded in a religious community, the central ritual in Islam is the call of the faithful to prayer five times a day. In the United States, the call from the minaret of the mosque that is the center of an Islamic community rarely exists, but the worship remains. Although noon on Friday is the traditional time for corporate worship, in the United States corporate worship usually occurs on Sunday. The service begins with a reading from the Qur'an that is the basis for the message of the day, but the service is organized around the second pillar of the faith: the call to regular individual and communal prayer. To underscore the oneness and majesty of God and the equality of all people before that God, Muslims face Mecca for prayer and then turn to their neighbors at the end of the prayer with the traditional greeting of Salaam, "peace."

Although most do not consider it absolutely necessary, corporate or temple worship is also common in Eastern religions. Services may include acts of teaching, devotion or meditation. In Buddhism and in some strains of Hinduism, the leader may engage the faithful in guided study and reflection on sacred texts. More often, however, worship centers on devotional practices—offering of gifts, bowing or prostrating before images of the Gods or to spiritual guides or teachers as their representatives. In some strains of Eastern religions, chanting facilitates communication with the Gods much as prayer does in Western religions. Like the prayers of Christians, some chants preserve and transmit core beliefs, while others facilitate communication with the divine or an infusing of the sacred. Meditation practices such as those popularized as "yoga" are another means of becoming one with the supernatural and opening oneself to divine guidance. In Christianity a similar ritual is the silent worship in Quaker churches.

While too numerous to describe, other religions also have their worship practices and rituals. Most are similar in form, though not necessarily in symbolism, to those of the major world religions. However, sometimes their regular services and their festivals mark the seasons rather than recall occasions in the history of the religion or the lives of their Gods. Where most religions hold their rituals indoors in a space made sacred, some alternative religions hold them outdoors. They may use naturally occurring materials such as plants or minerals in their rituals in ways that underscore the sacredness of all creation or an essential unity between the natural and supernatural world. Most notable of these are the Native American religions, some New Age and occult religions, and the resurrected practice of Druidism.

External Behaviors

Personal Expressions of Religiosity

Probably all religions expect their members to maintain contact with the sacred as a routine part of their daily lives. In some, such as Islam, it is mandatory. In other world religions, it is highly recommended. However, personal expressions of religiosity are not limited to those who identify with an organized religion the way corporate religious practices and rituals are. Many people who consider themselves religious rarely attend worship services. Some do not belong to any formal religious organization. Instead, they nurture their spirituality in the privacy of their homes or in small-group settings.

When those kinds of behaviors are confined to the home or occur only within small-group settings, they are purely private. But even those private expressions of religiosity can have a cumulative impact on the surrounding culture. Moreover, the beliefs often make it impossible to confine personal expressions of religiosity to purely private settings. These more public acts define and identify people as belonging to a particular religion. For the practitioner, they are a badge of commitment and identity that fosters a feeling of belonging to the group. To the extent the religious behaviors are visible to others, they separate people by their beliefs. Thus they serve the function of boundary maintenance.

The most common personal behaviors involve devotional activities, diet and dress. However, personal behaviors also include the countless religion-based decisions people make about how to order their life.

Many Christians have crosses, crucifixes or other religious artifacts in their homes as a constant reminder of their faith or to denote a spot set aside for prayer or religious study. Prayer at home in the morning, at bedtime and before meals is common, but Christians may also pray before meals in a restaurant, in the workplace, in schools and on athletic fields. In those places prayer is more common among Catholics who have learned to make the sign of the cross as a quick prayer and among conservative Protestants who take quite literally the biblical command to pray without ceasing than it is among other Christians who believe prayer should be a private matter between people and their God.

Like them, members of Eastern religions tend to confine their devotional activities to the home. Hindus often display religious artifacts in their homes or set up a shrine as a special place for devotional activity. Buddhists usually seek solitude for meditation.

As members of a religion with little inclination to convert or influence others' religious beliefs, Jews rarely pray in public places. Their devotional activities occur most often as rituals practiced in the home in connection with observances of holy days.

Like Jews, for whom those home-based observances are as important as corporate worship, Muslims consider their religion a way of life. Being a good Muslim requires practicing the Five Pillars of the faith: reciting the creed (There is no God but God [Allah], and Muhammed is his messenger); praying five times a day; almsgiving; fasting; and visiting Mecca at least once. Those requirements cannot be fulfilled solely by corporate worship, but neither can they be neatly confined to the home. Praying five times a day is an obligation that cannot be avoided simply because performing the act would be socially awkward.

Neither can the requirements for Muslims to avoid pork and alcoholic beverages and to fast from sunup to sundown during the month of Ramadan be confined to private spaces. Similarly, for those Jews who keep a kosher kitchen in their own home, following the same dietary restrictions away from home creates a public display of the faith. The same is true for Hindus who follow a vegetarian diet because of their belief in the sacredness of all animal life and for Mormons who abstain from drinking caffeinated beverages.

Neither can religion-based decisions about how one should dress be confined to purely private spaces. While Jews do not usually pray in public or wear symbols of their faith, the beards, broad-brimmed black hats and black garments worn by Hasidic men and the skull caps, or yarmulkes, worn outside the synagogue by Orthodox men clearly separate them from more liberal Jews and from those of other faiths. The challah or a modified form of it worn by many Muslim women, the traditional dress favored by some Muslim men and the red spot or bindi on the forehead of some Hindu women clearly express their belonging and commitment to their religion.

Among Christians, dress codes are less common, but they do occur. The Amish wear dark-colored clothes devoid of mechanical fasteners. Some Pentecostal women do not cut their hair. Short hair, white shirts and ties clearly identify young men as Mormon missionaries.

Because religious beliefs are deeply held, they color all aspects of life and show up in myriad ways. Beliefs that are related to a divinely created order translate into assignments of place on the basis of sex, marital status, race or ethnicity, or socioeconomic status. Those beliefs about what it means to follow one's God inform people's understanding of what each person or kind of person can, may or must do. Such decisions often influence family decisions such as who will pay the bills, who will or won't work and at what kind of job, what name to use upon marriage, what to name a baby and how to discipline children or resolve family disputes. They also inform decisions about what to do for recreation, what and how much to buy and from whom, how much to give away and to whom, and with whom to associate or avoid.

Public Religion

In most cases personal expressions of religiosity are just what they appear to be—purely private instances of people enjoying their right to the kind of free exercise of religion protected by the First Amendment. Sometimes, however, those individual expressions of religiosity are very public statements.

At the very least, expressions of personal religiosity that occur where others who do not share the faith can observe them identify a person as belonging to a particular religion. By implication, they label others as "outsiders." Praying, following a dietary code or wearing a particular kind of clothes or a symbol of the faith may also be an invitation to others to inquire about the religion or the first step in efforts to convert others. However, occasionally they can become, or even be intended as, attempts at intimidation or control as, for example, when an employer conspicuously engages in devotional activities and displays religious symbols in the workplace.

More often, however, religious beliefs become public behaviors with implications beyond the faith-life of the behaver when people take action, speak out or make political decisions that are linked to their core beliefs. They join causes or refrain from joining them, engage in civic or charitable work or choose to be uninvolved; they give to charities or decide to spend their money on something else.

They also take positions on issues and they vote. Therefore, religion has always been a force to be reckoned with. Disagreements about issues, policies, political parties and candidates often stem from different understandings of the Bible and different forms of moral reasoning.

Divisions stemming from basic beliefs occur within and among all religions, and probably also among atheists and agnostics. However, collectively those who are not Christian make up no more than 20 percent of all Americans. Fewer than 5 percent belong to any single non-Christian religion. Therefore, most attention to the role of religion in shaping opinions about divisive issues and in influencing voting decisions has focused on Christianity.

In strictly religious terms, labeling Christians as conservative or liberal makes little theological sense. However, the labels are appropriate for categorizing religious people according to their political preferences and behaviors. In general, conservative Protestants today take positions that, in political terms, are defined as conservative ones. More often liberal Protestants gravitate toward the politically liberal positions.

Those positions derive from core religious beliefs. Conservative Protestants look primarily to the New Testament command to save souls and to the Ten Commandments for guidance. Taking those Bible passages quite literally, they gravitate to issue positions and policies that will save souls by curbing the behaviors they believe are immoral. More liberal Protestants read the Bible less literally. They tend to take their cues from the Sermon on the Mount, the Book of James and the minor Old Testament prophets. Therefore, they more often see sin as manifesting itself in unjust structural arrangements and gravitate to issue positions and policies that would change social and economic arrangements.

Over a period of 50 years surveys have consistently shown that both the Protestant churches that are grouped under the conservative label and members of them give higher priority to morality issues than to other kinds of issues. For them, abortion, family values and education issues such as textbook selection and school prayer are the top concerns. In contrast, more liberal Protestant churches now give higher priority to matters of economic and social equity and diversity.

Where the tendency to read the Bible literally and consider it authoritative on all matters combined with a basically world-shunning and conversionist theology leads many conservative Protestants to believe that America should be a Christian nation, liberal Protestants find little biblical support for that idea. Liberal Protestants' interest in equity combined with their less literal reading of the Bible leads them, along with Catholics and Jews who suffered most under the *de facto* Protestantism that once prevailed, to oppose prayer in public schools. Conservative Protestants generally support it.

The relative weight they attach to the Sermon on the Mount versus the Mosaic Law leads liberal Protestants to favor equal rights for women and minority groups, including homosexuals. Conservative Protestants more often see inequalities, especially those between the sexes, as ordained by God. For them, homosexuality is primarily a sinful lifestyle choice.

On the matter of abortion, very few on either side of the debate are really "pro-abortion." In general, both sides recognize the fetus as human and agree that an abortion kills. Most would also agree that abortion is not an acceptable alternative to birth control. But where conservative Protestants take the commandment "Thou shalt not kill" literally, liberal Protestants more often base their pro-choice position at least partly on the Sermon on the Mount which adds to that commandment "whoever says, 'You fool!' shall be liable to the hell of fire."[4]

Where conservative Protestants believe killing an unborn baby is always wrong because the baby is innocent, they usually accept the killing that occurs through the death penalty, in wars and sometimes in self-defense. In those cases, they see the victim as living outside God's law and, therefore, guilty. Liberal Protestants more often consider the life of the mother and of the baby of equal importance. They reason by analogy from classic Christian distinctions between just and unjust wars to categorize abortions, wars and the death penalty as acceptable or unacceptable depending on circumstances.

The idea of just and unjust wars has its origins in Catholic theology, but to the Roman Catholic Church abortions are always examples of an "unjust war." At the same time, the Church links its stance on abortion to its positions on other issues in ways most conservative Protestants do not. Church teachings on abortion, contraception, the death penalty and war are part of a "consistent ethic of life" that also links them to concern for social and economic justice.

Catholic teachings about human sexuality and its purpose lead them to side with conservative Protestants on morality issues, but teachings about social responsibility as articulated in papal pronouncements and the bishops' statements on peace and justice often lead them to side with the more liberal Protestants on other issues. For similar reasons, Muslims and African American Christians usually side with conservative Protestants on morality issues. They tend to side with more liberal Protestants on economic and social justice issues.

Because of their religion's emphasis on engaging in charitable works and because of their long experience living as a despised people, Jews also attach more importance to the peace and justice issues than to matters of private morality. However, on Middle Eastern policy issues, their concern for a Jewish homeland more often coincides with the position of conservative Protestants whose millenarian views also give a special place to the nation of Israel. Muslims, of course, oppose an Israeli homeland for both religious and pragmatic reasons. For most liberal Protestants and Catholics, the existence of a Jewish homeland is, at best, a minor part of their theology.

Other Considerations

Personal expressions of private religiosity need to be interpreted with care. In some cases they may not be what they appear to be. For example, many conservative Christians wear clothing with Christian messages or logos as a symbol of their faith; many also wear jewelry bearing Christian symbols such as a dove, angel or cross. But Catholics have always worn crosses. Many more liberal Protestants also wear crosses, angel pins or clothing with Christian messages as do others for whom such things are little more than a fashion statement. Similarly, carrying or wearing a crystal is common among practitioners of New Age spirituality, but the practice is not confined to them. Christians often wear crystal jewelry simply because they find it attractive.

Even when personal expressions of religiosity are what they appear to be, motives can easily be misinterpreted or misrepresented. The same is true when religion enters the public arena. Patterns exist. But they are just that—patterns. Not everyone who belongs to a particular religion will exhibit the expected behavior. Moreover, patterns can change.

The influence of religion on party preference and on actual voting decisions, for example, is blurry at best. Historically, mainline Protestants aligned themselves with the Republican Party, whose positions most often coincided with establishment self-interest. But so did African Americans who, for many years, saw that party as the "Party of Lincoln" who freed the slaves. Partly because of the Republican policies during the reconstruction era and partly because of their generally lower socioeconomic status, conservative Protestants in the South gravitated to the Democratic Party, even though that allied them politically with Catholics and Jews who viewed the Democratic Party as the friend of the poor and the immigrant because of its social and economic policies.

Many religious people still vote in accord with those historic patterns, but over the past 20 years something of a religio-political realignment has occurred. As the Republican Party increasingly identified itself with morality issues such as abortion and "family values," it lost much of its image as the Party of Lincoln. Meanwhile the economic and civil rights policies of Presidents Franklin Roosevelt, Harry S Truman, John F. Kennedy and Lyndon Johnson identified the Democratic Party even more closely with the interests of those outside the economic and cultural mainstream. In response, Protestant African Americans moved into the Democratic Party while conservative white Protestants began to shift their allegiance to the Republican Party. Catholics became swing voters, sometimes siding with Republicans because of their platform on morality issues or out of economic self-interest as their socioeconomic status improved, but on other occasions preferring the Democratic Party for its positions on social and economic justice issues.

As those voting patterns suggest, religion plays a role, but human behavior is much too complex to be fully explained by any one factor. Both those people who are highly religious and those who are not are subject to cross-pressures. Equally compelling core beliefs or loyalties to family members or friends with different values may pull them in opposite directions, as may self-interest.

People who are tightly tied to their local church through leadership roles and activities beyond worship attendance and who have many friends within the church will usually take positions more in line with those of their church than will others with more casual church ties. However, motives for the ties also have their effects. People who become part of a religion for self-serving reasons—simply to make friends or to find an outlet for their leadership instincts, for example—may be less inclined to pay serious attention to what the religion actually teaches than those who are less active but attend out of a sense of commitment to their god or gods.

Patterns are at best a guide. Correlations found through statistical analysis of survey data do not prove religious beliefs cause observed behaviors. People do not always act on their beliefs. Even when they consciously connect their beliefs to their behaviors, they may find different ways to express their faith in the face of cross-pressures. Only careful study, observation and probing can determine whether events, actions and opinions are best explained by religion or by some other factor.

Notes

1 See Peter L. Berger, *The Sacred Canopy* (New York: Doubleday, 1967).

2 See Martin E. Marty, *A Nation of Behavers* (Chicago: University of Chicago Press, 1976).

3 For discussions of religion in public life, see A. James Reichley, *Religion in American Public Life* (Washington, D.C.: The Brookings Institution, 1985); Richard John Neuhaus, *The Naked Public Square: Religion and Democracy in America* (Grand Rapids, Mich.: William B. Eerdmans, 1984).

4 The quote is from Matthew 3:22, RSV.

For Further Reading

Fowler, Robert Booth and Allen D. Hertzke. *Religion and Politics in America: Faith, Culture, and Strategic Choices.* Boulder, Colo.: Westview Press, 1995.

    This basic textbook provides a good overview of the relationship between religions and politics. Helpful features include brief case studies set apart from the text and annotated lists of references at the end of each chapter.

Hart, Stephen. *What Does the Lord Require? How Christians Think about Economic Justice.* New York: Oxford University Press, 1992.

    This analysis of conversations with people from diverse Christian traditions nicely illustrates the variety of ways people can and do interpret the Bible and use it to make informed decisions. The book also provides a thorough discussion of the limitations of survey research as a way of understanding linkages between beliefs and behaviors. Its main weakness is a failure to link what people believe to the teachings of their churches.

Hunter, James Davison. *Culture Wars: The Struggle to Define America.* New

York: BasicBooks, 1991.

Although the author's terminology can create the impression that the "liberal" position is secular, Part IV provides a thorough examination of the way beliefs and styles of moral reasoning can lead to different positions in debates about family, education, the media and the arts, law and politics.

Jelen, Ted. G. *The Political World of the Clergy.* Westport, Conn.: Praeger, 1993.

Jelen, Ted. G. *The Political Mobilization of Religious Beliefs.* New York: Praeger, 1991.

The 1993 book describes the religious beliefs and political positions, teaching styles and authority of clergy from 15 Christian congregations. The 1991 book focuses on members of the same congregations.

Lenski, Gerhard. *The Religious Factor: A Sociologist's Inquiry.* Garden City, N.Y.: Anchor Books, 1963.

Changes in demographics make some of the findings obsolete, but the discussion of the effect of styles of attachment to religious organizations on people's opinions and behaviors makes this classic worth reading.

Marty, Martin E. *A Nation of Behavers.* Chicago: University of Chicago Press, 1976.

An "oldie but goody," this is the eminent theologian-historian's attempt to classify American religions according to behaviors and interests rather than strictly by doctrinal tradition. Embedded in the text are commentaries on journalistic practices and on mass media influence.

Noll, Mark A. (ed.). *Religion and American Politics: From the Colonial Period to the 1980s.* New York: Oxford University Press, 1990.

This is the handiest source of information about religious influences in elections prior to the 1980s. For the modern era, the chapter on Roman Catholics and the one examining voting patterns from 1948 through 1984 are most useful.

Stout, Daniel A., and Judith M. Buddenbaum. (eds.) *Religion and Mass Media: Audiences and Adaptations.* Thousand Oaks, Calif.: Sage, 1996.

Some chapters describe official church positions on the mass media and media use. Others present empirical evidence of how people from five Christian traditions actually think about and use the mass media.

CHAPTER 5

ORGANIZATION AND LEADERSHIP

A s Tocqueville noted more than a century ago, Americans have a penchant for creating voluntary associations, including religious organizations. His discussion of the ways they use the media for surveillance purposes and then to find allies and promote their causes[1] foreshadowed the resource mobilization approach many sociologists now use to examine religions and explain their influence relative to each other and to other organizations and social movements.[2]

From the resource mobilization perspective, success depends on being able to amass resources and then deploy them to accomplish goals. That is, people join together in groups and organize them into institutions that act as collection and dispersal agencies. With no religion assured of an automatic claim to legitimacy, each must attract members and then use the power that comes from numbers to further its goals. To accomplish those goals, some resources must continually be invested in activities designed to foster commitment to the organization and its goals so that members will willingly remain a part of the group and support it. Committed members create further resources for the organization by donating their money and their time to the organization. With committed members, the organization can use the money and the power of numbers they provide to further goals beyond mere survival. For religions, those goals range from saving souls to influencing public policies.

In recent years it has become fashionable to speak of the decline of organized religion. As people have lost their trust in all institutions, many more consider themselves conventionally religious but choose not to join a church. Others have joined alternative religions or created their own.

With so many options available and increasingly viewed as legitimate, all religions must work harder to attract and hold members than they might have had to do in the past. People now behave more like consumers picking and choosing their religion from among the many offerings in a giant religious marketplace. In fact, applying economic analyses to religions as a way of explaining their "market share" has become increasingly common.[3]

But none of that means that institutionalized religion is irrelevant. Traditional religious institutions such as the church or denomination are still important for many believers. People also join together to create and support religiously motivated special purpose organizations from which they may take their religious identity. The two kinds of religious institutions compete, but they also complement and supplement each other.

Privatized religiosity can have a cumulative impact; however, real power comes with organization. While many people consider themselves religious and find spirituality outside religious institutions, protecting and perpetuating a particular kind of religiosity and carrying out its other demands requires at least a modicum of organization. With organization religions gain the ability to deploy the members and money they accumulate in ways that can have far-reaching and long-lasting consequences.

But there is no single "right" way to organize. Instead, there are types of religious organizations and structural arrangements within them. Those structures and arrangements are the result of a religion's beliefs and the way it fits into the culture, but pragmatic concerns can also shape organizational structure and institutional tactics.

The Church-Sect Typology

Like other schemes for classifying religious organizations, the church-sect typology is partly theological and partly structural. In this scheme, orientations to the world create a background for the types, but the structural relationships between the religion and other aspects of the culture are more central.

In its original version, the typology had only two categories: the

church and the **sect.**[4] Religions of the *church* type had a monopoly within a nation such that citizenship and membership in the church were more or less synonymous. They were the "established church" that legitimated the civil order and were legitimated by it. *Sects* were those religions that arose when some members of the established church withdrew from it because they came to believe that the established church had "lost its way" by accommodating or adapting to the surrounding society.

In that form, the typology was useful for understanding the origin of new religious strains and differentiating them from the established religions in Europe, but it could not cope with the reality of religious diversity. To adapt it to the American experience, sociologists modified the definition of church and added two new categories: the **denomination** and the **cult.**

In this newer version, a religion is generally considered to be a **church** if it

1. claims universality and exclusivity.
2. has a bureaucratic internal organizational structure that transcends national boundaries.
3. relies on leaders with specialized religious training to transmit the essentials of the faith to a relatively passive and uninvolved laity.

As in the original typology, a religion is classified as a **sect** if it

1. separates from an existing religion in protest of its beliefs or practices.
2. sees itself and its members as an elect remnant of the true faith.
3. relies more heavily on an involved and highly committed laity than on highly educated religious leaders to accomplish its goals.

In between and overlapping the church and the sect are **denominations.** Each denomination has its somewhat distinctive beliefs and its own organizational structure. However, from the standpoint of the surrounding culture, all denominations are considered acceptable religious alternatives. They are also more or less acceptable to each other because they do not directly challenge each other's right to exist.

The **cult** is a category introduced to account for those new religions and new strains of religiosity within a nation that do not arise from a schism within an existing religion the way sects do. However, the actual definition of a cult varies. For some, a cult is any religion that is outside the cultural mainstream; for others, a cult is a truly new religion organized around a living, charismatic leader who claims to have a new revelation from the supernatural.

As those conflicting definitions suggest, the church-sect typology suffers from imprecise definitions. It is also inherently Western and Christo-centric even in its expanded and modified form. With the exception of *sect*, all of the terms have multiple meanings. Moreover, *church* and *denomination* are terms that have their origins in Christianity and do not translate well to other religions.

According to the definition of *cult* as a religion that is outside the religious mainstream, all religions are cults somewhere—Christianity in Asia, Islam in South America, Buddhism in Europe, Hinduism in Africa and Judaism almost everywhere except in Israel. As a theoretical construct, the second definition is useful, but by that definition Christianity, Islam, Buddhism, and arguably Hinduism and Judaism were once cults as were many variants within each of them. But because of its pejorative connotations, religions that currently match that second definition do not identify themselves as cults and those that once matched the definition are highly offended by those who would point out their cultic origins and characteristics.

As used in the typology, *church* and *denomination* also have multiple meanings, some of which differ markedly from those of the church-sect typology. According to dictionary definitions and everyday use, *denomination* most often means a particular theological strain within Christianity. As a synonym for a faith family, a denomination may include several groups that are denominations in their own right. Some of those may consider themselves a church or have the word *church* in their name. But *church* also denotes a local unit or place of worship.

Thus, we may speak of Methodism as a denomination. We might also call both the United Methodist Church and the Evangelical Methodist Church a church or a denomination; and, of course, we would call a local place of worship—First Methodist Church on Main Street—a church, but we would not call the place of worship a denomination.

As a further problem, both *denomination* and *church* carry with them certain assumptions about what a religion is and how religions fit into the broader culture. Strains within non-Christian religions may have denominational characteristics, but "acceptability" to the broader culture is problematic at best. *Church* is a word that grew out of the Christian experience. Therefore, it rarely can be used appropriately with non-Christian religions. Sometimes, it doesn't even fit ones that are usually considered Christian.

Eastern religions and many alternatives to the world religions do not really fit the definition of a church. The place of corporate worship for Muslims is usually a mosque; Hindus and Buddhists have temples; Jews worship in a synagogue, but their synagogue may have *temple* as part of its name. Jehovah's Witnesses worship at a Kingdom Hall. Quakers may speak of "going to church," but they also use *meeting* to describe their worship service, to refer to sessions at which they conduct their business, and sometimes for their local place of worship, although that place may have the word *church* as part of its official name. Roman Catholics may use *church* and *parish* almost as synonyms, although the parish is really the geographic unit served by a local church, where Catholics may say they "worship," "go to church" or "attend mass." Mormons also "go to church," but for them the equivalent of a Catholic parish is a *ward*. Several wards that use the same building for worship and other activities make up a stake; temples serve an even broader geographic region and are used for rites such as baptism and the sealing of marriages.

With so many multiple meanings, terms taken from the church-sect typology must be used with care. Religions that fit the technical definition of a cult, for example, are usually better described as "new religions" or "alternative religions" to avoid the implication that the religion is false or inherently dangerous. Because the church-sect typology is a categorization scheme imposed on religions by outside observers, in almost all cases the terms preferred by a religion should be used to describe it.

The typology is most useful for understanding writings about religions. But it is also important because it stands as a bridge between schemes that classify religions according to their orientation to the world and those that classify them according to their internal organization.

Church Polity: The Structure of Religious Organizations

Regardless of theology, some organization becomes necessary to protect core beliefs, transmit them to subsequent generations, and carry out the duties required of the faithful. The types of organization gener-

ally are consistent with core beliefs, but over time they can be shaped
or altered out of a pragmatic desire to accomplish certain goals, including attracting or holding members, or in response to impositions
from the surrounding political and social order. Because the structure
can be affected by forces external to the religion, the church-sect typology forms a backdrop for schemes that classify religions according
to their internal organizational structures.

In terms of their internal organization, Christian religions are frequently classified as **hierarchical, federated, congregational** or **associational.** The most churchlike tend to have organizational structures
of the hierarchical or federated types. The most sectlike religions usually have the simplest structural arrangements. Those religions properly termed denominations exhibit the full range of organizational
structures.

Those that have a *hierarchical structure* often see themselves as the
one true religion and teach that there is no salvation outside that religion. They usually have either a strong and distinctive doctrinal base
or believe that their leaders are the conduit for continuing revelations
from their god. In the Roman Catholic, Eastern Orthodox and Episcopal churches, and the Church of Jesus Christ of Latter-day Saints, for
example, there are levels of leadership, each with increasing authority
and responsibility. Although the details of the arrangement vary from
church to church, ultimate power is concentrated at the top. Congregations, as the basic units, have responsibilities but little real authority.

A hierarchical structure protects core teachings by centralizing authority within a structure that provides its own checks and balances.
Such a structure also gives visible form to belief in an all-powerful,
eternal god. But in the United States, where all religions are voluntary
association, hierarchical churches can be particularly vulnerable to defections. Lay members or clergy at lower levels often believe they
should have more influence over doctrine or practices than they have,
but within hierarchical churches they usually have few effective ways
to challenge teachings or practices with which they disagree.

To cope with those possibilities, the Roman Catholic Church makes
room for different religious orders, each with its own emphasis or purpose under the broad umbrella of a Catholic faith. Mormons rely on lay
leaders who are organized into various levels of priesthood and authority to which all male members can aspire. There are also parallel
organizations for female members.

In that arrangement, the Church of Jesus Christ of Latter-day Saints
resembles most Protestant religions more closely than it does the

Roman Catholic Church. Within Protestantism, the emphasis on members' ability to interpret and understand God's message without priestly mediators more often leads to a division of authority and responsibility between clergy leaders and lay members as well as between the local church and the institutional structure of which it is a part.

The more churchlike denominations often have a *federated organizational structure.* In that arrangement, national and regional leaders are usually responsible for protecting and promoting the faith, but their authority is balanced by rights and responsibilities reserved to the local congregation. Rights and responsibilities may be further divided between members of the clergy and lay members in congregations and also at higher levels within the institutional structure. Representatives of local congregations may meet regularly to elect regional and national leaders. Church leaders' decisions are often by majority vote, but they may become official only when they are approved by a vote of local representatives at the next national meeting.

Because of differences in how authority is divided, Lutherans and Presbyterians might be described as having a "democratic government" and a "monarchical gospel," while Methodists have a "monarchical government" and a "democratic gospel." In spite of their differences, vesting substantial authority within the leadership preserves and promotes the faith. Reserving some to local congregations and to the laity symbolically recognizes the essential equality of all believers and underscores the primacy of individual conscience. While that kind of division of power provides internal checks and balances designed to protect the faith, it also invites schisms and defections when those in the minority cannot accept the majority decision.

In *congregational polity,* all power is vested in congregations. Those congregations work together through the regional and national offices they have created in order to accomplish mutually agreed upon goals, but they do not cede any power to the institution they have created. Those elected or appointed to positions within the central institutional structure do not establish doctrine or set policy as leaders do in hierarchical and federated churches. Instead, their duty is to carry out those functions delegated to them by the congregations for their mutual benefit. However, congregations may also refuse to support regional or national programs and policies with which they disagree without risking loss of membership in the denomination. Congregations remain free to hire and fire their clergy leaders and to set their own policies.

Historically, the Southern Baptist Convention has had this kind of organization, with the central offices coordinating such things as missionary activity and preparation of educational materials. Because each congregation remains autonomous, the problem of schisms and defections from local units is lessened. However, as the recent history of the Southern Baptist Convention demonstrates, the practice of electing people to carry out delegated responsibilities on behalf of all congregations can produce battles for control. When that happens, losers may withdraw from the alliance, just as happens from time to time in religions with hierarchical or federated structures.

With *associational polity,* each congregation is truly autonomous and separate. That separateness occurs most often in noncredal religions of the sect type where it speaks directly to a core belief in the necessity of remaining apart from whatever could interfere with a direct relationship between people and their god. It is the structural arrangement of choice for many fundamentalist Baptist and Pentecostal churches as well as those evangelical churches that consider themselves nondenominational.

In associational polity, congregations or their members may join together in alliances through religious organizations made up of like-minded individuals or groups, but those organizations are separate from the local church. Church members may work in them or through them, but the local congregations do not have any official position in what are essentially parallel religious institutions. People move into and out of these organizations as their interests and priorities shift. Similarly, people move into or out of independent churches. But because there is no coordination of beliefs or practices among congregations, it makes sense to speak of schisms within a congregation but not within the broader religious strain.

While some congregations that choose to be autonomous may, in fact, be truncated hierarchies with authority flowing from God to the leader and thence to the laity, associational polity can also be highly democratic. In those congregations, it is an expression of the belief that people are equal and individually responsible to God. It can also be a powerful survival technique, as it has been for Judaism.

In Judaism diffusion of authority throughout the community underscores the belief that members are the people of God. Unity comes from cooperation among Jews, but the local unit or synagogue exists primarily to serve members and help strengthen them in their faith. For each congregation the rabbi functions relatively independently as the head teacher and local expert on ritual practices. However, primary responsibility for transmitting the faith rests with the family. Because any member can perform all of the rituals of the faith, the survival of the religion does not depend on access to a local congregation.

As a way of life, the practice and transmission of the Islamic faith is also primarily a family responsibility, but authority is more centralized than it is for Judaism. In Islam, the caliphs are the intellectual head of the religious community who interpret the Shari'a, or law, by consensus. While lacking the bureaucratic organization of a truly hierarchical church, there is an ecclesiastical line of authority resembling that of Catholic and Episcopal churches. However, Sunni and Shi'ite Muslims differ, just as Catholics and Episcopalians do, in their understanding of how church authority is transmitted from one generation to the next. In polity, Shi'ism is more centralized and hierarchical; the Sunni branch is more congregational.

Hinduism, Buddhism and most other minority religions in the United States also have relatively decentralized congregational or associational polities. As in the more decentralized Protestant denominations or sects, authority rests in the sacred writings or with the gods, not with an ecclesiastical office or institution. Therefore, leadership depends on the knowledge and charisma of the priests, teachers and gurus, whose primary functions are to maintain a connection to the sacred through devotion or service and to serve as guides and teachers to the faithful who gather around them in congregations or schools.

Those new religions that can properly be described as cults tend to vest authority in the founder, who is the transmitter and interpreter of the new revelation from God. Where the religion is able to attract a relatively large number of adherents in diverse geographical regions, something akin to a hierarchical organization may develop as with the Church of Scientology and the Unification Church.

Leadership in Voluntary Organizations

If sheer numbers and kinds of belief systems pose a problem, so do the variety and complexity of institutional structures. At the same time, no particular type of organization is inherently harder for reporters to cover than any other. Neither is structure necessarily related to newsworthiness.

Hierarchical and federated structures are, by their very nature, complex bureaucracies. Within them, divisions of labor and lines of authority can seem byzantine. In dealing with them, reporters may get the "bureaucratic runaround" just as they do when reporting on the phone company, an IBM or the government. At the same time, because they are bureaucracies, they usually have experienced, full-time staffs.

"Actually, because of the professionalism of many of its top communications people, the Catholic Church at times is easier to cover than some denominations with a high degree of democracy and sunshine laws," says *Pittsburgh Post-Gazette* religion writer Ann Rodgers-Melnick. The same is true for other large and highly centralized churches and denominations. With them, getting access to a religious leader who can speak on behalf of the religion is rarely a problem as it can be with denominations that have a congregational or associational polity.

Fairly large denominations that have congregational or associational polity may have a central office or there may be an umbrella group to which independent congregations belong. Many have a professional staff, but there may be no one willing or able to speak on behalf of the group as a whole. Smaller denominations may have no central office or only a small one with few full-time professionals on the staff. Where local units are truly independent and autonomous, religious leaders can speak for themselves or for their congregations, but not for others.

For those religions that rely heavily on leaders who also have another full-time job in addition to their religious vocation, access can be particularly difficult. That can be as true at the local and regional level for the hierarchical and bureaucratic Church of Jesus Christ of Latter-day Saints as for a tiny, independent Pentecostal or nondenominational church. "Sometimes I have trouble getting in the door, literally—the churches are locked around here—and contacting bi-vocational clergy in a timely way can be a big problem," says Marcia Z. Nelson, staff reporter for the *Aurora (Ill.) Beacon-News*.

But making contact is only part of the problem. Top leaders in highly structured religions may be accessible, willing and able to speak on behalf of their religion; but even the most hierarchical church is not a monolith. According to Sister Gertrud Kim, O.S.B., the Roman Catholic Church really has a structure akin to that of a gigantic multinational corporation, with its divisions, units, wholly owned subsidiaries and affiliates. Each has its own distinctive, and sometimes conflicting, purpose and outlook. The same can be true within the hierarchy itself. Because leaders come from different backgrounds and are generally appointed for life at different times and by different superiors, some Roman Catholic cardinals, archbishops, bishops and parish priests will agree with the official church position and with each other; others will vehemently disagree.

The same kinds of internal disagreements among leaders occur in other hierarchical churches. They also occur in denominations with federated or congregational polity where leaders may have staggered terms of office or be elected to fulfill different functions or to represent different constituencies, as is the case for many agencies both within the Evangelical Lutheran Church in America with its federated structure and the Southern Baptist Convention with its congregational polity.

In these arrangements, official positions and practices are newsworthy because of their consequences for the religion as a whole, but so are the internal differences that can lead to defection or schism. Regardless of the official outcome of those internal disagreements, some congregations and some members will accept the official position; others won't. Therefore, conflict and consensus at the local level is also important because ultimately the influence of any religion resides with its members who are its real power base.

In all religions, convincing people to accept a particular religious understanding and work on behalf of the institution's goals is a major problem. As a result, communication arrangements and styles can be as important for understanding the potential impact, and thus the newsworthiness, of institutional positions or activities as the actual institutional structure.

Religious institutions can issue statements, support causes or withhold support and lobby legislators in an effort to translate their vision of a good society into public policy, but impact often depends on being able to maintain and mobilize members who are also religious consumers and voters. Whether a religious institution can do that depends on how well it reaches local leaders and members. That varies across religions and even among congregations. At the local level, displays, books and magazines in the narthex or in a reading room, bulletin inserts, and even the choice of hymns or the leader's speaking ability may lead members of two congregations, located in the same town and belonging to the same doctrinal family, to behave in quite different ways.

In most cases, religious influence is strongest in cases where the religious institution speaks with a single, clear voice through a variety of channels that reach both leaders and members directly with the same message. It will be further strengthened if people are discouraged from seeking alternate sources of information while simultaneously being given help gaining access to supportive information sources that they are encouraged to use. Influence is usually weakest if the institution is silent, if it does not clearly present the linkage as coming from God or if it speaks too broadly across a number of issues without making a clear connection to scripture.

Centralized religions can issue official positions, but there is no guarantee that members will accept those positions and follow their leaders. Because of their size, their internal divisions and the very complexity and sophistication of their theology, both the hierarchical Roman Catholic Church and many hierarchical or federated Protestant ones have difficulty speaking with a unified voice in spite of an institutional structure that emphasizes the one-ness of the faith.

Regardless of polity, the more liberal Protestant denominations also have difficulty maintaining commitment or mobilizing members because their beliefs encourage a teaching style that relies on dialogue and discussion. The more conservative Protestant churches generally have an easier task because their communication style relies on local leaders who consistently link single passages from scripture to a handful of desired behaviors and actions. In the truly independent congregations, influence is further enhanced by the absence of an external bureaucracy. With no conflicting institutional demands, leaders can attract members who agree with them and channel them into supportive groups to accomplish their goals without running the risks of being officially linked to those groups should conflict or controversy arise or priorities change.

Special Purpose Organizations

Local congregations and the church, denomination, sect or cult of which they may be a part are only one kind of voluntary organization. Each of them will also have additional groups through which members and leaders may get involved. Congregations may have women's organizations, clubs for children or senior citizens, boards and task forces. Some churches and denominations operate hospitals and publishing houses. Both they and individual congregations may support social service agencies, relief societies, missionary groups and schools, either as "wholly owned" subsidiaries or as "affiliated" organizations.

Many other religious organizations draw support from more than one faith family but are attached to none. In cities, states and regions there are ministerial alliances or interfaith organizations to address mutual concerns and support causes favored by many religions. Some are exclusively Christian; others are not. At the national level, the National Council of Churches of Christ is the ecumenical organization for orthodox Catholic churches and the generally more liberal Protestant ones. Internationally the equivalent organization is the World Council of Churches, located at the Ecumenical Center in Geneva, Switzerland, which is also home to related intrafaith international organizations such as the Lutheran World Federation.

In the United States many of the more conservative Protestant churches cooperate through the National Association of Evangelicals or the American Council of Christian Churches. The National Conference includes representatives from Christianity and Judaism. Within Judaism, the American Jewish Committee, the American Jewish Congress and the Anti-Defamation League of B'nai B'rith are major organizations.

Historically, Christian missionary alliances and tract societies were the most influential parachurch organizations. Together, they spread both Christianity and literacy. Their publications mobilized people, channeling them into temperance societies and anti-pornography leagues and social service organizations. Both missionary alliances and tract societies still exist, but to a large extent religious magazines, radio and television have supplanted both.

Media-related organizations include the Associated Church Press, Catholic Press Association and the Evangelical Press Association, as well as the Religious Public Relations Council, which works on behalf of religious organizations and causes. For broadcasters there are the National Association of Religious Broadcasters, whose members are generally conservative, and the Protestant Radio and Television Center, whose affiliated members are theologically somewhat more liberal.

As allegiance to the institutional church has declined, media ministries have become increasingly effective ways of reaching both those who are church members and those who choose to be unaffiliated. Televangelists promoted the Moral Majority and then the Christian Coalition. James Dobson's radio programs, newspaper columns and his *Citizen* and *Focus on the Family* magazines support and draw on work from the Family Research Council.

In a climate of culture wars, but with institutional allegiance declining, religion-based special purpose groups from the conservative Concerned Women for America to IMPACT, which is much more liberal on economic and social issues, have proliferated. Many of these groups also act as lobbying groups or political action committees. Although many churches and denominations have their own lobbyists, working through special purpose groups can relieve the churches which channel people and money to them of any overt ties to politics which could jeopardize their tax-exempt status, offend their members or risk organized opposition to the church itself.

Just as the missionary and tract societies effectively mobilized people a century ago, today religious media and religion-based special interest groups are often more influential than churches and denominations. But finding the underlying religious dimension to these groups often requires looking carefully at what is going on in local churches or inquiring carefully of those who promote or join causes because they often do not call attention to their underlying beliefs, their affiliations or their sources of support.

Notes

1 For Tocqueville's analysis of how voluntary organizations amass power, see Alexis de Tocqueville, *Democracy in America*, Vol. 1 (New York: Longmans, Green & Co., 1989), 189-197, 304-312.

2 For an explanation of the resource mobilization perspective, see J. McCarthy and M. N. Zald, "Resource Mobilization in Social Movements: A Partial Theory," *American Journal of Sociology* 82(1977):1212-1239.

3 For a discussion of the strengths and weaknesses of an economic marketplace approach to studying religion, see "Symposium on the Rational Choice Approach to Religion," *Journal for the Scientific Study of Religion* 34(1995):76-120.

4 For the classic version, see Ernest Troeltsch, *The Social Teaching of the Christian Churches* (New York: MacMillan, 1931), 331-343. For reviews and alternative formulations, see Benton Johnson, "A Critical Appraisal of the Church-Sect Typology," *American Sociological Review* 22, no. 1 (1957):88-92; Rodney Stark and William S. Bainbridge, "Of Churches, Sects and Cults," in their *The Future of Religion: Secularization, Revival and Cult Formation* (Berkeley: University of California Press, 1985), 19-37.

For Further Reading

Bromley, David G., and Anson D. Shupe, Jr. *"Moonies" in America: Cult, Church, and Crusade.* Beverly Hills, Calif.: Sage, 1979.
　　　This book illustrates the usefulness of the resource mobilization

approach for understanding nontraditional religions.

Bruce, Steve. *Religion in the Modern World: From Cathedrals to Cults.* New York: Oxford University Press, 1996.

In addition to being a thoughtful study of religious change and the changing place of religion in culture, this book has a nice chapter on the structure of religious organizations based on the church-sect typology. It also provides a useful discussion of the world views and organization of some New Age and privatized religions.

Gilbert, Christopher C. *The Impact of Churches on Political Behavior: An Empirical Study.* Westport, Conn.: Greenwood Press, 1993.

Unlike most studies of religion and politics, this one focuses on the influence of local congregations and interpersonal communication networks within them.

Hertzke, Allen D. *Representing God in Washington: The Role of Religious Lobbies in the American Polity.* Knoxville: University of Tennessee Press, 1988.

This is one of the most thorough empirical examinations of the role of national religious lobbies. Groups examined represent a broad range of Jewish and Christian interests.

Hofrenning, Daniel J.B. *In Washington But Not of It: The Prophetic Politics of Religious Lobbyists.* Philadelphia: Temple University Press, 1995.

This book examines the interactions among religious beliefs, goals, tactics, organizational structure, leader-member relationships and effectiveness of religious lobbying and interest groups. Tables of organizations, their interests, and budgets are particularly helpful.

Liebman, Robert C. and Robert Wuthnow. (eds.). *The New Christian Right: Mobilization and Legitimation.* New York: Aldine Publishing Co., 1983.

Some of the information is a bit dated, but several chapters document the alliances and interlocking leadership arrangements among conservative religious parachurch organizations, interest groups and political action committees. Others examine communication and mobilization strategies and their effectiveness.

Scherer, Ross P. *American Denominational Organization: A Sociological View.* Pasadena Calif.: William Carey Library, 1980.

Church mergers since this book was published make some of the organizational charts obsolete, but this is still the best available guide to church polity. Part One provides information on organization structures within Protestantism, Catholicism and Judaism. Part Two examines religious agencies, including missionary organizations, Bible societies and seminaries.

PART II
UNDERSTANDING
RELIGION NEWS

CHAPTER 6

TRENDS IN RELIGION NEWS

The mass media have always provided news about religion, but the coverage has changed over time in response to changes in American culture and in journalistic practices.

Early American journalism was religious journalism. Publishers understood their papers to be performing both informational and religious functions. Religious language and arguments infused the news as writers interpreted events and issues from a religious perspective intended to promote and defend true religiosity as they understood it. Arguments rooted in religious belief fueled hostility among religions but also provided religious justification first for separation from England and then for the American experiment in self-government.

More than a century later, much journalism was still rooted in religion. In his examination of the yellow press, Robert Park detected two schools of thought. One school, represented at the turn of the century by journalists from established newspapers, believed that "if God let things happen that were not in accordance with their conceptions of the fitness of things," it was their duty to protect public morals by suppressing news about "things that they knew ought not to have happened." The other, represented by the increasingly popular Hearst and Pulitzer newspapers, thought it their right and their duty to report "anything that God would let happen."[1]

While newspapers remained the creation of and the mouthpiece for individual owners/publishers, reporting news about religion to uphold a particular understanding of God's will remained an option. But changing audience expectations and professional norms now make religious journalism of the kind practiced openly by earlier generations the province of specialized religious publications. Today, religion journalism is the norm. For media owners, editors and news directors, news about religion is a commodity like any other kind of content—a subject of interest reported and packaged to attract the widest possible audience. Because that audience is religiously diverse, journalists today apply the same news values to religion news that they do when reporting on other subjects. In religion reporting, the same widely accepted standards of fairness and objectivity also apply.

The Birth of Modern Religion Reporting

The change from religious journalism to religion journalism began with the penny press. Soon after the Revolutionary War industrialization led to an increasingly urban, immigrant and religiously diverse population. In that climate of social, economic and religious change, James Gordon Bennett began publishing his *New York Herald* in 1836 as a cheap alternative to the party papers. Recognizing that people cared about religion, Bennett began the practice of covering religion as news.

In his *Herald,* virtually every religion received attention, but the coverage ran the gamut. Bennett provided extensive neutral to favorable attention to human interest stories about individual instances of charitable and moral behavior, church histories, worship services, revivals and other events, but his paper also carried thorough and highly critical stories about sexual and fiscal improprieties on the part of the clergy and of ecclesiastical interference with individual and congregational affairs and with politics. Individual items could be quite personal and polemical, but taken as a whole, Bennett's religion journalism was essentially neutral and evenhanded. No church was singled out for criticism. None got only favorable attention.

To a society accustomed to the serious political news and commentary provided by the party press, the penny press approach to news was truly revolutionary. As a Scot and a Catholic in a predominantly Protestant America, Bennett wrote as an outsider. Instead of upholding or defending a particular religion or religion in general, he defended religious freedom for all at both the individual and social levels.

Although few journalists today take Bennett as their role model, his approach to religion news foreshadowed modern coverage. Today

Bennett's satire and fiction would be unwelcome in most mass media. Biblical allusions would be lost on many. However, his thorough coverage of local congregations, religious events and people was the prototype for the church pages that became increasingly common after the Civil War. His serious attention to the interplay among religion, politics and money paved the way for treating religion as hard news. But his policy of providing both features and hard news coverage was not quickly adopted by other papers.

In the years leading up to the Civil War, religious beliefs informed public debates over slavery. Because those beliefs divided the nation, coverage of them in papers, which usually reflected the views of their owners, produced divisive religion news. But after the war, people sought peace and stability.

While people generally agreed that personal religiosity is beneficial and should be encouraged, they gradually came to see overt expressions of personal beliefs as unnecessarily divisive. Religious language in public discourse became less common. Gradually the accepted wisdom became that religion and politics don't mix and that neither should be discussed in polite society. Of course the mass media never gave up discussing politics, but the conventional wisdom about religion and its place in society shaped religion news coverage.

For most of the 20th century, religion news has been a product of a three-way division of labor with responsibility for coverage, to the extent anyone was or is responsible, shared among religion specialists, reporters assigned to other beats, and columnists. If religion has often been a second-class beat at newspapers and magazines, historically it has not even achieved that status in broadcasting.

On radio and in television, less reliance on the beat system, a tendency toward more passive newsgathering and a very limited news hole compared to the space available in print media combine to make most coverage haphazard at best. Although broadcast journalists were much slower to recognize religion as news than were their counterparts in print media, cultural shifts and audience demands are producing changes in all media.

Therefore, religion news can look quite different depending on whether one examines print or broadcast media, newspapers or magazines, radio or television or some subset of them. Coverage also differs depending on whether only stories that focus on religion are counted as religion news or whether any story that includes some attention to it also counts. It also matters whether those stories must be produced by a religion specialist and appear in space set aside for religion or whether they can appear elsewhere or be reported by someone who is not designated as a religion reporter.

Newspaper Coverage of Religion

Before the Civil War, religion stories were scattered through the newspaper, but as newspapers became larger, stories began to be segregated by subject matter. Since about 1900 weekly religion pages have been a regular feature of at least four-fifths of all daily newspapers. Until the 1970s almost all religion pages, or "church pages" as they were usually called, were devoted primarily to relatively short stories about local people and events.

Because newspapers frequently provided coverage for churches according to their size and influence in the community, most attention went to well-established Protestant or Catholic churches. Coverage of Christian churches serving ethnic or racial minorities was left primarily to the newspapers serving those communities. Except in urban areas with large Jewish populations, there was little mention of non-Christian religions.

At newspapers, initial efforts to broaden religion coverage came from churches. By the late 1920s most churches and religious organizations had public relations or public information offices. In 1929 they created the Religious Public Relations Council to improve church public relations practices and supplement individual efforts to garner favorable publicity. In 1934 the National Conference of Christians and Jews established Religious News Service to provide the media with an unbiased, alternative source of news about religion.[2]

Both developments led indirectly to more thorough, balanced coverage by increasing the number of available sources and stories from which religion journalists could choose. Those choices were further increased after World War II when religion news became regularly available through the wire services. In 1950 George Cornell wrote his first bylined religion story for Associated Press. A few years later Louis Cassels began covering religion for United Press International.

However, religion remained primarily a local beat at all except the elite papers with large national circulations. Newspaper coverage of national and international religion stories came primarily from reporters working other beats. But those stories were relatively rare.

Most were quite short. Where the church pages created an image of peace and harmony among the dominant churches in the community, coverage in other parts of the paper emphasized conflict or treated religion as a joke, as in the case of sensationalized and inflammatory coverage of the Scopes trial.

That pattern began to change in the 1960s in response to Vatican II, religious involvement in the civil rights and anti-Vietnam War movements and the interest in alternate forms of spirituality spawned by the counterculture. However, the real impetus to treating religion as an important cultural and political force came in the mid-1970s with the rise to power of the Ayatolleh Ruhollah Khomeini in Iran and the election as president of the born-again evangelical Christian Jimmy Carter, the advent of the electronic church, and the rise of the New Christian Right in the United States.

In the early 1980s the *Denver Post* abandoned its eight-page weekly religion section as part of a move to treat religion news more like other kinds of hard news. But other papers added religion pages or expanded them to assure space for stories and to satisfy reader interest. In 1994 the *Dallas Morning News* began offering a weekly section to meet reader interest in serious religion news coverage. A year later, the *Ashland (Ky.) Independent* launched its monthly religion magazine.

By the 1980s routine coverage of meetings had decreased. Religion stories became longer and more issue-oriented, both on the religion pages and in other sections. Journalists began to allocate space according to a diversity approach that provided more information about smaller Christian and non-Christian groups. As conflict and consequence replaced consensus as the dominant news values, attention to mainline Protestant churches decreased, while coverage of conservative Protestants increased.

In 1985 few newspapers set aside more than a single page for religion, but a decade later two or three pages had become quite common. During that decade most papers also redefined religion news. Instead of a narrow institutional definition that emphasized coverage of national religious organizations or local congregations, the new definition was much broader. It made room for more coverage of non-Christian religions and, indeed, for almost anything connected to people's search for meaning and purpose in their lives. Where once the space set aside for religion news was commonly called the "church page," the more generic "religion page" became the common designation. Some newspapers went even further. By 1990 designations such as "religion and ethics" or "faith and values" began to appear.

In spite of a trend to take religion more seriously, many newspapers still treat religion as an expendable beat. Fewer than a dozen papers have ever had as many as two religion reporters. Although they still write the majority of the local stories about religion, religion reporters no longer find themselves confined to producing stories for religion pages. Most religion reporters also write hard news stories that run on the front page or in other sections. Both on and off the religion page, their work is increasingly being supplemented by substantive stories about religion produced by colleagues whose primary responsibility is for other kinds of news.

While both specialists and nonspecialists concentrate on religion news, religious journalism has never entirely disappeared from newspapers. Traces of religious influence show up in all papers. In reporting about religion, that influence most often manifests itself in subtle ways through story framing and word selections that tend to marginalize both sectarian Christians who present a challenge to the religious and cultural status quo and those outside the Judeo-Christian mainstream. For the most part, however, religious journalism is the province of columnists. Cal Thomas, for example, writes opinion columns from a conservative Protestant perspective; Catholic influence can sometimes be detected in columns by William F. Buckley, Michael Novak and George Will; Donna Brigg often weaves religious values into her work. From time to time, leaders from religious organizations contribute their opinions to op-ed pages. Religion pages often feature syndicated columns written from a religious perspective. Many also feature columns by local clergy.

Magazine Coverage of Religion

Even before newspapers began devoting serious attention to religion, news magazines covered religion as hard news. From its beginning in 1923, *Time* magazine devoted a regular section to religion and often featured religious subjects on the cover. Other news magazines followed that lead.

At first, *Time's* religion section was a weekly roundup of short items about religion. Although the section now appears less regularly, stories have became longer and less people- and event-oriented. However, *Time* style still emphasizes action.

Conflict and church-state tension have always been the dominant themes in news magazine stories when religious people or organizations participate in national and international politics or are parties to court cases. After World War II attention to conflict within and between churches became increasingly common, but stories about interchurch cooperation and personality profiles of religious leaders still appear rather regularly. Most stories focus on Catholicism or mainline Protestant religions with membership concentrated in the Northeast or with offices in New York City. Stories about religion in other areas of the United States are less common. Most news sources are theologians or church leaders, not local clergy or laypersons.

Although *Time* and *Newsweek* employ talented religion writers, reporting at those magazines is usually a team effort. Stories are heavily edited to conform to the magazine's editorial position and style. At *Time,* in particular, all coverage, including that of religion, still bears traces of the predestination and manifest destiny predilections of its founder, Henry Luce, who was the son of Presbyterian missionaries to China.

Other general circulation magazines do not have religion reporters or religion columns, but that does not mean they do not carry religion news. Qualities, including *Atlantic Monthly, Harper's* and *The New Yorker,* frequently feature in-depth reports on religious issues and personality profiles of religious leaders. Many other stories that are not specifically about religion include meaningful information about it. Some of the earliest reporting on the growing influence of televangelists, for example, appeared in *Harper's.*

In contrast to the issue-oriented reporting in the qualities, stories emphasizing the role of religion in people's lives began appearing in women's magazines with increasing regularity during the 1990s. *Family Circle* and *Woman's Day* have published holiday features that recognize the religious dimensions of Christmas and Hannukah for years, but during the last decade they have published many more stories than they once did that pay tribute to the place of religion in women's lives.

Radio Coverage of Religion

Radio stations have rarely made religion coverage a priority, although some obtain religion news by purchasing special feeds from wire services, such as the UPI Radio Network, which has had a religion editor only since the 1980s. "The World of Religion" is available to CBS radio affiliates, but only a few large stations such as WINS in New York have ever produced their own religion news programs.

With television, radio lost much of its news audience. Therefore, the trend over the past 40 years has been toward producing 5-minute segments of headline news instead of longer news programs. Most of the time religion finds its way into the newscast only when there is a major event, such as the visit to the United States by Pope John Paul II, or when a person closely associated with a religion is accused of wrongdoing. Because most stations today serve a narrowly defined local market, radio news usually consists of more local than national or international stories. Information for national and international stories comes primarily from the wire services. For local stories, newsgathering commonly consists of a cursory check of local newspapers or some phone calls to government sources.

In contrast to the newscasts, many talk shows do devote attention to religious concerns. In many cases the programs are little more than forums for expressions of public beliefs and opinions that can be supported or contradicted by the host's commentary. However, some include interviews with religious leaders or book authors. In quality, they run the gamut from pure puffery to truly excellent journalistic endeavors.

Some of the best interview segments are on National Public Radio. With its longer newscasts, other kinds of informational programming and a history of active newsgathering, NPR is also the one major exception to radio's general pattern of perfunctory coverage of religion news. In 1993 National Public Radio assigned Lynn Neary to a newly created religion beat. But even before that, NPR aired substantive stories about religion.

Television Coverage of Religion

On national network television newscasts, about 5 percent of all news stories mention religion, but most of those stories are shorter than 20 seconds and are not really about religion. While the numbers are very low, they are not significantly different than those for other kinds of specialty news including news of business, education, science or sports.

With the exception of holiday features, which are often selected more for their visual appeal than for their news value, mentions of religion occur primarily in coverage of political conflict. Because the newscasts concentrate on national and international political news, more than half of all mentions come in reports from religious trouble spots such as the Middle East and Northern Ireland and, more recently, Bosnia. Domestic attention occurs primarily in stories about major court cases or political activities of the New Christian Right.

Television did not make any special effort to cover religion news until the early 1990s when *Time* magazine's religion editor, Richard Ostling, began providing occasional religion coverage for public television's "The MacNeil-Lehrer News Hour." ABC and CBS began running in-depth stories about religion as a regular part of special segments of their nightly newscasts. On CBS those stories are about 4 minutes long; typically they are either "Eye on America" or "Sunday Cover" segments. On ABC they are part of the "American Agenda."

In 1994 ABC became the first television network with a religion specialist when it hired Peggy Wehmeyer who had previously covered religion news for WFAA-TV in Dallas. Wehmeyer's contributions to the "American Agenda" are at least 4 minutes long and are aired, on average, about once a month. Most focus on issues or trends, but some also explore the meaning of religion in people's lives.

Only NBC does not routinely set aside a portion of time on a feature segment for in-depth religion coverage. Its in-depth segments tend to be somewhat shorter than those on ABC or CBS, but they are also more integrated into the newscast. While the feature-segment approach at ABC and CBS has added some depth to the reporting in comparison to what was available 10 years earlier, neither that approach nor the presence of a religion journalist in the newsroom at ABC has had much effect on the overall pattern of coverage. Routine stories still tend to be relatively short ones that simply mention religion without providing much information about it.

At the local level, religion news is usually even less informative. Churches may serve as the backdrop for newsworthy funerals or weddings. People involved in accidents and disasters are captured attributing their survival to God's intervention more frequently than they once were. But as with network coverage, the penchant for live coverage of breaking news sometimes leads to breathless, but shallow and sometimes erroneous coverage as happened in connection with the siege of the Branch Davidian compound at Waco and the bombing of the federal office building in Oklahoma City. Most actual coverage of religion consists of features devoted to local events or projects sponsored by religious organizations.

Only a handful of local stations have religion reporters. Until 1993 WFAA in Dallas and KSL in Salt Lake City were the only VHF television stations with religion reporters. In 1993 KOTV in Tulsa hired Howard Licht; in 1994 WFLA in Tampa-St. Petersburg persuaded Michelle Bearden, religion reporter for the *Tampa Tribune*, to provide one religion package each week and WKYT in Lexington, Kentucky, assigned Hillary Wicai to a newly created religion beat.

Although network newscasts provide some longer analytical or investigative stories and some features explaining particular religions and religious practices, much of the issue-oriented coverage appears as occasional segments on magazine-format shows. Examinations of the place of religion in people's lives and in American culture have, for the most part, been the province of public television, largely because of the work of Bill Moyers.

Content and Meaning

Patterns of religion coverage have changed over time with shifts in public interest and journalistic practices. For those reasons, the patterns also differ among media in any given time period. But along with those ever-changing patterns, another more subtle shift has occurred.

According to classic libertarian philosophy, freedom of speech and press was meant as a guarantee there would be a marketplace of ideas. People would put their information and their ideas into that marketplace and from what was available, people would find their truth. But over time, responsibility has shifted. Where people once expected to find truth by picking through multiple sources, today they more often expect every mass medium to provide them with Truth.

That shift in public understanding of the proper role of the media places a responsibility on journalists that they did not have even 50 years ago when multiple newspaper towns were common. But it places an especially heavy burden on those who report on religion because the truth of any religion and the truth about its meaning for individuals and for society depends in large measure on whether or not one has first made the leap of faith to accept its claims as true.

When religious journalism was the norm, people understood the explanations of religion and its connections to events, issues and issue positions were the views of newspaper editors and writers. With the exception of Native Americans and a few thousand Jews, all readers were at least nominally Christian. Therefore, they generally knew the Bible and were in a position to judge for themselves the "correctness" of the meanings conveyed to them through the media to which they had access.

The idea of the media conveying meaning according to the beliefs of the owners, publishers and contributors remained acceptable as long as there was also agreement that people were responsible for finding truth. But over time, the shift from media as the mouthpiece of their owners and publishers to a less personal style of journalism produced a change in understanding about the locus of truth in news content.

At first journalists saw themselves primarily as stenographers. Truth and meaning came from their sources; the journalist's duty was to report accurately what sources said. In the wake of the McCarthy anti-communist witch hunts of the 1950s, however, the limitations of that approach became apparent. Increasingly both journalists and the public began to take the Hutchinson Commission's recommendations seriously. Where once merely transmitting information from well-connected sources seemed enough, eventually journalists came to recognize that surveillance necessarily means providing a "representative picture" of minorities. Being a watchdog requires telling "the truth about an event" by placing information "in a context which gives them meaning."

Much as Bennett had reported religion news more than a century earlier, meaning, for journalists, became largely a matter of the consequences of beliefs and behaviors of leaders for those who were part of a religious tradition and of one tradition's actions for other religions and for society. However, a search for meaning always raises the question of whose meaning counts. With conflict and controversy the dominant news values, both the meaning of religion in people's lives and the possibility that religion could be a benign or even a positive force for individuals or for society received less emphasis.

Today most journalists consider the move away from local, feature-oriented coverage and toward a more hard news, issue-oriented approach appropriate because they have come to see religion news as serving surveillance and watchdog functions. But the current approach to news has created its own problems. As journalists adopted the recommendations from the Hutchinson Commission, the public came to believe that it is the duty of newspapers to provide them with Truth, rather than their responsibility to examine the various bits of information and reach their own conclusions.

Faced with information that displeased them or interpretations that did not match their own, people lost their trust in the news media and, indeed, in all institutions. In response, some media scholars and practitioners began searching for ways to reconnect with the public. Sensing that conventional news practices may foster a sense of alienation that is inimicable to democratic self-government, some now advocate "civic" or "public" journalism.

Although it is too early to tell whether that kind of journalism will become the norm, the attention it has received suggests that the news values journalists look for in their effort to provide meaningful news may be changing. In religion reporting, renewed emphasis on faith and values in everyday life may be a part of that change.

While civic journalism has merit, no extant model for religion news coverage is without its problems. A hard news approach can overemphasize conflict and controversy even as a more feature-oriented approach underestimates them. Where investigative reporting can make journalists appear to be religion's adversary, a stenographic one can make the media its ally. Taking meaning from believers easily ignores the impact of beliefs and subsequent behaviors for others; but seeking it primarily in the impact of a religion on its dissidents, on outsiders to the faith or on society misses the reality of religion as believers experience it. Apportioning news coverage among religions according to their size in a community presents an image of religious diversity that is quite limited. A diversity approach that seeks out minority faiths can easily inflate their power and influence.

Notes

1 Robert E. Park, "The Yellow Press," *Sociology and Social Research* 12(1927):3-11.

2 Religious News Service is now owned by Newhouse Publications. In 1994 the name was changed to Religion News Service to better indicate the kind of stories about religion it produces. The proper name for the National Conference of Christians and Jews is now The National Conference.

For Further Reading

Buddenbaum, Judith M. "Analysis of Religion Coverage in Three Major Newspapers," *Journalism Quarterly* 63(1986):600-606.

This article compares religion news coverage by specialists and nonspecialists for the *New York Times, Minneapolis Star* and *Richmond Times-Dispatch*. For information on the way religion journalists define and select stories, see Judith M. Buddenbaum, "Religion in the News: Factors Associated with the Selection of Stories from an International Religion News Service by Daily Newspapers," Ph.D. diss., Indiana University, Bloomington, Ind., 1984.

Buddenbaum, Judith M. " 'Judge...What Their Acts Will Justify': The Religion Journalism of James Gordon Bennett." *Journalism History* 14(Summer/Autumn 1987):54-67.

This article provides information on Bennett's religion coverage and on the strengths and weaknesses of his approach to religion news.

Buddenbaum, Judith M. "Network News Coverage of Religion." In *Channels of Belief: Religion and American Commercial Television,* ed. John P. Ferre', Ames: Iowa State University Press, 1990, 57-78.

This chapter provides information on religion news provided by ABC, CBS, and NBC for the period 1976-1986. Other chapters examine the image of religion in other genres.

Hart, Roderick P., Kathleen J. Turner, and Ralph E. Knupp. "Religion and the Rhetoric of the Mass Media," *Review of Religious Research* 21(1980):256–275.

This is the best available research on religion news coverage by news magazines. Data are for *Time* magazine and cover the years 1947-1976. Another report of Hart, Turner and Knupp's research can be found in *Journal of Communication* 31(1978):58-68.

Mason, Debra L., "God in the News Ghetto: A Study of Religion News from 1944 to 1989." Ph.D. diss., Ohio University, 1995.

This dissertation is the best source for detailed information about newspaper coverage of religion since World War II. The newspapers examined include the *Dallas Morning News, Minneapolis Star-Tribune, New York Times, Orlando Sentinel, St. Louis Post-Dispatch,* and *San Francisco Chronicle*.

Nordin, Kenneth D. "Consensus Religion: National Newspaper Coverage of Religious Life in America, 1849–1960." Ph.D. diss., University of Michigan, 1975.

This is the best source for detailed information about religion news coverage between the Civil War and World War II. Newspapers examined include dailies from large and small cities and weeklies from urban and rural areas in the Northeast, Northwest, South and West.

Silk, Mark. *Unsecular Media: Making News of Religion in America.* Carbondale, Ill.: University of Illinois Press, 1996.

In this cultural history of religion news, the author, who is a former writer for the *Atlanta Journal and Constitution,* makes the case that journalists draw on certain forms and assumptions rooted in the culture to report religion in a way that supports conventional beliefs and values.

Sloan, William David. (ed.). *Media and Religion in American History.* Tuscaloosa, Ala.: Vision Press, in press.

The chapters in this book comprise the best available collection of research on religious influences on American journalism in the United States from the colonial period through the modern era.

CHAPTER 7

THE AUDIENCES FOR RELIGION NEWS

P eople probably do not turn to the mass media specifically for news about religion, but that does not mean whether or how the news media cover it is of little consequence. People consider religion news much more important than other kinds of specialty news on which most media lavish far more attention.

In a national survey, people ranked religion news second in importance—just behind news about education, but well ahead of sports which they said is the least important of nine kinds of specialty news.[1] However, when the same people were asked how likely they are to read religion news, the ranking for it fell to sixth place. Education news moved up to first place. For readership, sports moved up to seventh place among the nine kinds of specialty news, but it took first place in audience satisfaction. In terms of satisfaction with the coverage, education news fell to fourth place. Religion news ranked last.

In general, people said it is somewhat more important for newspapers to cover religion than for television to cover it, but the importance people attach to religion news is not related to how particular media cover religion. However, the way media cover it does affect audience attention and satisfaction.

Because of the nature of television, it is almost impossible to gauge audience attention to particular kinds of stories within a newscast. However, viewers probably attend to religion news on television much as they do with newspapers. Where there is a good match between audience interests and coverage in daily newspapers, almost everyone reads religion news. When media pay little or no attention to the subject, reported readership is very low. In most towns, about one-third of a newspaper's readers always or almost always read religion news. Others read news about religion whenever the subject or writing style captures their interest. However, about one-third rarely if ever read news about religion.

For the most part, people are reasonably happy with the amount of religion news. Although they are about twice as likely to say they want more coverage than to say they want less, nationwide most people say the media give enough attention to religion. The problems of audience attention and satisfaction stem from the ways people see the media covering the subject.

Journalists' Perceptions of the Audience

Part of the disparity between the importance people attach to religion news and their actual attention to and satisfaction with it stems from the low importance journalists have historically attached to religion news. Stories of editors and news directors who spike any story even alluding to religion are legion. Although times have changed, as recently as 1980 newspaper editors and reporters ranked religion news 18th in importance out of 18 content areas.

A few religion journalists may overestimate the importance of religion news. Others, taking their cues from their workplace environment, still consider religion an unimportant beat to be endured until it can be escaped. But most religion journalists take the subject more seriously than do those who work other beats.

Studies conducted over the past 15 years clearly indicate journalists are more knowledgeable about religion and more likely to take it seriously than they once were. However, they have been hampered in their work by a lack of solid information about their audience. In a survey of religion reporters conducted in 1985, many said their newspapers conduct readership studies, but very few had ever seen any data about the audience for religion news. When they were asked to describe the audience they served, most admitted they could only guess.

Reporters at small papers guessed that elderly people, shut-ins and those looking for a church home read religion news. Reporters from larger papers thought most of their readers had above average education and income. But very few were able even to guess about the demographic makeup of their audience. Only one-fourth of the reporters, most of whom worked for large papers, thought their readers included people other than clergy and church members. More than two-thirds thought people read religion news primarily to keep tabs on what is going on. Fewer than one-fifth said that people are interested in the spiritual aspect of religion or that they read religion news to learn about political issues and issue positions.

At one level journalists' perceptions of the audience for religion news were quite accurate, but at another level their perception was quite limited. Capitalizing on the general importance people attach to religion news requires understanding that there is no single audience for religion news. There are really multiple audiences, each with somewhat different interests.

Audience Demographics

Studies of the audience for religion news conducted for the American Newspaper Publishers Association in the mid-1960s showed that readers were more likely than nonreaders to be older, female, highly religious and conservative in lifestyle, religion and politics. Most newspaper subscribers said they liked the traditional church page, although only about one-third read it regularly.

The core audience is still made up of older, conservative women with lower socioeconomic status, who are religious and active in their church. But buried within the demographics there is a second audience made up of people who are usually younger, better educated and less conservative than the "typical" audience. Some are not religious. Others are. Where the first audience includes many conservative Protestants, the second audience is more likely to be made up of more liberal Protestants and non-Christians.

Most people, regardless of their demographic characteristics, are generally satisfied with the amount of religion news in newspapers and on television. Older people, those with lower socioeconomic status and conservative Protestants are somewhat more likely than younger people, those with higher levels of education and those from other religious traditions to say religion news is very important and to want more of it. People with no religious affiliation, and especially those who consider themselves atheist, are more inclined to say religion news is irrelevant and to think the media pay too much attention to it.

News Preferences

The two audiences have very different news interests. The traditional audience has what might be called a "localite" orientation to news. The second audience has more "cosmopolite" interests. Although both share an interest in some kinds of news, **localites** are more likely than cosmopolites to want soft news about local events, people's faith experiences and ongoing church programs and projects from familiar religions. The **cosmopolite** audience is more likely to want news about unfamiliar religions, issues and trends.

The localite-cosmopolite distinction has little to do with whether people live in a small town or a big city. Rather, the distinction stems from differences in worldviews that are, at core, religious (Table 7.1). Religious activity is positively correlated with a localite orientation, as measured by agreement with the statement "Despite all the newspaper and TV coverage, national and international happenings rarely seem as interesting as events that occur in the local community in which one lives." However, because conservative Protestant churches have worship services more than once a week and are more likely than other religions to encourage the kinds of religious activities that are easily measured in survey research, religious activity is often little more than a surrogate measure for conservative Protestantism.[2]

As members of a religion with a worldview that teaches both the importance of avoiding the temptations of the world and redeeming individuals, many conservative Protestants prefer localite coverage because it is most consistent with their underlying religious beliefs and values. Similarly, mainline Protestants, members of most non-Christian religions, and those with no religion generally prefer cosmopolite coverage because it is more consistent with their worldviews.

For many members of the localite audience, attending to religion

TABLE 7.1. DEMOGRAPHIC AND RELIGIOUS CORRELATES OF INTEREST IN LOCALITE AND COSMOPOLITE RELIGION NEWS

Correlate	News Preference	
	Localite	Cosmopolite
Gender	Female	Female
Education	Lower	Higher
Income	Lower	Higher
Importance of religion	Very high	High
Church attendance	Very high	High
Religion	Protestant	Mixed

news serves a quasi-religious function. Therefore, they want stories about faith experiences and things people do because of their religion that can serve as a model for or a test of their own religiosity. For cosmopolites, attention to religion news depends primarily on its instrumental value for making informed decisions. Therefore, they value stories that serve surveillance and watchdog functions. Many pay attention to religion news primarily for the insight stories can give them about other people or to help them understand and make up their mind about social and political problems and issues.

Catholics do not fall neatly into either the localite or cosmopolite camp. Although they often dislike issue-oriented coverage because they see much of it as harming their church, their general approach to the world makes them more comfortable with cosmopolite news than with an approach that equates religion news with spiritual guidance.

No matter how the media cover religion, criticism is inevitable. When most newspapers practiced religious journalism, writers with one understanding of God's commands openly and bluntly argued that those who promoted a different understanding were both a threat to true religiosity and a detriment to society. James Gordon Bennett's religion journalism was, in part, both cause and effect of a Moral War waged against him by religious, political and business leaders of his day. In 1912 the Seventh-Day Adventist Church established a public relations office as part of an effort to counter media coverage that portrayed Adventists' lack of support for Sunday-closing laws as un-Christian and, therefore, suspect.

Nothing much has changed. People still take positions on religion news coverage that are informed by their own religious beliefs. Criticisms of religion news both influence and mirror public attention to it. They also influence the climate in which journalists work and help shape their understanding of how they should cover the news.

Religious Criticisms of Religion News Coverage

In a 1994 survey, 65 top leaders who responded to a mail survey of all Christian churches listed in the 1993 *Yearbook of American and Canadian Churches* gave the mass media an average grade of D+ for the way they cover news but only a D for their coverage of religion. For general news coverage, there were 13 B's, 11 C's, 26 D's and 21 F's. For religion news only two leaders awarded a B. Thirteen gave religion news a C. There were 33 D's and 15 F's.

Leaders were generally more critical of television than of newspapers and of "the media" rather than their local media. However, their judgments were not affected by how much coverage these leaders said their churches received, by whether they saw their own religion being portrayed more or less favorably than other religions, or by how much contact they had with media representatives. Three-fourths of the leaders said their own relationship with reporters was either amicable or very amicable. Leaders from all Christian traditions said the media are too sensational and focus too much on fringe elements in ways that denigrate religion and the value it holds for many people and for society. But beyond the general agreement that many newspapers and most television stations refuse to treat religion seriously, there were religious differences that underscore and support people's preferences for localite or cosmopolite coverage.

For the most part, the conservative Protestant criticisms have received the most attention. Claims of bias and calls for a kind of religious journalism to replace the secular humanism they believe infests the media have been widely disseminated through religious television and in newspaper columns written by conservative Christians. National leaders such as the Rev. Donald Wildmon frequently mount protests and boycotts against the media.

Although they use religious media less often to criticize mass media and rarely advocate boycotts against them, the views of mainline Protestant and Catholic leaders are usually well known to members of their churches. Both mainline Protestant and Catholic churches advocate "media literacy" programs designed to encourage "responsible" media consumption. And just as conservative Protestants often learn about their church's criticism of the media through religious communication channels, mainline Protestants and Catholics learn their church positions and recommendations through religious magazines, church newsletters, sermons and study groups.

Across all religious traditions, lay members' criticisms of the media mirror those of their leaders and they act in accordance with their beliefs about what religion news could and should be.

Conservative Protestants often say journalists promote secular humanism. Many are loathe to believe there are any Christian journalists.[3] Instead of news about minority religions, issues, conflict and controversy, they want stories that emphasize the good parts of religion and they want them told in a way that supports and promotes their own beliefs.

Mainline Protestants more often want a broad definition of religion news that gives serious attention to the faith dimension of religion and to its meaning in people's lives but that also includes hard news and investigative reporting about religion and its consequences for everyone. They want coverage of religion to be fair and balanced, but they also generally accept as a fact of life that not all news will be as well reported as it could be. Although many can point to individual instances of biased stories and they do lament instances of bias against their own beliefs, most do not want religion news told from any particular religious perspective.

Catholics often share the conservative Protestant opinion that journalists are biased against their religion and that the media's emphasis on conflict and controversy undermines their Church and its teaching authority. But, like mainline Protestants, they usually accept and want hard, issue-oriented coverage even when it points to wrongdoing on the part of Catholics. Like members of other religions that are, or have been, outsiders in a *de facto* Protestant America, most Catholics do not want reporters to act as apologists for or promoters of any particular religion.

Members of minority religions most often criticize the media for ignoring or marginalizing them. Muslims, in particular, regularly complain about frequent references to "Muslim terrorists." Their concerns about media stereotyping are echoed by members of new religions who worry that their right to believe as they choose is threatened by stories that leave the impression that all non-Christian religions are dangerous cults.

Where religious leaders, regardless of their own religious beliefs, complain that journalists fail to take religion seriously, treat it as a joke, or fail to show its beneficent effects, atheists such as Don Barker, director of public relations for the Freedom from Religion Foundation, more often complain that the media take religion too seriously. In their opinion, the media accept at face value and perpetuate meaningless claims about the existence of a god. Barker, for example, asks why the media routinely find people who survived a disaster and attribute their good fortune to god without asking why a supposedly all-powerful god would let others who claim to believe in him perish in the same disaster.

The Problem of Mismatches

Because the mass media do not serve homogeneous audiences, mismatches between coverage and the interests of at least some people are inevitable. Sometimes reactions to those mismatches can be severe. When religion news does not meet with their approval, people aren't at all shy about complaining.

Lack of substantive reporting about religion can cause cosmopolites to ignore what little is available. Often they supplement their mass media use by also attending to more specialized sources, including religious media. However, most drop newspaper or magazine subscriptions or stop watching television news only when they believe they are not getting enough news to make attention to mass media worth the time or money. When they discover they did not get information about religious involvement in issues that concern them in time to act or react, they feel betrayed by the media. In the case of television, a few will push for reinstatement of the fairness doctrine.

Although cosmopolites rarely react strongly to one or even a few stories that displease them, many who prefer localite coverage do react very strongly to a single story. Those who believe the mass media in general undermine religion and promote immorality often turn to the "700 Club," Christian radio stations or to religious magazines for their news. Those who do use mass media may stop believing anything they learn from it or even drop their subscriptions or turn off the television in response to individual stories. Such strong reactions sometimes occur in response to casual coverage, pickups from the wire services or even to stories that, on the surface have nothing to do with religion, but they are more likely when the media cover religious scandals or wrongdoing on the part of religious people. When the *Charlotte Observer* broke the story about the PTL scandals, the paper received nearly 2000 critical letters; 189 households dropped their subscriptions.

Content and Consequences

Much public concern about religion news coverage is related to the public's growing suspicion of all institutions, including the media. But that distrust, in itself, stems at least in part from media practices. Underlying both audience orientations to religion news and criticisms of it is a general concern for media effects.

Those who prefer localite news generally fear that media coverage of religious conflict and controversy undermines support for religion and that attention to diverse religions will lead people astray. Cosmopolites, however, are more inclined to see bad news about religion as something akin to a prophetic warning. They fear that too little diversity or too many soft features at the expense of hard news will leave them without the information they need in order to make informed decisions.

Both fears are real. Although the threat from mass media may be overblown, that does not mean the concerns are without merit. Messages do have consequences. To argue otherwise would, in effect, be tantamount to saying journalism is a meaningless activity.

Research conducted over the past 25 years clearly indicates the most important effect may be the ability of the mass media to set the public agenda. Although the strength of the effect can differ among the media and vary according to the nature of the issue, the amount of coverage the media devote to people, subject matter and issues and the way they display that coverage does teach people what is important and what is not. The coverage also teaches them the language to use in describing people and issues. However, people's opinions are usually closer to those advocated by their churches or by their friends and family than to those emphasized in news or favored in opinion columns.

Although there is little evidence that mass media messages have strong, direct effects, at one time or another most people have decided what to do on the basis of something they have read or seen on television. Almost everyone has heard accounts of someone who watched a violent movie and then committed similar mayhem. But even in those cases, there are almost always other influences besides the mass media.

The few studies that directly address the effects of religion news indicate that people do learn about new religions and gain some new ideas about their own religion from the mass media, but they provide little evidence that media coverage alone causes people to become more committed to their current religion, abandon it or join a new one. Consistent with findings from agenda-setting research, some studies indicate that negative coverage of a religion can affect people's perceptions of that religion, but often the effect is more one of re-enforcing pre-existing beliefs or opinions than changing them. Other studies show that people may learn about a new religion and attend an event it is sponsoring because of media coverage, but whether they decide to join that new religion depends less on the nature of the media coverage than on their pre-existing religious beliefs and levels of religious commitment, previous knowledge about the new religion, motives for attending an event, the persuasiveness of the program and the way people who are already members of it treat them.[4]

In most cases personal needs and experiences, along with interpersonal communication, are more influential than mass media messages. Therefore, reporters who cover religion news need not worry unduly about the effects of individual stories. At the same time, because there is an agenda-setting effect, they should be concerned about the consequences of their overall pattern of coverage of all news, including religion news.

In the case of religion news, no approach to the subject will totally satisfy everyone. Almost anything can offend someone. Because people who prefer localite coverage are the ones most likely to complain and even drop their subscriptions or turn off the television in response to individual stories they dislike, the media are often tempted to avoid controversy by ignoring religion or by providing purely localite coverage. But that is an easy out that is unlikely to be in the long-term best interest of the media or the public.

"No coverage" has an agenda-setting effect just as surely as heavy coverage does. Most people in every community consider themselves religious and are more likely to attend worship services each week than attend a sporting event. Therefore, absence of coverage invites people to accept an image of their community and of the world that is misleading at best. Because people attach so much importance to news of religion, failure to cover the subject sends clear signals to the public that journalists are not concerned about their audience and have no interest in meeting their needs. Such an image feeds many localites' belief that the media promote a liberal, secular humanist agenda and, therefore, are best shunned.

Purely localite coverage can counter that belief about the media. But that kind of coverage serves one segment of the public at the expense of another, sometimes larger, audience. The localite emphasis on one-time events, church projects, and religious people takes seriously the role religion plays in many people's lives, but it often creates the impression that there is less religious diversity than there really is. It also can create a false impression of religious harmony. Neglecting minority religions or failing to cover serious differences among religious people invites feelings of betrayal that can lead those who are religious but want cosmopolite coverage to look elsewhere for their news.

Because there is no homogeneous audience for religion news, deciding how to cover it is a difficult task. Community demographics can provide a clue. In communities where people fitting the description of a localite audience are the majority, emphasizing localite coverage may be appropriate. In more diverse communities or in ones where the majority fit the cosmopolite profile, emphasis on hard news about religion can be appropriate.

But demographics are only a clue. Neither localites nor cosmopolites are a homogeneous audience. Localites may like some issue-oriented stories or stories about new religions. Cosmopolites may be bored by trend stories or offended by too much investigative reporting. Atheists may consider religion irrelevant but still want to know what religious people are doing.

Therefore, the best approach is usually a broad one that makes room for all belief systems, giving serious attention both to the meanings they have for individuals and to their positive and negative consequences. Within that broad coverage, some stories will appeal more strongly to some readers than to others. Some will offend one group or another. But a total package that respects the sensitivities of those with different understandings of news and its purposes and that builds bridges among the diverse audiences by taking advantage of areas of mutual concern and interest is most likely to create a win-win situation for everyone.

Notes

1 For further details, see Stewart M. Hoover, Barbara M. Hanley and Martin Radelfinger, *The RNS-Lilly Study of Religion Reporting and Readership in the Daily Press* (Philadelphia, Pa.: School of Communications and Theater, Temple University, 1989); and Stewart M. Hoover, Shalini Venturelli and Douglas Wagner, *Religion in Public Discourse: The Role of the Media* (Boulder, Colo.: Center for Mass Media Research, School of Journalism and Mass Communication, University of Colorado, 1994).

2 The localite-cosmopolite distinction was first introduced by the sociologist Robert Merton in his book *Social Theory and Social Structure* (Glencoe, Ill.: Free Press, 1957). For other studies of its relevance in understanding audiences, see Wade Clarke Roof and Dean R. Hoge, "Church Involvement in America: Social Factors Affecting Membership and Participation," *Review of Religious Research* 21(1980):405-4260, Supp.; Garrett Ray, "So Who's Parochial Now?" *Grassroots Editor* (Spring 1986):3-7.

3 The most commonly quoted source is a survey of journalists working for

elite media in the northeastern United States conducted by Robert S. Lichter, Stanley Rothman and Linda S. Lichter published as *The Media Elite* (New York: Adler & Adler, 1986).

4 For details, see Rodney Stark and William S. Bainbridge, "Networks of Faith: Interpersonal Bonds and Recruitment to Cults and Sects," *American Journal of Sociology* 85(1988):1376-1395; Robert Abelman, "Influence of News Coverage of the 'Scandal' on PTL Viewers," *Journalism Quarterly* 68(1991):101-110; William H. Swatos, "Getting the Word Around: A Research Note on Communicating an Evangelistic Crusade," *Review of Religious Research* 33(1991):176-185.

For Further Reading

Fore, William F. *Mythmakers: Gospel, Culture and the Media.* New York: Friendship Press, 1990.
    This book is most concerned with the entertainment media, but it does a good job of presenting a mainline Protestant perspective on mass media content.
"God in the Newsroom." *Nieman Reports* Summer 1993.
    The 15 articles in this special issue examine religion news from religious, scholarly, journalistic and audience perspectives.
Olasky, Marvin. *Prodigal Press: The Anti-Christian Bias of the American News Media.* Wheaton, Ill.: Crossways Books, 1988.
    This critique of the mass media and impassioned plea for a return to religious journalism is highly influential in conservative Protestant circles.
Parker, Everett C., David W. Barry and Dallas W. Smythe. *The Television-Radio Audience and Religion.* New York: Harper & Brothers, 1955.
    Although the focus is on religious broadcasting, this very early multi-methodological study is still one of the best attempts to understand how people think about and use the mass media. Chapter 5 explores clergy attitudes toward the media in the 1950s; Chapters 7 and 8 provide historical data on radio and television ownership and use.
"Religion and the Media: Three Forums." *Commonweal* February 24, 1995.
    This special issue contains reports from three national forums in which journalists and clergy discussed religion news.
Said, Edward W. *Covering Islam.* New York: Pantheon Press, 1981.
    This book critiques media coverage from a Middle Eastern and Muslim perspective.
Stamm, Keith R. and Robert Weis. "The Newspaper and Community Integration: A Study of Ties to Local Church Community." *Communication Research* 13(1986):125-137.

This article examines the relationships among Roman Catholics' religious commitment, use of a diocesan newspaper and use of a general circulation newspaper.

Stout, Daniel A. and Judith M. Buddenbaum. (eds.). *Religion and Mass Media: Audiences and Adaptations.* Thousand Oaks, Calif.: Sage, 1996.

Chapters in Part 2 describe church teachings about mass media and mass media use. Other chapters examine the relationship between people's religions and their uses of news media. One chapter on public attitudes toward religion news includes a review of the literature, national survey data and case studies of audience reactions to local religion news coverage in three communities.

CHAPTER 8

RESPONSES AND RESPONSIBILITY

Journalists themselves have long been among the most vocal critics of the way the media report news about religion. A few advocate something approaching religious journalism. Joseph Duggan, an editorial-page editor for the *Richmond (Va.) Times-Dispatch,* for example, once accused journalists of being "vulgar Marxists" who exhibit "antipathy or indifference toward the spiritual side of man and to that which transcends earthly life and human nature." That, he says, "concedes secular humanism ... to be the common ground of the American experience."[1]

Although most would not share that opinion, surveys of religion journalists indicate an occasional reporter shies away from covering religions outside the Judeo-Christian mainstream "for fear they will lead people astray." Others complain of editors who won't let them cover stories about controversial religions or that cast generally accepted religions in a bad light. While they freely admit that some journalists may be biased against religion and that the public can mistake critical stories for biased ones or "coverage of" for "support for," most see problems with missed and mishandled stories stemming primarily from a lack of resources.

In many places the newsroom culture remains a serious obstacle. Many religion reporters still have editors and news directors who fail to see the importance of religion or to take news about it seriously. But if their specialty has neither the prestige of covering a presidential election campaign nor the glamor of reporting on sports or the world of entertainment, neither is it a moribund beat fit only for the lazy or inept journalist.

In quick succession, religious involvement in civil rights and anti-war demonstrations gave way to a time of religious experimentation within the counterculture movement of the 1960s and then to the advent of the electronic church and resurgent fundamentalism in the United States and abroad. As religion's public face re-exerted itself, the media responded with more hard news coverage of religion.

Increased coverage began as a half-hearted response to events that could not be ignored, but today change is also market-driven. News is shaped as much by audience demands as it is by journalists' interests, their socialization to professional norms or the demands of a particular workplace.

For most of this century newspapers have struggled to hold their audience in the face of competition first from radio and then from television. Now both print and broadcast media see their place threatened by specialized media and by new communication technologies. That kind of heightened pressure has caused mass media to ask people what they want. In letters to the editor, surveys and focus groups, people say they want serious attention to religion and values.

In the current climate, religion sells. The 1994 issue of *Newsweek* with Kenneth Woodward's report of new scholarly theories about the death of Jesus as the cover story tied with one featuring the life and death of Jacqueline Kennedy Onassis as the top-selling issue of the year. In 1996 Woodward's Easter cover story on academic controversies surrounding Christ's resurrection made that issue the second highest seller.

Religion is no longer an "orphan beat." Now, "it's one child in a large, competitive family of beats," says Marcia Z. Nelson, sections editor for the *Aurora (Ill.) Beacon-News*. In a 1995 survey, almost two-thirds of all religion reporters said top management was more interested in religion news than they had been five years earlier. At both print and broadcast media the response to events and audience demands can be seen in new and expanded definitions of religion news, allocation of resources and staffing arrangements for covering it.

Rethinking Religion News

The traditional church-page approach to religion news underplayed religion's public face, and so journalists who had never noticed or had forgotten the way religion influenced passage of anti-pornography leg-islation and blue laws in the 19th century but also social reforms from child labor laws to equal rights legislation were surprised in the 1970s to find religion mixing with politics. They responded by giving new attention to religion's public face.

But the new emphasis on religion as hard news also missed part of the story. Stories framed as political conflict over social policies and preferences told the "who, what, where and when" but could not adequately explain the "why" or the "how." In dealing with religious sources and in listening to criticism from them and their supporters, journalists found they needed to devote more attention to religion's private face.

"Religion news has moved beyond denominational reports and simple events coverage to include lifestyle explorations of all forms of personal spirituality," says religion page writer-editor Bill Broadway. "At the *Washington Post,* we've almost—but not quite—trained everyone from copy editors to reporters to advertising reps to call our Saturday page the 'religion page,' not the 'church page.' "

Increasingly the preferred name for dedicated space is even more inclusive. The "church page" has given way to sections devoted to "religion and ethics" or "faith and values." The ethics, faith and values are those of people who are conventionally religious and those who are not. As journalism professors Gary Atkins and William Rivers point out:

> ... The perfect accord that once existed in medieval thought about the nature of the universe, the canons of the social order, and the good of the individual lie shattered by the experiences and knowledge of contemporary man. ... Out of the disintegrated center [between the traditionally religious and the truly secular] will rise either beneficial intelligence or, as cultures struggle to maintain forms that have comforted them for so long, horrors beyond the scale to which we have already been subjected in this century. ...
>
> To us [journalists] falls the task of covering the daily expression of this "age of longing," ...
>
> Event coverage is needed, but so is a more illuminating examination of this subject matter of values themselves, particularly their acquisition and development, their humaneness or inhumaneness, their appeal to human emotions, and their importance in human existence. What is required is a more comprehensive tying together of the links between issues such as abortion, euthanasia and nuclear weapons.[2]

In a world where change seems too rapid and problems appear unsolvable, uncertainty abounds. In a culture that fosters individualism and teaches people to question authority, people still seek certainty, purpose and meaning in their lives. Some people have found them in a set of religious beliefs that puts them on one side of an issue. Others have found certainty, purpose and meaning in another set of beliefs that puts them on the other side. Still others remain skeptical or behave as consumers, intent on finding their own way by piecing together bits and pieces from among the options readily available in the religious marketplace.

"Meaning," then, is central to current thinking about the importance of religion news and the way it should be covered. The new approach has its roots in the Hutchinson Commission's call for a "free and responsible press." Initially the Commission's insistence that the media provide "the truth about the facts" and also "full access to the day's intelligence" led to investigative and sometimes adversarial journalism. That kind of reporting is still appropriate on all beats, including religion. But it also has its limits, especially in religion news. In response to audience demands, today the goal in religion reporting is to provide a "representative picture of the constituent groups of society," a "mechanism for the presentation and clarification of the goals and values of the society," and also for the "exchange of comment and criticism."

Explaining beliefs and exploring meanings take more space and time than covering people and events, or even issues for which the journalist can consult a few well-placed official sources. It also requires finding good journalists, using their talents wisely, and giving their efforts the play they deserve. But implementing change is often more a matter of reallocating existing resources than spending additional money.

Faced with the challenge of deciding whether or not to add a new subject to the mix of media coverage or change the approach to covering a topic that has long been included, media managers and the reporters who are on the front line always have questions about the benefits and costs associated with change. The information needed to answer those questions can come from the experiences of those media that have implemented change and from research data that reveals industry trends.[3]

Allocation of Space

Very few newspapers have added extra pages. Most television stations have not expanded their newscasts. In fact, the trend has been in the opposite direction. Faced with increasing costs for newsprint, many newspapers trimmed the size or number of pages. Network news lost about 1 minute of time to advertising from 1976 to 1986. Yet space for religion news has increased.

Some papers have never had a religion page. Others have abandoned them in an effort to treat religion like other kinds of news. However, the absence of dedicated space for religion may or may not mean less religion news coverage. In 1981 the *Denver Post* had a weekly religion tabloid. Now veteran religion reporter Virginia Culver can count on space for only a story or two on Saturday. Although there is no longer room for routine coverage of religious events, she still writes substantive stories about religion just as she did when she had a section to fill each week. Today more of her stories appear on the front page or elsewhere in the newspaper. When the pope visited Denver, the paper gave her the resources to travel with him on his plane from Rome to Denver and back to Rome.

The rival *Rocky Mountain News* killed its religion section a few years later but continued to carry a weekly syndicated column by its former religion reporter, Terry Mattingly. However, after several years of relying on staff writers and pickups from the wire services for more substantive stories, it assigned Jean Torkelson to write a weekly column. In 1997 it reinstituted a religion page.

The decision to make sure there is space for religion news can be seen even more clearly in the expansion in religion pages at other daily newspapers. By 1995, at least nine out of every 10 newspapers set aside space for religion news. In 1985, the religion page was just that—a page. Typically only newspapers with circulation over 50,000 set aside as much as two pages for religion. Except at the larger papers, almost all stories written by religion journalists appeared on the religion page. Ten years later religion reporters still complained they needed more space for religion news even though two-thirds said their paper had increased the space for religion news over what it had been five years earlier. In 1995, the average amount of space set aside for religion news was three pages.

The *Dallas Morning News* became the leader with its six-page section, but by then sections of three and four pages were common even at relatively small newspapers. The much smaller *Ashland (Ky.) Daily Independent* began publishing a monthly religion tabloid that sometimes had as many as 50 pages.

As space set aside for religion news has increased, so has story length. Until the mid-1970s, only about 8 percent of all stories about religion published in daily newspapers were at least 30 column inches in length. Only a handful were much longer than that. By the mid-1980s, newspapers managed to find room for twice as many long stories. In 1980 very long stories rarely exceeded 40 column inches. But by the mid-1990s, stories with accompanying graphics that filled an entire page and spilled onto a second began finding their way into papers. By 1995, even some newspapers with circulations under 50,000 published that kind of very long story almost every week.

Because television has a smaller and less flexible news hole than newspapers have, similarly dramatic increases in number or length of stories have not occurred in television coverage. On television, religion may get mentioned in a story several times a week. Some of those stories include substantive information about religion, but more often religion is simply mentioned in a story that focuses on something else. The longest stories have always been under 5 minutes. Most run less than 2 minutes.

At networks and local stations that have made a commitment to religion news, however, time is now set aside for religion. But as is true for most newspapers, religion news is rarely confined to a special segment. Since at least 1990, ABC and CBS have aired special segments on religion about once a month. A few local stations have them weekly. Those special segments get between 3 and 5 minutes of air time, but most stories about religion are integrated into the main news segment and are relatively short—anywhere from 10 seconds to 1 minute.

Staffing Arrangements

At media where news coverage is organized along beat lines, divisions of labor are a fact of life. Media that are committed to thorough religion coverage have hired specialists to cover the beat, but even so the lines dividing reporting about religion by specialists and nonspecialists are increasingly becoming blurred. Both specialists and nonspecialists may produce hard news coverage and features about religion. Both may find their work published anywhere in a newspaper, including the front page, in the body of a television newscast or even in the sports segment. But they also may have more space specifically set aside for religion available to them.

Through surveys, focus groups and conversations with religious leaders, the *Dallas Morning News* learned its readers wanted more and better religion news coverage. The paper responded by creating almost a newspaper within a newspaper. The religion beat is part of the city or metro desk, but the section has its own editor, and also an assistant editor, three staff writers, a religion researcher, an artist and a part-time clerk.

The religion specialists produce most of the stories for the weekly six-page religion section, but they also write stories that appear on the front page, on the metro page, or in other sections of the newspaper. In spite of having more staff specifically dedicated to religion news coverage than many smaller publications have to put out an entire newspaper, religion editor Sharon Grigsby often publishes stories written by free-lancers and columns contributed by local religious leaders. Other staff writers also cover religion and their stories may appear anywhere in the newspaper, including the religion section. Says staff writer, Christine Wicker, "The problem hasn't been finding enough news; it has been finding time enough to cover all the news."

A repeat winner of the Schachern Award, given by Religion Newswriters Association annually to the best religion section in the country, the section has received both critical acclaim and popular approval. According to Bob Mong, managing editor for the *Dallas Morning News,* the religion section has created more excitement than any other project he has launched in his career.

Located in a city where religion is an important part of the culture, the *Dallas Morning News* could hardly afford to ignore audience interest in the subject. With a weekday circulation of over 500,000 and a Sunday circulation almost half again as large, the paper could afford to devote substantial resources to the beat. But its approach to religion news is hardly typical.

More typical, especially for smaller papers, is the approach taken by the *Reading (Pa.) Eagle-Times,* with its combined Saturday circulation of about 70,000.[4] As the paper's religion editor, John W. Smith writes a weekly column for the paper's religion section but spends most of his time working his "other job" as copy chief. Because of his twin positions, Smith can assign other reporters to cover local religion stories, check their work, and also select stories from the wire services and syndicates. At the paper, all reporters are encouraged to find religion stories which they may offer first to Smith, or "sell" to the news or feature editors. Therefore, Smith has little trouble providing a thoughtful mixture of stories for a Saturday religion section consisting of three pages, including one that is devoted primarily to a church directory and other religion-related advertising.

Even though Smith works the beat only part time and does little active religion reporting, his work is taken seriously. "We use design tools to create an interesting-looking page, offer thought-provoking columnists and give as much variety as we can," he says. The paper also airs 1-minute spots on a local television station to promote stories in the next day's paper. According to Smith, the managing editor uses the time to highlight religion stories whenever they warrant that kind of publicity.

While part-time religion reporters are common at all but the largest papers, even part-time specialists are rare in broadcasting. ABC, National Public Radio and a handful of local stations have religion reporters. In one of the most creative arrangements, WFLA-TV in Tampa-St. Petersburg, Florida, and the *Tampa Tribune* share one. There, Dan Bradley, the WFLA-TV news director, convinced Michelle Bearden, the award-winning religion reporter for the *Tampa Tribune,* to cover religion news for television as well as for the newspaper. It was, he says, easier to teach a religion reporter about television than to teach a general assignment reporter about religion.

Although she was reluctant at first to move into television, Bearden now says she has the "best of both worlds." With almost complete freedom to choose her stories for the *Tribune's* religion pages and for the television station's weekly stories plus the ability to do breaking news or other stories that fit into the regular news hole, the two kinds of reporting complement each other nicely. "TV is the appetizer; the newspaper is the full banquet. I did a Hindu wedding for both," Bearden says. "On TV religion news can be much more vivid—hearing the music, seeing the costumes and dancing captured people's attention. I could show the rituals and then explain them in the newspaper."

The Tampa venture into sharing a reporter was possible because both WFLA-TV and the *Tribune* are owned by Media General, but according to Bearden, there is no reason similar arrangements couldn't be worked out between a newspaper and a television station with different owners. In many cities separately owned media already share a meteorologist, a consumer reporter or a media critic. That kind of sharing of expertise and personalities may also be the wave of the future in religion reporting.

Currently four-fifths of the newspapers with circulation over 100,000 have full-time religion reporters, but at papers with circulation under 30,000 the situation is more similar to that at the typical television station where almost all reporters are generalists rather than specialists. Although a reporter at smaller papers may be assigned to the religion beat, only about one in 10 spends even half of the time covering religion. At small papers a common arrangement, and one that can work quite well, is to assign one person to coordinate the coverage but deputize all reporters to find and report the stories.

At the larger papers, the religion reporter usually reports to a city editor. At smaller ones, religion is more often an adjunct of the lifestyle or feature desk. At the very smallest, everyone, including the person responsible for religion news, reports to the editor-in-chief or publisher. Partly because of those arrangements, reporters at the smallest papers and those who report to the lifestyle or feature editor most often produce the kind of stories long associated with traditional church pages and they find most of their stories published in the space set aside for religion news. Although that arrangement can work well, assigning the religion beat to a news editor rather than to a feature editor is usually a clear signal that the paper considers religion real news. At papers where religion is attached to a news desk, the specialist more often engages in active newsgathering, writes hard news stories and finds the stories compete quite successfully for space on the front page or in other sections.

At the same time, other reporters produce more stories for the religion page than was true even five years ago. Even at the handful of large papers with several pages set aside for religion news and more than one full-time religion reporter, more than half of all stories about religion are covered by reporters from other beats or picked up from the wires. However, at the larger papers, religion reporters rarely have much responsibility for those other stories about religion.

At newspapers and television stations, religion reporters can usually decide what stories they will cover for the religion sections. At almost all papers, they can also choose stories from the wire services or from syndicates for use on the religion page. At both large and small papers, they can sometimes collaborate with other reporters on complex stories. But fewer than one-fourth, regardless of the size of the newspaper they work for, can assign other reporters to cover a story or check wire service stories about religion or those produced by other staffers for accuracy and clarity.

The Religion Journalist

Although trend data indicate the media have begun to devote more space to religion news, at first glance some of the staffing arrangements would seem to indicate religion news is still a poor stepchild. But first impressions can be misleading.

Not too long ago, editors assigned reporters to the beat without much thought. Reporters plotted ways to escape it. The experience of Steve Chambers, religion writer for the *Newark (N.J.) Star-Ledger* is typical of the more than three-fourths of all religion reporters who were surprised to find themselves assigned to the beat but now say they enjoy religion reporting. According to Chambers:

> My jaw almost hit the floor when my boss [Jim Willse] asked me to cover the religion beat. I thought, "What did I do wrong?" What I quickly realized is that in some ways this is the hottest beat in America, and in others it's very much like any other news assignment.
>
> Religion is one of the few areas of reporting that attracts a wide, varied audience. The stories really seem to get noticed. I've had more letters to the editor written in response to my religion stories than I have to other more "typical" front-page stories about crime, politics and natural disasters.
>
> My stuff goes out front or on section covers. It isn't relegated to a religion section buried somewhere in the back pages. In fact, I was specifically told not to write for our Faith page. ... I was expected to get religion on the front page. I think that's what large, progressive papers are doing today in America.

Because of experiences like that, many more reporters are asking for the beat. However, they are less likely to get the assignment simply because they are interested in religion, are religious, or are a member of the clergy or have a clergy relative than was the case even 10 years ago.

In assigning people to the beat, the most common concern—and one taken quite seriously—is the question of whether a religious person or one without a religion should cover the beat. Although many people believe journalists are irreligious or anti-religion, reporters are as likely to identify with a religion and be active in it as are members of the publics they serve.

Just as people who are athletic are more likely than couch potatoes to cover sports, people who are religious are more likely than those who are not to gravitate toward the religion beat. Nine out of 10 religion reporters identify with a religion. With few exceptions the number identifying with any particular tradition pretty closely mirrors that tradition's strength in the population as a whole. About one-third of all religion reporters are Roman Catholic. Of the approximately two-thirds who consider themselves Protestant, most are Methodist, Baptist or Lutheran. Among the approximately 5 percent who identify with a non-Christian religion, half are Jews; the rest identify with other world religions or with new religions.

In most cases, the religion reporter does more than just identify with a religion. Two-fifths describe themselves as very active in their religion; an equal number describe themselves as somewhat active. Only about one-fifth say they are either relatively inactive or not at all active. Although about 10 percent of all religion journalists received clerical training, the number of ordained clergy who cover religion has steadily declined. Almost all of them are no longer on the clergy roster for their faith.

In spite of the potential for conflicts of interest, complaints about clergy journalists are uncommon. However, neither religion reporters nor media managers believe a member of the clergy is the ideal candidate for the religion beat. But neither do they believe that people who are lay members of a religion or those who have no religion are necessarily ideal candidates. Both having a religion and having no religion are attitudes toward religion that can lead to good reporting or that can cause problems.

Journalists who are not religious may have difficulty understanding how people make the leap of faith necessary to commit themselves to a truth that seems unprovable. If they can bring an outsider's perspective to their work, they may notice things that insiders would take for granted. But being outsiders, they may find it difficult to establish rapport with religious people. Their outsider's perspective may also lend a touch of cynicism to their reporting.

Religion journalists who are religious may understand religion. They may initially find it easier to establish rapport with their sources, but their own beliefs can also creep into their work. Some highly religious reporters may see the beat as an opportunity to proselytize; others may simply find it difficult to cover religions they consider false.

Because of federal civil rights laws, employers cannot make staffing decisions on the basis of religion. However, they can fire employees or change their assignments if their religion creates an undue hardship for the business or interferes with job performance. Therefore, many appropriately restrict their religion reporters' religious activities beyond regular worship just as they place limits on partisan activities by political reporters. Even where workplace rules would allow other kinds of religious activity, journalists often limit their own involvement. In surveys, for example, many religion journalists who select the "somewhat active" or "not very active" categories to describe their religious activity explain their choice by noting they refuse leadership positions in order to avoid, as much as possible, the appearance of a conflict of interest.

In general, religion reporters are opposed to having a member of the clergy cover news about religion and ambivalent as to whether or not a religious person should cover the beat, but their opinions do not reflect a lack of concern. To them, the question of whether a religious person or one who is not religious should cover religion ought to be a nonquestion. The ideal religion reporter, they say, should be evenhanded, nonjudgmental and fair.

Because many religious people believe the media are biased against religion, they also say those who cover religion need good "people skills" such as empathy and the ability to get along with all kinds of people, including those with whom the reporter disagrees. According to experienced religion reporters, a thick skin and a sense of humor can also help. Religious people take their religion so seriously and are so easily offended by stories about other religions or by stories about their own that do not live up to their opinions about how religion news should be reported that religion reporters quickly acquire a drawerful of letters promising them eternal damnation.

There are so many different religions that even the best religion reporter occasionally makes a mistake or unthinkingly produces a story that is less sensitive and fair than it should be. Therefore, experienced religion reporters also say that, ideally, reporters should have a degree in journalism, have studied religion and also have some reporting experience before being assigned to the religion beat.

The very complexity of religion makes good reporting and writing skills imperative. Finding the connection between religion's private and public dimensions requires superb interviewing and investigative skills. Beliefs, their consequences and connections cannot easily be communicated in the standard inverted-pyramid style. Making religion news meaningful to audiences with diverse interests requires combining the accuracy and faithfulness of a stenographer with the artistry of the poet or novelist.

In short, they say, appointments to the religion beat should be made on the basis of the reporter's temperament, knowledge, and talent. Increasingly, those are the qualifications that matter in deciding who will cover religion.

Because most journalists begin their careers at small media outlets and work their way up, there are real differences in the qualifications of religion reporters at small newspapers and those who work for larger newspapers and for the television networks or larger stations that have made a commitment to religion news. However, even at the smallest papers there is an unmistakable trend toward professionalism. Those who work at papers with circulation under 30,000 have lower levels of education and professional experience than those who work at larger media, but most of them are at least as qualified as most of the reporters who covered religion news for the largest papers 15 years ago.

Almost all religion journalists have a college degree; almost one-third have graduate training. Over half studied journalism in college or graduate school; almost half studied religion or theology alone or in combination with journalism. Except at small papers, few are true beginners. Although just over half have covered religion for fewer than five years, even at small papers most now have over five years of reporting experience before they are assigned to the religion beat. At both very small and very large papers, almost one-third have more than 15 years of reporting experience.

Points to Consider

The trends in the past few years attest to the changing status of the religion beat. At those media that have made religion news a priority, audience response and critical acclaim attest to the benefits. But they also point to areas of concern.

For journalists, the most important concern is whether or not they have the interest, temperament and knowledge to cover religion accurately and to treat all religions fairly. Just as those who truly do not like sports should not pursue a career in sports reporting, those who are uninterested in religion or do not believe they are temperamentally suited to religion reporting should consider tactfully refusing the assignment should the religion beat be offered to them. Although reporters from other beats may not be able to avoid covering stories about religion or ones that have a religious dimension to them, consultation or collaboration with other reporters can alleviate problems.

While religion journalists do need to know about religion, knowledge grows with study and experience. Those who are uncertain of their expertise can, in many cases, start small by covering those stories they feel competent to handle and gradually increase the depth and complexity of their work as they learn.

For the media the major decisions involve the amount of resources to be allocated to the beat, including whether or not to set aside space for religion news. Those media operating in places like Dallas where there are many religious organizations and many active congregations will undoubtedly want to devote more resources to the beat than those located in areas where religion is not such an integral part of the local culture. At the same time, people in areas where religion appears to be quiescent will still be affected by religion and may be very interested in the subject.

Audience research can be a useful gauge. However, if the local paper or local television stations have little history of religion reporting, it can be an uncertain guide. Most people have a very hard time saying they want a kind of news they have never seen.

In most cases, people like serious attention to religion, but whether religion should have its own section is an open question. On television, a separate segment for religion can ghettoize it and invite people who are not interested to switch channels, particularly if the segment comes at the end of a newscast as is often the case. The same thing can happen in newspapers because the audience for a religion section is somewhat different from the audience for other sections. At the same time, a section for religion does clearly signal a paper's recognition that most people are religious and that religion is a part of community life. It also makes it possible to group together those little stories that are important but might get lost if they were scattered throughout the paper.

Whatever decisions are made about resources and space, media managers must also consider carefully their staffing arrangements. At too many small papers and television stations there still is no one with a title reflecting understanding of and responsibility for religion news. At small papers, those who do cover religion now may be required to fill two or more pages each week but have so little time to devote to the task that they cannot produce the kind of sensitive features and in-depth reports the public wants. While larger papers more often have adequate staffing on the religion beat, their specialists may have too lit-tle authority. Because many religion journalists cannot routinely check wire stories or those produced by journalists with less knowledge of re-ligion and empathy for religious understandings, errors and ambigui-ties that might be caught at smaller papers where journalists do work more closely with each other may go undetected.

Notes

1 See Joseph P. Duggan, "Is the Media's Language a 'Marxist Vulgate'?" *Vital Speeches of the Day,* August 1, 1981:635-637.

2 Gary Atkins and William Rivers, *Reporting with Understanding* (Ames, Iowa: Iowa State University Press, 1987), 196-197.

3 Data for 1995 are from an unpublished survey conducted for Religion Newswriters Association by Debra Mason, Judith M. Buddenbaum and Guido Stempel, III; data for earlier years are from surveys conducted by the author for Lutheran World Federation and for the National Press Foundation.

4 In 1996 the morning *Times* had a Monday-Friday circulation just under 50,000; the evening *Eagle's* weekday circulation was about half that.

For Further Reading

Buddenbaum, Judith M. "The Religion Beat at Daily Newspapers," *Newspaper Research Journal* 9(Summer 1988):57-70.
    This study reports 1985 data on the qualifications of religion journalists and on allocation of resources to the religion beat at newspapers in all circulation categories.
Hoover, Stewart M. "Finding Religion." *Quill* January/February 1996:36-38.
    This article explores some reasons behind the trends in religion news coverage as well as common concerns about religion news coverage.
Hynds, Ernest C. "Large Daily Newspapers Have Improved Coverage of Religion." *Journalism Quarterly* 64, no. 2-3 (Summer/Autumn 1987):444-448.

This article discusses journalist qualifications and resource allocation at the largest daily newspapers.

Ranly, Don. "How Religion Editors of Newspapers View Their Jobs and Religion." *Journalism Quarterly* 56, no.4 (Winter 1979):844-849.

Although written before many newspapers began to take religion news seriously, this article is worth reading for background.

Shephard, Alicia C. "The Media Get Religion," *American Journalism Review* December 1995:18-25.

This article discusses media's changing attitude toward religion news. It includes quotes and comments from print and broadcast reporters and their supervisors.

Weaver, David H. and G. Cleveland Wilhoit. *The American Journalist in the 1990s.* Mahwah, N.J.: Lawrence Erlbaum, 1996.

This is the authoritative source for data on the qualifications, news orientations and working conditions of journalists from all media. Information on journalists' religious backgrounds can be found in the chapters on demographics and on values and ethics.

PART III
REPORTING
RELIGION NEWS

CHAPTER 9

RECOGNIZING AND REPORTING RELIGION NEWS

ecause there is so much going on and so much of what is going on appears routine, even experienced religion reporters sometimes have a hard time defining religion news. In response to open-ended questions asked of them in surveys conducted since 1980, many initially produce tautologies of the "religion news is news about religion" variety. Others claim not to be able to define it but say they know it when they see it.

As unhelpful as those "I know it when I see it" responses may appear to be, the kinds of stories experienced reporters cover and the importance they attach to them illustrate, as well as anything, what religion news is and what it can be. Besides profiles of people and groups, holidays, local events and church anniversaries, there are, says *Hartford Courant* reporter Gerald Renner,

> trend stories such as the decline of denominationalism ... and the growth of "nontraditional" religions.
>
> Money stories, about how much the church needs for maintenance ... and how it goes about raising money.
>
> Stories of redemption, such as the heroin addict who found God and now runs the local teen center.
>
> Religious-choice stories such as yuppies with growing families looking for a church home.

And there are the stories of conflict, scandals and squabbles.

Religion reporters define religion news broadly. As one anonymous survey respondent explained:

> [Religion news] consists of two very distinct varieties. [First there is] what's happening within religious institutions *per se*—as they change and reflect the surrounding culture, what they and their members are doing and how they represent themselves to the outside world and maintain cohesion and survive.
>
> Then, there's other news that's not institutional ... ways in which people attempt to find meaning and order ... anything that touches on beliefs, values, ethical concerns and how they affect people and culture.

Studies of religion news coverage have identified upwards of a dozen kinds of stories ranging from simple announcements or short stories about local events to complex and sophisticated ones about beliefs, trends and issues. Each kind of story can be covered as a local story, or it can be developed as a regional, national or international one. Each might involve any of the innumerable religions represented in the country. Each might also be reported as hard news, presented as a news analysis, given a feature slant, or covered in a column. As a result, there are an almost infinite number of story possibilities.

News Values

If experienced religion journalists find so many ideas that their major problem is figuring out what to do first, the problem for most journalists is finding any real news about religion. As in covering all kinds of stories, the news values journalists use to guide them in their work can help reporters recognize religion news and set priorities for covering it. But in religion reporting, those values can also blind journalists to stories that are worth covering.

Because there is never enough room for all the possible news of the day or enough time to cover it, experienced religion journalists look primarily for the stories that are most likely to be important to the audience. Says the *Pittsburgh Post-Gazette*'s Ann Rodgers-Melnick:

> I look for stories that have a direct bearing on the religious belief, practice and commitment of some significant portion of my readers, or which may help explain events on the national or international scene. Stories that deal with the official teachings of religious bodies that are strong in my re-

gion or that deal with significant challenges to those teachings are very important.

I look for stories that have wider implications, that will be of interest both to those whose religion is at issue and to those outside that religion.

"Readers care," adds Rebekah Scott, the religion editor for the *Toledo Blade*. "People like details on what is vaguely familiar, so I try to cover trends, ethics, beliefs with *local* applications."

In a conventional sense, the least important stories are the routine ones about people and events that have long been associated with religion news. Still, they are an important part of religion reporting.

Those who are involved in the religious community know about them, look for them and miss them if they are absent. People not directly involved sometimes know about them from other sources. They may scan religion news looking for ideas they can use in their own organizations or to stay in touch with a part of the community or to keep tabs on what is going on. Newcomers to a community also use them to find a suitable congregation.

Individually each of those little stories is relatively unimportant, but collectively they help create a representative picture of society. Because of the media's agenda-setting and cultivation effects, their absence can imply that religion is absent from the community or unimportant in spite of the significance people attach to their beliefs and the time, talent and money they invest in support of their religion.

Ironically, if it is the abundance of those "little stories" that leads nonspecialists to overlook religion as news, it is the compulsion to cover them all that stands in the way of opening up religion pages to other kinds of stories. Because newspapers and television stations serve a local market, the religion beat is almost always defined as a local one but that doesn't mean every local event deserves its own story. Little stories can be grouped into a roundup column and events can be listed in a calendar.

Coverage that serves a local audience does not have to be parochial. In small towns, reporters can redefine "local" to include surrounding areas where people worship, send their children to parochial schools, shop or work. They can also insert a local angle into national and international news.

Searching for stories that are important and that have real consequences almost guarantees some stories about religion will focus on controversies and conflict because both their existence and their resolution impact individuals and shape society. But contrary to popular opinion, most news about religion does not have conflict as its dominant news value and religion reporters do not go out of their way to find it. Although proportions vary from time to time and medium to medium, it's rare for conflict to be the main news value in even one-third of all stories about religion. Only about 10 percent of experienced religion journalists say it is something they really look for.

They cover intrachurch and interchurch battles over doctrine, practices and leadership. Both religion reporters and reporters from other beats report on religion when it fuels political debates or gets caught up in policy decisions. They also find religion-based conflicts when they cover arts and entertainment, business, crime and the courts, education, lifestyles, medicine, science, the environment and sports. But if they find news in conflict, they also find "importance" and "relevance" to their audience in stories about conflict resolution or cooperation.

They also find news value in the new and different, especially when the unusual may signal a trend or provide insight that others can learn from. Most, however, shy away from the oddball story that amuses without enlightening because that kind of story is relatively unimportant. It can also be both misleading and highly offensive.

Finding Story Ideas

When religion news was simply a matter of reporting on local people and institutions, finding it was easy. Religion reporters relied heavily on newsletters and news releases from local congregations and from other religion-related organizations in the community as well as ones from their regional and national offices. With them and a quick phone call to get a quote or set up a photo opportunity, they could easily fill the space allotted to them. By the best estimates, 20 years ago religion reporters received, on average, 40 pieces of mail each day.

Their mail boxes are still overflowing and religion reporters like it that way. "We sent a letter to every place of worship inviting them to put us on their mailing list and telling them how to get their stories in the paper," says Sharon Grigsby, editor of the *Dallas Morning News'* award-winning religion section. Although much of the material sent to newspapers by congregations or other religious organizations has very little news value, about one-fourth of all religion reporters use several items from them each week. Very few ignore them.

Newsletters and news releases are still one of the best ways to survey the religious community, find story ideas and get information. Those from church and denominational headquarters and from regional and national parachurch organizations are one of the best sources of information about current developments, issues and leadership changes within a particular religion. Because organizations often take positions on public issues, mailings from ecumenical bodies such as the National Council of Churches, parachurch organizations such as missionary societies and television ministries and special purpose ones such as the Christian Coalition, the Rutherford Institute and the Family Research Council are also important.

However, as a source of information and ideas, mailings from religious organizations are declining in usefulness and in actual use because much of the information in them is now on-line. Local congregations and most religious organizations have websites where information about activities and current concerns is readily available. The Vatican distributes news releases via the Internet. Worldwide Faith News posts news releases from religious organizations authorized to use the service by its advisory group and also maintains an archive of those postings.

Religion reporters check the Internet regularly to find out what is going on in the world of religion, to find facts and gather background information for their stories. Some of the material available on-line is, of course, suspect, but much of it is excellent—full texts of scripture, church teachings, position statements, and calls to action. For alternative religions, the Internet may be the only readily available source as it was when reporters needed to find information about Heaven's Gate in a hurry when 39 of its members committed suicide in March 1997.

For ideas and information, savvy religion reporters also turn to religious media and to the academic and scholarly literature. Religious media can alert reporters to situations that otherwise might go unnoticed or give them the background they need to help put local developments into a broader perspective. For nondenominational churches, smaller religions and ones with an associational polity, monitoring the religious media church leaders and members use regularly can be virtually the only way to spot trends or to determine whether what is going on locally is typical or atypical.

Academic journals keep religion reporters abreast of current religious scholarship and help them monitor church-state relations. Those from the field of sociology of religion alert reporters to religious change and to the latest findings concerning the effect of religion on everything from people's personal lives to their political behavior. Although some of the works are so theoretical or technical that they are of little use for journalistic purposes, other research, such as Ball State University Professor Stephen D. Johnson's investigation of "Religion and the O.J. Simpson Verdict among the Elderly," has both significance and obvious appeal for a general audience.

But as helpful as newsletters and news releases, the Internet and publications can be, passive newsgathering goes only so far. "The best advice in journalism, whether the subject is religion or anything else, is to get out of the office," says Steve Chambers, religion editor for the *Newark Star-Ledger*. "There are a lot of powerful, spiritual things going on in churches, mosques, temples, soup kitchens, urban streets, suburban homes and numerous other places in America. If you witness them, the results can be very powerful, both through your words and on film."

Using the phone book as a guide, reporters need to identify all the local places of worship and then visit as many of those organizations as possible as quickly as possible. In the *Hartford Courant*'s guidebook for its reporters, Gerald Renner advises his colleagues to

> get to know who is who in the predominant houses of worship and schmooze with them straight off. In most Connecticut towns, for example, that means: Congregational, Catholic and Episcopal.
>
> Pay a visit to that white-spired Congregational church and say hello to the pastor. The Congregational minister is unusually tuned in to the community and is ecumenically minded. He or she can give you pointers about the other churches, not to mention scuttlebutt about what is going on in town. ...
>
> Also say hello to the Catholic pastor. ... There may be several Catholic churches, and, if it is a heavily ethnic town, you are likely to find ethnic Catholic churches (Italian, Polish, Lithuanian, Slovak, etc.). With them you get a bonus, gaining an insight into what might ordinarily be a closed community.
>
> The Episcopal Church is usually also in the middle of community stuff, and ... its membership probably includes some of the town's movers and shakers and the wannabes.

In other towns, the major players might be the Methodist Church and a Baptist one or Lutherans and Mormons. The number and nature of the entries under each subheading in the local phone book will provide a feel for the relative size and probable influence of each religion represented in the community. Although it is important to establish contacts within the congregations that appear to be most influential, covering religion thoroughly also means making contacts within the local ministerial alliance, if there is one, and also reaching out to those groups that may not be part of the religious establishment—storefront churches, synagogues, mosques and alternative religious communities.

Besides visiting local places of worship, one of the best ways to get to know the religious community and to find story ideas and sources of expertise is to visit different kinds of bookstores in different parts of the community, observe what is on the shelves and talk to the owners, store managers or bookbuyers about their customers, their interests, and changes they have observed in audience tastes.

In bookstores that serve a general clientele, titles shelved under "Religion," "Philosophy," "Metaphysics," or "Spirituality" are good for generating story ideas about how people are satisfying their quest for meaning; those under "Current Events" or "Current Nonfiction" offer possibilities for story ideas connecting religion to other concerns. At used book stores, multiple copies of the same title often are the byproduct of religious study groups. Asking who brought those books in for resale can produce leads about institutional concerns. Really old books can lead to stories illuminating the community's religious past.

Christian bookstores usually have a clientele made up primarily of conservative Protestants. The books are a clue to their beliefs and also to their concerns, but most Christian bookstores sell much more than books. Fashion or lifestyle reporters can get ideas from clothing, household items and cookbooks. Business writers might check out the computer software or inquire into marketing and promotional strategies. Entertainment reporters can get ideas by comparing the CDs and tapes sold in Christian bookstores to those available in other music stores.

Alternative bookstores can be the only clue to new religions in a community. These bookstores are usually listed in the phone book, but their clientele may be individuals unaffiliated with any religion or members of small, tightly knit groups that have no real need for listings in the phone book. They may also be somewhat fearful of attracting attention to themselves. Therefore, the only way of finding story ideas or sources for stories about those who practice alternative forms of spirituality may be to develop a rapport with the people who operate businesses catering to their religious needs.

After that, religion reporters can branch out to other agencies in the community. Local colleges and universities may have faculty with expertise relevant to religion reporting. Phone book listings for day care centers, schools and social service organizations will include ones that are religious or at least religion-affiliated. Entries under more specialized business headings may turn up some that advertise themselves as Christian businesses and some that suggest other religious influences. Separate Christian business directories can be useful sources of story ideas for both religion reporters and business reporters. Some larger cities also have Chinese yellow pages that are useful for finding possibilities for stories about Eastern religions.

Talking to as many of the religious leaders and the principals from other agencies in the community as possible will point to many story ideas and sources of information. But, whenever possible, it is best not to rely exclusively on the telephone.

"I never interview people on the telephone unless I absolutely have to," says Laurie Goodstein, whose reporting for the *Washington Post* made her a repeat winner of the Templeton and Supple awards for religion reporting and writing. "I try very hard to go where they are, meet them on their turf." Much of what goes on within congregations and other organizations may initially be hidden from public view. "Good reporters have to use all their senses. Observation," she says, "is critical." In many cases, knickknacks, artwork, books and magazines, brochures and items on bulletin boards provide a better feel for what people are really like and what organizations care about than anything the person might say.

Similar clues to what religious people think is really important can be detected by observing who speaks up in public forums. The presence at meetings and hearings of people who use religious language or wear religious symbols—clerical collars, a cross or yarmulke—show that religion is present and that the religious concerns need to be reported and explained.

Stories for Dedicated Space

Religion reporters still cover the new minister at First Baptist, revivals and box socials. They also cover religious leaders, church conventions, pronouncements from denominational headquarters, organizational programs and projects.

However, those stories that focus on religious institutions do not receive the emphasis they once did. At newspapers where there is a real commitment, stories in the religion section create a picture of the local religious community but they also serve as a window on the world.

Institutional stories about what the late Louis Cassels, longtime religion reporter for United Press International, once called the "grinding and clanking of ecclesiastical machinery" are still important. Those "grindings" and "clankings" establish institutional policy and sometimes signal mobilization efforts. The more traditional stories about people and events help flesh out the picture of the religious community. But they are what *Dallas Morning News* religion editor Sharon Grigsby calls "agate stories."

Because no community is an island, papers committed to thorough coverage emphasize stories that connect religion to people's lives and to the life of the community. That kind of story also functions as a bridge between the local community and what is going on elsewhere. They bring to public attention events, trends, issues, situations and ideas from elsewhere that may have local repercussions. They also put local news into a broader context.

The best religion sections do not cater to a single audience. Instead, they provide variety—in religions, subject matter, levels of coverage and story types. Their reporters cover religions that are making news, but also seek out those that seem quiescent. They look to institutions, but also to people who are not part of any organized religion. At local media, they cover their region but also pay attention to what is going on elsewhere. At national media, reporters always keep one eye on local communities and the other on the world.

With six pages set aside for religion news each week, the *Dallas Morning News* carries more religion news than most papers, but the kinds of stories it contains and the way space is allocated among them is fairly typical. On Page One, religion gets a thematic treatment, marking a radical shift from the traditional notion of religion news. The theme could be megachurches, the marketing of Jesus, the role of women in religions, church architecture, religion and single-issue voting, crystals, candles, an interfaith dialogue or a debate between a religious person and one with no religion about a topic such as the relationship between religion and ethics.

Ideas come from everywhere. "We make a deliberate effort to be inclusive," says religion editor Sharon Grigsby. "We try to make sure the coverage gives the big picture, but we also must reach people." The

theme may be developed in a single long story accompanied by photos, art work or infographics or told through a cluster of closely related
stories. Most weeks the coverage spills over to Page 4 which is also the
space for other kinds of stories of more than transitory local importance.

On Page 4 there are usually regional or national stories from
churches, denominations or other religious institutions, perhaps a
roundup column devoted to short religion-related news from around
the country or around the world and, on rare occasions, an important
story from a news service or the wires that didn't make it into the paper's regular news columns.

Occasionally Page 4 may also have a guest column by a religious
leader or one may appear on Pages 2 and 3, which are set aside for the
"agate" stories. On those pages, stories about people and about events
are clustered together under their own standing heads. There is also a
section for stories of "community needs." Those short stories about local programs or projects end with "contact information" for people
who want to get involved. On Page 2 there is also a calendar of holidays and holy days that mark special occasions within each religion.
Page 3 usually has a day-by-day listing of events.

People told the *Morning News* that they wanted more good news
about religion, so there is also space for readers to share "acts of kind-
ness" that have touched them. Because people respond to the religion
section, some space is also reserved for letters to the editor that were
addressed to the religion section or its staff.

Page 5 consists of advertisements and announcements from
churches and other religious organizations. Page 6 is for arts and entertainment. There are reviews and listings of books, music, television
programs, art shows and museum exhibits, CD-ROMs, computer
games and computer programs that are religious or that have religion-
related themes.

Most newspapers do not have the resources to set aside as many
pages for religion news as the *Dallas Morning News* does, but those
that are committed to thorough coverage find ways to provide the same
kind of diversity.

In smaller communities, the institutional kind of local religion news
may take up as much as half of the total space set aside for religion
news. But regardless of community size, good sections feature several
stories each week about local congregations, people and events. Those
stories may be abridged to create roundup columns or they may be

grouped together under standing headings such as "Where We Worship," "People of Faith" or "This Week in Religion." To flesh out the picture of the local religious community, many also include a "What We Believe" column written by local clergy.

Usually featured stories about local religious organizations and people are rotated among the religions in a community so that each gets coverage in rough proportion to its strength in the area. In most cases, the religion page will not feature both a place of worship and a person from the same religion in the same week. But events may alter the normal rotation. If for example, a church will celebrate its 100th anniversary, it may be featured out of turn even though another church from the same denomination was covered only a few weeks earlier; if the Buddhists break ground for a new temple the same week a Buddhist is chosen to lead the local ministerial alliance, both will get coverage in the same week.

But in addition to covering institutional news, good sections also find ways to include in-depth stories similar to those the *Dallas Morning News* features on the front page of its religion section. For this expanded kind of coverage, subject matter and storytelling style vary. Some in-depth stories are features; some are hard news. They may be about people, religious organizations, doctrine and practices, projects, trends, issues, programs and events, but their goal is to convey the many facets and meanings of religion from as many perspectives as possible.

Because these stories often weave together the connections between beliefs and behaviors across many religions or explore consequences for the religious organization, for individuals and for society, they take more time than reporters who cover religion on a part-time basis can devote to them. Therefore, smaller papers, in particular, often use pickups from the wire services or from specialized news syndicates such as Religion News Service for at least part of their coverage.

The best papers, however, include as many locally written in-depth stories as possible. They are also careful not to relegate national or international stories to the religion section when that would unduly delay or detract from attention to important developments. Instead, they select carefully, taking into account what they contribute to public understanding of religion, and also add to them. By including some information comparing the situation in the local community to what is going on elsewhere or by localizing stories from outside the community, good sections effectively act as a window on the world.

Local television stations usually cannot cover religion news as thoroughly as newspapers can, but those committed to religion reporting do cover all of the kinds of religion news typically found in newspapers. Because of its limited newshole, local stories about people, religious institutions and events are the hardest to include, but where there is a commitment to religion reporting, a station can still provide a representative picture of religion in the community as well as some in-depth coverage.

Those stations that have a segment set aside for religion news sometimes divide that time among short interviews with a religious newsmaker, stories about major events within the religious community that are open and likely to appeal to many people, service projects undertaken by religious organizations, and longer segments devoted to issues or trends. Those same kinds of stories can also be incorporated into regular news segments. Attention to people, organizations and events can also be rotated among religions just as it is at many newspapers.

Religion Stories for Other Beats

Even though religion journalists now think of religion news as more than just stories about what religious people and their organizations are doing and their employers now set aside more space for religion news than they once did, more than half of all stories about religion are the work of nonspecialists. However, nonspecialists who fail to see the connection between religion and what is happening on their beat also miss many stories.

Because some portion of the audience always knows that such a connection exists, stories where the religious dimension is misrepresented, ignored or incompletely covered can greatly affect media credibility. Both stories that misrepresent and those that overlook the religious dimension are common and often most troubling in political reporting.

As a result first of the activities of the Moral Majority and then the Christian Coalition, reporters who cover national politics have learned that religion can be a political force. In the 1996 presidential election, they regularly noted that Republican candidates felt compelled to cater to the interests of the Christian Right. For them, stops in Colorado Springs to visit influential spokespersons such as James Dobson, whose radio programs and magazines are highly influential in conservative religious circles, became something of a "must do." At the same time, most failed to get input from religions that are not aligned with the Christian Right.

Political concerns often appear to be those of people acting out of their own self-interest rather than because of beliefs that may be widely shared, but wherever there are issues, there is going to be religion. Because the formulation of policy and passage of legislation addressing issues are usually the province of the political reporter, they need to be on the lookout for any connections to religion. In politics, religion is most often a part of the story when people's positions and candidate preferences are passionately held ones. That is as true at the local and state level as in national politics, but the connection is more often missed because the mobilization is less visible.

In international reporting, religion gets mentioned most often in stories from the Middle East, Ireland, Bosnia and occasionally India and Pakistan. Religious influence in other areas is neglected or misrepresented, but it is there and it makes itself known in the same ways it does in the United States. Foreign correspondents might not have been so surprised at how quickly communism appeared to crumble if they had noted the thousands of East Germans who turned out each year for Kirkentag (Church Day) and then inquired whether churches throughout the region were being used much as black churches in the American South and white ones in the North were used to provide moral and organizational muscle to the civil rights movement.

Inquiries into the religious climate can also add depth to reporting on business practices, tourism, entertainment and education. On the education beat, prayer and observance of religious holidays in public schools and state standards for parochial schools and home schooling are the most obvious examples, but religion can also be at the core of disputes over academic freedom, parental authority, discipline, curricular content, teaching methods and taxation.

Different religion-based understandings inform opinions about the relative merits of government authority versus institutional prerogatives versus individual rights that show up on the business beat in stories about employer-employee relations, management techniques, housing, equal opportunity and equal access, just as they do on the education beat.

Because laws must be enforced, many religion-related stories also show up in crime and court reporting. Religious people and their institutions sometimes become victims of crime; sometimes they are charged with wrongdoing. In this litigious society, they also file civil complaints or find themselves defendants in a civil case. Even when they are not directly involved, religious organizations file *amicus curiae* briefs when cases touch on their interests.

Because religion provides answers to the purpose and meaning of life, stories about the beginning, preservation and end of life that are at the core of much reporting about science, medicine and the environment also have their religious dimensions. Science can tell when a life is viable, when it can be saved or when it is threatened. However, only religion can answer whether a particular life—an unborn baby, a spotted owl, or a person needing a blood transfusion—must be saved at all costs or whether some other good may take a higher priority. Therefore, many stories from science-related beats are incomplete if the religious, moral or ethical dimensions are omitted.

Issues gain their strength from religious convictions, but on some beats, religion's private face more often dominates. Personality profiles of athletes and everyday people paint an incomplete picture when questions about the core influences in people's lives are left unanswered. Some art and entertainment is obviously religious, but religious beliefs and beliefs about religion find expression even in art, books, dance, music and plays that may at first appear to be entirely secular. On the lifestyle beat, notions about fashion, food, family and fun vary across religious traditions. As in art and entertainment, trends in each may influence or be influenced by the religious climate.

Building Bridges

At best, specialists and nonspecialists supplement and complement each other. But often their work is unconnected.

Religion reporters may fail to notice or may lack the time to follow up on leads suggested by stories from other beats. Reporters from those beats often fail to include appropriate information about the religious dimension of stories they cover because they fail to keep up with the work of their colleagues whose job it is to keep abreast of developments within the religious community.

When journalists fail to follow through with stories, public understanding suffers. But public understanding also suffers when members of the audience attend to some stories but not to others. That problem can be quite severe in the case of religion news because the localite and cosmopolite audiences have such different news interests.

Localites have always been the core audience for the stories covered in space set aside for religion news, but their favorite stories are those about the churches, organizations, events and people who are conventionally religious. Because they see religion news as fulfilling a quasi-religious function, they may not read much else in the newspaper or watch much television. Moreover, they are likely to be offended by or skip stories about alternative religions or about issues and trends they find unsettling.

Localites are often quite vocal about their likes and dislikes. Therefore, it can be tempting to cater to their wishes. But that would fail to serve cosmopolites who are, in many cases, the silent majority when it comes to religion news. Although cosmopolites are often news junkies, historically many of them did not read the religion pages because there was nothing on the traditional "church page" that they found interesting. They like coverage of alternative religions and in-depth stories about ideas, trends and issues.

Different opinions about those ideas, trends and issues can divide a society. In a climate of culture war, the media must be concerned about their own freedom and prerogative to cover the news as they see fit. But they also must be concerned for their audience and for the whole community. Because so many of the issues that can tear societies apart are religious, the media must cover religion and religion-based viewpoints.

Because they cannot afford to serve one audience at the expense of another, media committed to good religion reporting try to provide something for everyone. They also take steps to build bridges between stories and between audiences.

Fortunately, for all their differences, localites and cosmopolites do share some interests (Table 9.1). Both audiences are interested in local news, including news of local people. They also like opinions and commentary and advice columns. Those shared interests suggest ways to reach both groups and entice each one to pay attention to stories they might otherwise overlook.

Whenever possible, complex regional, national or international stories can be given a local angle. A sidebar story about a person with expertise or insight can give the story greater appeal by putting a human face on the subject. Personality profiles and personal experience stories add depth and invite understanding, as do stories or invited columns in which people with diverse perspectives share their thoughts.

Space set aside for religion conveys a sense of importance and dignity to the subject. It also allows for more flexible and creative packaging of news. To build connections among stories and between stories that appear in space set aside for religion and those that appear elsewhere, some newspapers run a hard news story on the front page and a related personality profile in the religion section. Conversely, they sometimes carry the feature story on Page One or in some other section and the hard news story on the religion page. With each story, they include a box with "related story on Page xx" as a way of encouraging readers to find stories or parts of the paper they might otherwise skip.

TABLE 9.1. NEWS INTERESTS OF LOCALITE AND COSMOPOLITE AUDIENCES

	Audience	
Subject Preferences	Localites	Cosmopolites
RELIGION NEWS		
Church positions/policies		yes
Doctrine and practices (Judeo-Christian)	yes	
Doctrine and practices (other religions)		yes
Ecumenism and cooperation	yes	yes
Ethical issues	yes	
Faith experiences	yes	
International religion news		yes
Local congregations/one-time events	yes	
Missionary activity	yes	
National denominations/groups	yes	yes
Ongoing projects and programs	yes	
Opinions and commentary	yes	yes
Religion and politics		yes
Religious issues	yes	yes
Social issues		yes
Surveys and trends		yes
GENERAL NEWS		
Accidents and disasters	yes	
Advice columns	yes	yes
Arts and entertainment		yes
Business and the economy		yes
Editorials page		yes
Education news	yes	yes
Environmental news		yes
International news		yes
Lifestyle	yes	
Local government	yes	yes
Local people	yes	yes
National news		yes
Science news		yes
Sports		yes
Weather	yes	yes

Similarly, television stations can run one story at the top of the news-cast and tell viewers to stay tuned for an interview or an in-depth analysis in the religion segment.

For Further Reading

Buddenbaum, Judith M. "Predicting Religion Reporters' Use of a Denomi-national News Service," *Newspaper Research Journal* 8, no. 3 (Spring 1987):59-70.

    This study examines the relative influence of a reporter's own beliefs, newsroom constraints and audience characteristics on use of information sources.

Buddenbaum, Judith M. "Religion Journalists' Perceptions of Religion News and Its Audience," ERIC ED 283189. August 1987.

    This study uses survey data to explore how religion reporters de-fine religion news and decide which stories to cover.

Buddenbaum, Judith M. "Source Dependence and Story Production," ERIC ED 257132. August 1985.

    This paper compares the sources used most frequently by spe-cialists and nonspecialists for stories about religion.

Ruehlmann, William. *Stalking the Feature Story.* New York: Vintage Books, 1979.

    Although this text book is not directly related to religion report-ing, Chapter 1 "Vision" and Chapter 4 "Ideas" have much to say about finding story ideas.

Walsh, Mary Ann. "Meeting the Call for Better Religion Coverage," *Editor & Publisher* August 24, 1996: 48, 37.

    In this article, the associate director of communications for the U.S. Catholic Conference presents ideas for stories about the Roman Catholic Church, most of which are equally applicable to other reli-gions.

CHAPTER 10

CHOOSING AND
USING SOURCES

F inding story ideas is only half the battle. Stories require information and that means finding the sources that can provide information that is accurate, credible and meaningful. Much of what is wrong with religion reporting is the result of failures to find that kind of information. Too often journalists consult just a few widely recognized and readily available sources and report what they say instead of digging deeply enough to discover whether the angle they chose is really appropriate or taking the time to uncover the information that would add perspective and answer people's questions.

Journalistic norms demand objectivity. For simple stories, that usually gets translated into an accurate report of what sources who appear to be credible say, do and believe. Even in situations when the journalist should have been aware that the source was not in a position to have all of the relevant information or might have ulterior motives, journalists often take their story idea and their angle from the source who first alerted them to the story or that first sent a news release. That first interpretation often lingers even when subsequent stories provide countervailing information.

In one city, people living near the House of God's Love called local media in hopes reporters would reveal that the group headed by a black ex-convict was a dangerous cult. During sweeps week one low-rated television station picked up the story. The three-part series passed on the neighbors' beliefs and juxtaposed them with scenes from Waco to support the angle that the group was a virtual "time bomb" in spite of the police department's inability to turn up any evidence of illegal or even suspicious activity. Notably missing from the stories were any efforts to find out from group members or from their leader why they invited street people into their home, what they actually believed or why they wore the flowing white robes and sandals that so aroused neighbors' suspicions.

That kind of reporting is not limited to stories about unfamiliar religions. "Too often we listen to the loudest voices, not the most discerning ones," says John W. Smith, religion editor for the *Reading (Pa.) Eagle-Times.*

Stories announcing revivals and rallies are often followed up with ones taken directly from press releases announcing "thousands turned to Christ" without any further checking to determine how the figures were gathered. Most newspapers ignored the Re-Imagining conference organized by women from moderate to liberal Protestant churches until after conservative Protestants seized on the women's use of female terms for God in their worship service as evidence of "goddess worship." That interpretation persisted for months in spite of efforts by those who had organized the event to explain the historic and biblical roots of their belief that the God of Christianity transcends all human categories, including gender.

For stories involving conflicts and controversies, "objectivity" means finding sources with opposing views and reporting those views, but doing so in a way that is both accurate and fair to all. While reporters for print media are not immune to the tendency, on television time restrictions and storytelling conventions quickly reduce "opposing views" to "both sides." In religion, however, "both sides" can be meaningless. With so many religions, there are almost always multiple perspectives, both among religions and within any single congregation, denomination or religious tradition.

Balanced coverage requires telling those sides through use of equivalent sources while also taking into account the extent to which those sources' positions are representative ones. Stories about abortion nicely illustrate the problem.

Because they are highly visible and easily accessible, both specialists and nonspecialists almost invariably turn to conservative Protestants or Catholics for the "pro-life" side and to Planned Parenthood or medical professionals for the "other" side. Those sources are appropriate, but they are not equivalent. Relying on them captures the religious dimension of one position but ignores it for the other side even as it misses the possibility that people might oppose abortion for reasons that have little to do with religious beliefs. Too often stories oversimplify the controversy by making it appear there are only two positions—one Christian and one not religious. Yet simple reflection on the proportion of people who identify themselves as religious with the proportion of those who are truly opposed to abortion in all circumstances should indicate there must be religious people on "both" sides, as well as many who, for a variety of reasons, hold intermediate positions between the two extremes.

Finding "secular" sources for the "religious" positions, "religious" ones for the "secular" positions, and multiple perspectives for both sides takes more work than relying on conventional sources, but it is possible. Checking *amicus curiae* or "friends of the court" briefs filed with court cases involving abortion would turn up religious groups and ones that are not religious on both sides of the debate. Simply contacting people or organizations whose views are not usually taken into account—Native Americans who adhere to traditional beliefs, New Agers, Druids and goddess worshippers, organizations representing Judaism, Islam, Hinduism, Buddhism—would counteract the tendency to polarize disputes.

In covering religion, reporters might well take their cue from social scientists. Just as scientists create a hypothesis that is capable of being supported or proven false, journalists should treat their story idea and their initial angle as an hypothesis and then gather evidence until they are convinced either that their initial hunch was correct or that it must be rejected. Rejecting the angle does not mean there is no story. Although it may take some convincing of skeptical editors, a story that controversy within a church is overblown, for example, or that a cult is not recruiting large numbers of unsuspecting children is important intelligence.

In religion reporting, gathering information from multiple sources and multiple perspectives and then triangulating the evidence much as social scientists do is the key to writing stories about complex subjects. Only in that way can journalists produce stories that will approximate reality instead of passing on easy assumptions that may be wrong.

"It starts with the reporting process," says Laurie Goodstein, the award-winning religion reporter. "I throw the net very wide. I never know what I'm going to catch that's going to be useful or where I might catch it." Doing that requires seeking out many kinds of sources and many sources of each kind, as well as understanding the kinds of evidence each source may provide and its strengths and weaknesses.

For journalists, evidence is the information they gather in order to write stories. The goal is an accurate report of information that is true, but truth can be a troubling concept in religion reporting. Information may consist of facts, opinions, or some hybrid of them. All may rest as much on beliefs as on anything that is empirically verifiable. In any case, the evidence obtainable from any source may depend on that source's vantage point and motivations.

Facts, Opinions and Religious Truth

Ordinarily facts are those statements subject to empirical verification through independent observation or experimentation. In contrast, opinions are statements of personal preference that are not subject to verification and, therefore, can be neither right nor wrong. Some information about religion is factual—when a church was built, how many people belong to a particular religion, for example. Other information is opinion, as when a person says she cannot accept church authority. Other statements, however, are more complex and sometimes troubling blends of fact and opinion.

Beliefs are both fact and opinion. It is a fact that Hindus believe in reincarnation and that the Roman Catholic Church teaches that Mary was assumed bodily into heaven. But accepting those beliefs rests on a faith that is akin to personal opinion because one cannot prove reincarnation to the satisfaction of a Catholic or convince a Hindu that Marian doctrine is correct. As a result, religion can appear to be entirely a matter of personal opinion. But if those teachings cannot be proven true to the satisfaction of those who choose not to accept them, the statements themselves can be verified. By pointing to sacred writings and to the testimony of Hindus or Catholics, even those who cannot accept either belief can come to accept as fact the reality that Hindus and Catholics do believe them. It is that kind of factual accuracy, not whether a particular belief can be proven through empirical evidence, that is important in reporting about religion.

At the same time, it is important to remember that knowledge about any religion and the meanings and evaluations attached to its beliefs and practices will vary across religions and within religions just as government officials may differ in their knowledge about particular laws or in their evaluations of them. Both people who are members of a religion and those who are outsiders to it have opinions about religion in general and about particular religious beliefs and practices. Those opinions may differ and yet be equally important, but in reporting, as in libel law, people's opinions should not be considered protected "fair comment" if the underlying facts are wrong.

Primary and Secondary Evidence

Primary evidence is based on firsthand observation or experience or is gathered through original research. Secondary evidence is more akin to hearsay. Courts consider hearsay evidence inadmissable.

Journalists, too, should treat it with a healthy skepticism. In fact, like everyone else, they usually assume primary evidence is better than secondary sources. Television stations tout their eyewitness reports. When they cannot be on the scene themselves, both print and broadcast journalists usually go first to people who were directly involved. But as every reporter who has tried to find out how an accident happened knows, eyewitness accounts can differ so radically that it is often impossible to tell what happened. Even police investigations or a trial may not clear up all the ambiguities.

If there is no reason to believe religious people are more likely to lie than any other source, neither is there much reason to assume they will always tell the truth. Like everyone else, they may not know or may have forgotten crucial information. They may also tailor their accounts according to what they think is required or appropriate in a given situation or to protect themselves and their causes.

As on all beats, journalists who cover religion must take into account the competence, reliability and credibility of those who saw, experienced, or gathered the information that qualifies as primary evidence and of those who pass on secondary evidence. People who are unhappy with some aspect of their religion's doctrine or practices will almost always overstate the problem and overestimate the number of people who, like them, are dissatisfied. Those who are satisfied may downplay conflict.

Over time those who leave one religion for another tend to forget the good parts of the religion they left and exaggerate its horrors, particularly when their new religion encourages that kind of personal testimony. Therefore, testimony from heretics and apostates needs to be checked carefully for reliability and validity. But so does information from those who happily remain a part of a religious community. Clergy differ in their training and thus their knowledge. Some laymembers of a religion may also be highly knowledgeable about church doctrines and practices and others may understand little about what their church teaches or why it does things a particular way. People who know they will be called on to give testimony more often prepare in advance and have information available than those who are suddenly asked for an opinion. Those who had time to prepare may concoct a plausible story. Those who did not have time to prepare their testimony may later have second thoughts about it.

Data collected by one organization for its purposes may not be comparable to that from another. Church membership figures, for example, are rarely comparable across religions. Some religions count as members anyone who ever attended; they rarely purge names from lists unless specifically asked to do so. Others have strict membership requirements and purge their lists frequently to remove people who do not meet established levels of activity or demonstrate sufficient commitment. In either case, data are only as good as the data collection and reports are only as good as the reporter. Both may vary from religion to religion or from congregation to congregation within the same religion.

People as Sources

It is a truism that "every person is a story." Often that story is worth telling. For simple stories about events and some stories about people, a single source may be enough. But in most cases, even stories about one person's faith will be more complete if journalists seek out multiple sources each of whom can add something to the telling.

Where stories cut across religious traditions or where conflict is involved, multiple perspectives are almost always required. "Reporting on religion is talk intensive," says Gustav Niebuhr, religion writer for the New York Times. "I'm always talking to people, filing away ideas and names. Religion is a multifaceted part of people's lives. Like religion, people are complex and good religion reporting has to reflect that."

Occasionally finding sources to represent the time-honored leader-follower, conservative-liberal, or Protestant-Catholic-Jew categories may be enough. Background information about religious beliefs, orientations to the world, religion-inspired behaviors and institutional structures discussed in Part I can serve as a useful guide to viewpoints that must be included in a particular story. But in many cases, reporters who rely too heavily on typologies will fail to capture the full range of possibilities, overinflate conflict or miss its most important dimensions.

In selecting sources for complex religion news stories it is often more useful to think of people as insiders and outsiders, and then to categorize them within each group according to their levels of authority, expertness and credibility and also to their perspective, or vantage point, and to their possible motivations.

In religion, everyone is simultaneously an insider and an outsider. Both insiders and outsiders may be leaders or followers who may or may not have authority and/or knowledge in any given situation. The person who is an insider with authority and vast knowledge in one situation may be an insider but have less authority or expertise in another situation and be a completely uninformed outsider for other purposes.

Journalists rely on church leaders or heads of parachurch and special purpose religious organizations for information about matters of church doctrine and practices, to explain programs and policies and to comment on issues and issue positions. Although their level of authority varies depending on theology and organizational structure, most national and regional leaders can speak with authority. Divisions of labor within the most churchlike organizations often mean that leaders may be more knowledgeable on some topics than others, but their backgrounds and vantage points can produce disagreements among them even though theirs is usually the institutional perspective.

That institutional perspective is important, especially in religions where the leadership is charged with protecting and promoting correct beliefs and behaviors among members. Official spokespersons and other knowledgeable sources with positions of authority can be found by consulting general directories or directories for each individual religion. Names of other sources, including clergy, who can provide a local perspective can usually be found by consulting phone books.

However, stories about lay members and ones that include their perspectives are just as important as ones about religious organizations, institutional activities and those that are told from the institutional perspective of religious leaders. Overreliance on institutional sources can miss the meaning of religion for those who believe. At the same time, overreliance on lay sources can, in some instances, overinflate controversy. In some religions, lay members in effect set theology through their power to call clergy and elect regional or national leaders. In other religions where they have no such role, overreliance on lay opinions can create the false impression that correct theology is a matter of majority vote.

Church leaders and laity alike are insiders to their own religion, but they are outsiders to everyone else's. Their perspectives on those other religions need to be included, but in a way that makes their perspective clear.

Insiders who are knowledgeable about their own religion may have at best limited information about others. Their views may also be colored by their current position. Just as insiders may differ depending on how they see themselves being affected by matters internal to their own religion, outsiders' viewpoints will also be colored depending on whether or not they see themselves as being directly affected. Their reaction may also depend on the extent to which they see others as engaging in activities or holding opinions that support their own beliefs or that are inimicable to them.

Although strict neutrality on matters of religion may be too much to hope for, the best safeguard against passing on religious sources' limited knowledge or biases is to cross-check information obtained from religious outsiders with that from religious insiders and check both against information from outsiders whose positions impose a degree of detachment. For most purposes, experts in comparative religion, religious history or the sociology of religion are the most knowledgeable and neutral outsiders. They can be found by consulting the public information office of universities, checking membership lists of professional organizations, or looking through books and journals to find authors of works relevant to a particular story.

For their authority, those outsiders depend on creating and maintaining a reputation for good scholarship. However, their perspective may be influenced by research traditions, choice of methodology, and sometimes their own religious beliefs or beliefs about religion. Therefore, they, too, should be checked. In particular it is important to distinguish between theologians and other experts who work within, and often on behalf of, a religion and those with employers such as state universities or nonsectarian private schools that have little vested interest in any or all religions. Publication by major book publishers, by university presses and in refereed scholarly publications is usually an indicator of work that meets professional norms for reliability and validity, but asking scholars about their own orientation to religion, why they study a particular subject or what they hope to accomplish with their work can be an equally useful way to detect potential biases.

Dealing with People

For journalists, the major problem is always one of obtaining access to people whose information or viewpoints are potentially useful. Outsiders are usually welcome to attend Christian and Jewish worship services, but as private organizations, religious institutions are under no legal compulsion to allow access to their services or meetings.

Most leaders from ecumenical organizations and those at the national, regional and congregational levels within Judaism and from the more churchlike Christian denominations readily grant interviews. However, leaders of new religious movements, those from other religions outside the Judeo-Christian tradition, and from the more conservative and sectlike segments of Christianity may be reluctant to speak to journalists. In some cases, that reluctance is simply because they have so seldom been asked for their views that they don't quite know what to expect. In other cases, the reluctance stems from having seen too many poorly reported stories that distort their beliefs in ways that make them seem weird or even dangerous.

Because many clergy assume that all journalists are biased against religion, even leaders from religions that are most inclined to deal with the press may be reluctant to talk to a journalist with whom they have not established a working relationship. Stressing the benefits of being able to tell their own story or of getting publicity for their cause may work, but simple appeals to the "public's right to know" are rarely very successful.

In the long run, continuing access to religious sources depends on developing a reputation for accurate and sensitive reporting about many different religions. That kind of reputation can also help a reporter gain initial access to groups that are generally inaccessible, but in many cases working through trusted intermediaries provides the only entry. Therefore, it is important for journalists to develop working relationships with many different people because each one may have among their friends some who are members of those difficult-to-reach organizations. Here, scholars who have gained access to religious organizations, business people such as the owners of religious bookstores or those who practice alternative medicine can be very useful.

Because so many religious people are suspicious of journalists, questions about the reporter's own beliefs are inevitable. Neither religion nor a lack of religion should be a barrier to good reporting. In any case, there is no way a single journalist could have religious beliefs matching those of every possible source. Therefore, no way of answering the question honestly will be universally useful.

If company policy prevents reporters from revealing their religious beliefs, simply referring to that policy is the only viable option. Where there is no policy, some reporters routinely tell their religion whenever asked, others never reveal their own beliefs, and still others decide on a case-by-case basis. But regardless of strategy, all strongly caution against challenging sources' beliefs or engaging them in theological debates. The best way to deflect what is often a source's attempt to uncover biases is simply to point to the variety of stories that have been covered and covered well.

Although religious sources may be suspicious of the reporter's motives, there is no reason for journalists to change their interviewing style. Depending on the purpose for the interview, hard questions, thorough investigation, and even some badgering of reluctant religious sources can be as appropriate or inappropriate on the religion beat as they are in any other kind of reporting.

At the same time, it is always appropriate to show a certain respect for sources' religious sensibilities by observing those customs common to each religious tradition. In most cases that requires little more than dressing modestly or, perhaps, removing shoes or covering one's head upon entering a place of worship. On those occasions when reporters must attend worship services, they should not participate in any part of the service if taking part would offend either their own beliefs or those of the religion whose service they are attending. However, to the extent possible, they should stand, sit or kneel as appropriate. Although they may, with permission, discretely tape the service, taking notes can be disruptive except in those congregations where members also regularly take notes.

More difficult problems of access and reporter-source relations occur in situations where the reporter is trying to elicit commentary from those who are not accustomed to being news sources or who come from religious traditions that have generally been outsiders to a particular debate. Although both clergy and lay members are usually willing to talk about their own faith, they may be reluctant to comment on issues that are not particularly salient to them. In many cases lay members are most concerned about saying something "wrong" that will affect their standing within their religious community. Leaders are more often reluctant in situations where their organization could be perceived as rife with conflict, as being a party to controversies that do not directly concern it, or as being allied with groups with which the institution agrees on a particular issue but with which it otherwise has little in common.

Even when religious sources may be willing to comment, differences in rhetorical styles may make it difficult for them to explain their positions. Preaching and teaching styles within conservative Protestantism make both clergy and laity quite adept at quoting scripture and connecting religion to issue positions and behaviors, but rhetorical styles in most other religions may make it difficult for members of those faiths to provide connections even where they exist. To guard against overestimating religious influences for some religions and underestimating them for others, journalists may have to interview multiple sources. They may also have to probe carefully to elicit thoughts, then paraphrase the source's comments, trying out various interpretations of it to elicit whatever meanings may exist.

Problems may also arise in eliciting information from those outsiders whose positions and vantage points do not readily identify them with any religious interest. Gathering information that includes religious identity is appropriate when interviewing lawyers who routinely handle cases on behalf of religious organizations, legislators who advocate positions or sponsor bills that reflect religious interests, people who testify about legislation or policies with implications for religion, or business persons expressing views on workplace rules relating to religion. However, if people are acting in a professional capacity that demands neutrality—a policeman arresting an animal rights protester, a judge hearing a driving-under-the-influence case—asking about religion would more often distort the story than reveal anything meaningful.

Documentary Sources

When journalists think about sources, they naturally think first of people, but they should not ignore the possibility that some of the evidence they need may come from documents. In some situations news releases or other kinds of documentary evidence can substitute for interviews. Often they are necessary to supplement, corroborate or refute evidence gathered by interviewing people or through the journalist's own observations.

As with people as sources, documents may be classified according to whether they are produced by insiders or outsiders and then according to varying levels of authority, expertness and credibility and as to the vantage point and motivations of those who created them.

The information in documents can be as complete and thorough as that obtained from people or it may be just as selective. As sources, their strength lies in the fact that, regardless of why they were created or how self-serving the information in them may be, documents are not readily changed. People's words are fleeting; documents are timeless. However, it is not always easy to interpret documents or to determine when one document has been replaced by another, especially because some relevant documents may not exist or they may not be accessible to journalists.

Examining documents over time can be the best way to detect changes. Those fixed records can also be an effective way of documenting official teachings, policies and positions and detecting discrepancies between them and actual behaviors. For new religious movements as well as the independent Christian churches and those that have a strictly congregational polity or have sectlike characteristics, religious publications may be the only source of information that can put local concerns in a broader perspective.

Magazines, books, sermons, other printed material, teaching materials, audiovisuals such as movies, and music can be useful as sources for story ideas and information. However, care needs to be taken in relying on them because some are official materials produced under the imprimatur of a religion and some are not.

Magazines are a case in point. Most of the larger churches and denominations have official publications, but official publications may have quite different editorial policies. Lutheran editors, for example, usually make a sharp distinction between religious matter and news. Their publications are usually more open to varying viewpoints, and news in them is more likely to be about conflict, deviant beliefs or inappropriate behaviors than is true of most other official Christian publications, which practice a kind of religious journalism intended to promote and defend the religion's understanding of correct beliefs and behaviors.

Some religious media are nondenominational or ecumenical in nature and, therefore, not wholly representative of any particular church's doctrinal positions or policies. Other publications are independently produced. Within the Roman Catholic Church, most Protestant denominations, other world religions and many of the larger new religious movements, publications freely circulate that support official church positions, attack them or seek to change them. Within Catholicism, for example, there are both church-produced and independently edited diocesan newspapers. There are also many newspapers and magazines that more closely reflect the views and interests of individual religious orders than those of the church itself.

These religious sources may be considered insider documentary sources in some contexts and outsiders in others. More neutral information from an outsider perspective can be found in many encyclopedias, books, public opinions polls and research reports. Some are authoritative and expert. Others may be of dubious quality, but all provide ways of tapping into a range of views and of cross-validating information.

Because open record laws do not apply to religious organizations, information collected and published by outsiders may be the only source of data about some religions. However, almost all religions willingly share their scriptures, other doctrinal writings and official policy statements. One notable exception is the Church of Scientology, which considers its scriptures to be trade secrets. The Church of Scientology also uses copyright law to guard against unauthorized publication of material in them. It often files lawsuits even when the documents were legally obtained from court records and when use of information from them is clearly fair use under copyright law.

Where such material is available, however, scripture and other official statements are the most authoritative sources for documenting religious teachings, policies, practices and, in some cases, issue priorities and positions. Although quoting from scripture sometimes strikes editors as promoting religious beliefs, that view should be resisted. The documents can be complicated and subject to varying interpretations, so journalists should not pick and choose information in them to make a point. However, there is little difference between including people's references to them or quotes from them and similar uses of quotes from or references to court decisions, statutory law, corporate annual reports or party platforms. The information simply gives readers a way of judging the source's understanding and credibility. Without that information people can be baffled as to why those who are ostensibly members of the same religion take different positions on important issues such as abortion or school prayer.

Although not all religions publish them or make them available to outsiders, yearbooks and other reports can be useful sources of data about religions and information on religious priorities. Where they exist and are accessible, they can be considered official documents although the material in them can be somewhat unreliable.

Data, such as membership figures, that come from self-reports can be especially misleading. Religions have different membership requirements. They also differ in the diligence with which they keep records. Local congregations may have reasons for underreporting or overreporting their membership but their parent organizations usually have a vested interest in inflating their figures. Because of social pressures, people overreport their identification with and attendance at worship services within the mainstream Judeo-Christian religions and tend not to report their identification with other religions.

Although membership figures obtained directly from religious institutions are seldom completely accurate or reliable, they can be checked against similar figures compiled by outside agencies. The censuses conducted by the U.S. government in the 19th century and less frequently during the first half of the 20th century included information on religious affiliation. More recently public opinion surveys have replaced the census as the best independent source for figures on religious identification and attendance.

Although the federal government no longer collects census data about religion, all levels of government hold some information about religious organizations and religious people. Information may also turn up in government reports on education or welfare or in records of hearings or legislative deliberations. Other government information can be found in police or court records, records of registered lobbyists, and IRS and state lists of tax-exempt charitable organizations. Although churches do not pay property taxes, their property holdings and sales are matters of public record. *Amicus curiae* briefs filed with court cases can be an excellent source for identifying religious interests on both sides of legal disputes. If a religion has been labeled as deviant or as a cult or if its members have been involved in protests, information about them or about government surveillance of them may be obtainable by filing requests under federal or state freedom of information laws.

The Internet

With a computer and a link to the Internet, journalists now have access to sources that once would have been beyond their reach even if time were not a factor and travel and phone budgets were unlimited. As a resource for journalists, the Internet has such potential for providing both valuable information and dangerous misinformation that it deserves its own mention.

The Internet can be a quick way to find general information or an answer to almost any question, but postings should be treated as coming from anonymous sources unless the site has previously been checked for authenticity. The major problem with the Internet is that anyone can post almost anything. Sometimes sites that appear to be those of reputable organizations are really copies of them. A more common problem is that authentic home pages and bulletin boards often have links to other sites on similar topics. Those sites often contain information that is inaccurate or does not reflect the viewpoints of the organization whose home page or bulletin board was used to access the other sites.

Although some home pages and bulletin boards have features that allow sending e-mail directly to the organization, taking the trouble to track down an address and phone number and then calling the organization sponsoring the site is the best guard against unwittingly misrepresenting the source of the information. In any case, a phone call may be necessary in order to contact someone who can provide additional input for a story. Home pages and bulletin boards can have information that is problematic, but as long as they are treated with caution they can be an effective way to get access to documentary sources and also to find people who can serve as sources for stories. However, information gathered by tapping into chat rooms must be treated with even more caution. There really is no effective way to determine if participants are who they claim to be. In most cases, chat rooms are best treated as windows into the world of religion-related discourse rather than as credible sources of information.

For Further Reading

Bromley, David (ed.). *The Politics of Religious Apostasy: The Role of Apostates in the Transformation of Religious Movements.* Greenwich, Conn.: Praeger, 1997.

Chapters in this edited volume examine from a social science perspective the motives and roles of those who leave a religion and those who remain within it while challenging its beliefs and practices. The chapters on stories apostates and heretics tell and on assessing their credibility are particularly useful.

Bromley, David G., and Anson D. Shupe, Jr. *"Moonies" in America: Church, Cult and Crusade.* Beverly Hills, Calif.: Sage, 1979.

Parts of this book, written from a resource mobilization perspective, show how a religion and its opponents can co-opt the media into promoting their causes. The book is also one of the best studies of the Unification Church.

Buddenbaum, Judith M. "Of Christian Freedom Fighters and Marxist Terrorists: The Image of SWAPO and the Namibian Independence Movement in the Religious and Secular Press." In Yonah Alexander and Robert Picard, eds., *In the Camera's Eye: The Media and Terrorist Events.* Washington, D.C.: Brassey's, 1990, 131-150.

This chapter examines the implications of relying primarily on religious sources or on official and political ones.

Clark, Lynn Schofield, and Stewart M. Hoover. "Controversy and Cultural Symbolism: Press Relations and the Formation of Public Discourse in the Case of the Re-Imagining Event." *Critical Studies in Mass Communication,* in press.

This study points to the dangers of missing a religious event, of expecting religious organizations to be equally skillful public relations practitioners, and of accepting one side's framing of a story.

Jensen, J. Vernon. *Argumentation.* New York: D. VanNostrand, 1981.

This basic textbook has a good chapter on gathering, classifying and evaluating various kinds of evidence.

Strentz, Herbert. *News Reporters and News Sources: Accomplices in Shaping and Misshaping the News,* 2nd. ed. Ames, Iowa: Iowa State University Press, 1989.

This little book provides practical advice on finding and evaluating sources. It also serves as a reminder of the ways sources and reporter-source relations shape the news.

Webb, Eugene T., Donald T. Campbell, Richard D. Schwartz and Lee Sechrest. *Unobtrusive Measures.* Chicago: Rand McNally, 1968.

This classic research methodology book provides helpful tips for gathering information and triangulating evidence to check out assumptions.

CHAPTER 11

WRITING STORIES

G ood religion reporting requires both a steady stream of ideas for obvious stories and for those that are of potential importance but less obvious. It also requires a large enough network of contacts to gather and cross-check information from sources each with their own strengths and weaknesses.

For the audience, however, the proof of good reporting comes with the story that is actually published or broadcast. At that level, even the best idea and the most careful and extensive research can be defeated by the way the story is actually told.

Journalists are usually quite good at reporting the who, what, where and when of news, but reporting with depth and understanding requires probing further. Religion is as much about meaning and purpose as it is about events, pronouncements, and strategies.

The religious dimension most often is missed or misinterpreted when nonspecialists accept without question the meaning provided by sources on their own beat with whom they are familiar and then use conventional news angles and themes to tell the story from an outsider's perspective. If religion journalists do not as often miss the religious dimension, the need to provide meaning in stories about religion is no less troublesome for them. The recent shift from covering religious institutions and religious elites to a broader focus that includes people's quest for meaning and purpose, the kinds of spirituality that occurs outside organized religion and matters of ethics and values makes meaning a matter of paramount importance. But the shift creates its own dilemmas because it raises new questions about whose meaning counts most.

In order to capture the faith dimension, religion journalists now turn more often to religious people with whom audiences can identify and from whom they can gain insight or guidance in their own search for understanding and purpose in their lives. In telling their stories, journalists for print media frequently abandon the inverted-pyramid style in favor of a feature approach that relies more heavily on narrative and literary conventions than on those associated with a traditional hard news approach.

That approach to religion reporting requires greater empathy for religion and religious people on the part of religion journalists than was necessary when journalists focused on religious institutions and leaders. Empathy is necessary if reporters are to avoid telling stories that appear biased against religion. At the same time, the new approach to religion reporting can easily miss the consequences of religiously inspired beliefs and behaviors for outsiders, for the culture, and for religion itself. In cases where stories are told from the perspective of lay members, and especially where those members' understanding or preferences conflict with institutional norms, overreliance on average religious people can easily foster the impression that lay opinion counts for more than that of religious leaders. It can also create the impression that matters of belief and behavior are and should be determined by majority rule or even subject to individual veto.

Because of the variety of religions and of opinions about religion in general and of particular religions, no way of telling a story is likely to satisfy everyone. Nevertheless, effective communication requires some awareness of how audiences may perceive storytelling conventions and of the problems associated with language use.

The way journalists frame their stories and organize the information can miss the point, baffle readers or lead them to see bias where none was intended. Their words can enlighten, but they can also misinform, foster stereotypes, and create the impression that the reporter is ignorant, if not biased.

Framing Stories

For print media, the first few paragraphs are the key to story framing. From a writer's perspective, the lead can make it more or less difficult to provide a complete or balanced account. From the reader's perspective, the lead provides the initial impression of what the story is about. Because readers have learned through experience that journalists often use the inverted pyramid to organize information, many may read no further. Therefore, whatever is in the first few paragraphs will give those casual readers their only understanding of a person, situation, event or issue. Even if people read the whole story, those first few paragraphs set up expectations that can affect their understanding or lead them to see bias if subsequent information seems to stray from the theme established by the lead or introduces contradictory information or perspectives.

Consider the framing of four stories written in connection with Pope John Paul II's October 1995 visit to the United States:

> Filling the wooden pews to overflowing on Sundays, the faithful at Ellicott City's Church of the Resurrection look like a suburban monolith—well-educated parents of mostly young children, dangling keys to the vans and station wagons that are the hallmark of middle-class families. ...
>
> But in the pews, around the dinner table or at night before bed, each at times has drawn strength from the conviction that whatever their struggles, they are somehow united with the suffering of Christ on the cross. Two weeks from today, 594 of them will ride buses to Camden Yards to see Pope John Paul II celebrate Mass. Twenty others will join a papal parade through the streets of Baltimore that afternoon. Seven youngsters will perform at the stadium in a pre-Mass celebration.
>
> Why are they going? The answers come out slowly—and different every time: John Paul II is the vicar of Christ. He is an unequivocal defender of life. He is a tireless advocate for the world's downtrodden.
>
> –Debbi Wilgoren, *Washington Post*

> Their spirits hardly dampened by steady rain, nearly 83,000 area Catholics transformed Giants Stadium into an open-air cathedral Thursday evening, giving a warm and long-awaited welcome to their pope at a windblown Mass in the Meadowlands.
>
> Pope John Paul II, his white and gold vestments billowing as he stood on the red-carpeted altar, responded enthusiastically to their cheers, but struck a serious note in his sermon, calling on the American church of immigrants to resist the national mood toward self-interest at the expense of the downtrodden.
>
> —David Gibson, *Bergen Record*

Central Park was transformed into a giant open-air cathedral Saturday as Pope John Paul II celebrated Mass before a flock of 130,000 urging Americans to stand up for family life and side with the homeless, the disabled and people with AIDS.

"Do not be afraid to search for God. Then it will truly be the land of the free and the home of the brave," the pope said at the end of the service. "God bless America."

The celebration was the pope's farewell Mass in the New York region during his five-day U.S. trip, and the city the pontiff describes as "God's playground" did not disappoint.

—David Briggs, Associated Press

The several thousand people who gathered in a private area of Newark International Airport seemed unaware of the intermittent drizzle yesterday as they waited for a rare opportunity— the chance to see the president of the United States and the head of the country's 60 million Catholics side by side.

—Julia I. Martin, *Staten Island Advance*

Although the stories were written on different days to tell about different stages of the pope's visit, the perspective chosen for each story could have been used appropriately on any day for an account of any part of the visit. For a major event such as a papal visit, which deserves and almost always receives sustained coverage, there is little reason to choose among perspectives. Different framings can be used and each one will complement the others so that over time even those readers who simply skim story leads will acquire a multifaceted understanding of the event's significance and meaning.

The first two examples illustrate the trend toward reporting religion news from the perspective of average people. Both the September 24 advance story by Debbi Wilgoren for the *Washington Post* and the October 6 account of the Mass in the Meadowlands written by David Gibson for the *Bergen Record* give readers a sense of the importance of the event for Catholics and their feelings about it.

Wilgoren's approach is well suited for exploring the place of religion in people's lives, the role of a religious organization in fostering religiosity, and individuals' religious motivations. Her approach could easily have been adapted for coverage of the Mass itself by following the parishioners to it and then incorporating their reactions to the pope's message.

Gibson's story captures the feel of being there in a way that allows bringing in more of the pope's message and of people's initial reactions to it. His approach shows something of the power of religion and of a religious event, but it also lends itself to examining the place of religion in people's lives.

Because in this case the people who attended the event and who were the focus of the story were devout Catholics, the lay perspective provided by Wilgoren and Gibson does not differ significantly from the institutional one provided in the third story, written by Associated Press reporter David Briggs. However, his more conventional summary lead followed by the pope's description of New York as "God's playground" makes it possible to include significant information about the pope's message and about the power and significance of the event to Catholics as well as oppositional readings. Information about protests by atheists and feminists, which would seem out of place in the first two stories, can more comfortably be blended into Gibson's story.

Where the more feature-oriented approach used by Wilgoren and Gibson keeps the focus squarely on religion, Briggs's summary lead signals a less feature-oriented approach that allows some attention to nonreligious implications. Those implications can also be used to frame a religion story, as Julia I. Martin's account for the *Staten Island Advance* illustrates. By mentioning a secular and non-Catholic, in this case the president of the United States, before the pope in her lead, she clearly signals that the papal visit is more than just a purely religious event. That framing opens up the possibility of exploring the political, cultural and social implications of a seemingly purely religious event, but at the risk of missing its religious dimension both from the perspective of the institutional church and that of the faithful.

In cases where there will be only one or two stories on a subject instead of the kind of sustained attention given to major religion stories, journalists must make a choice among the possibilities. "Each story is an opportunity. Sometimes you get only one chance, so you need to get it right," says religion writer Laurie Goodstein.

To understand more fully the implications of story framing for readership and for public understanding, consider the leads for two March 25, 1997, stories reporting Rep. Ernest Istook's plans to introduce a religious freedom amendment to the U.S. Constitution:

> Ellen Pearson was shocked when a principal barred her 9-year-old daughter from reading her Bible during 90-minute bus trips to and from a Dumfries, Va., school.

The ban was required by laws that mandate the separation of church and state, the principal said. ...

The case and others like it show that Americans need a constitutional amendment to protect them from judges and officials who mistakenly believe the Constitution requires them to stamp out all public religious expression, Rep. Ernest Istook, R-Okla., said Monday.

—Cassandra Burrell

A Republican congressman, backed by a coalition of conservative Christian groups, Monday unveiled new language for a proposed constitutional amendment that would knock down what he said is the needlessly high wall of separation between church and state.

The Religious Freedom Amendment proposed by Rep. Ernest J. Istook, R-Okla., would, if adopted, permit states and municipalities to fund private religious schools, to allow prayer in public school classrooms and graduations and to place religious symbols on government property.

—Laurie Goodstein and John E. Yang,
Washington Post

Both stories tell readers that the proposed amendment is a new version of ones proposed in the past and that there is disagreement within the religious community over the need for such an amendment and over whether this version will accomplish the goals attributed to it by Rep. Istook or whether it will cause new problems. Both also include the opinions of secular sources.

With its anecdotal lead, the first version, written by Cassandra Burrell and distributed by the Associated Press, captures readers' attention, but at the risk casual readers may mistake the principal's understanding of the law for the law itself. Because the anecdote is so powerful, even those who recognize that the problem is not with the law but with people's interpretation of it may find it difficult to understand why some religious leaders quoted further down in the story seem to oppose the amendment so vehemently.

To prevent those possible problems, Laurie Goodstein and John E. Yang chose to risk the possibility that readers would ignore their story for the *Washington Post* by using a more conventional summary lead. By presenting the new development as part of an ongoing religio-political debate, readers could not as easily dismiss the serious arguments for and against the amendment.

In print media, most readers realize that, except in cases where graphic elements clearly signal that several stories are part of a news package, each newspaper story or magazine article stands alone. In most cases they also interpret pictures and infographics as illustrating parts of stories.

With television, however, that is not the case. Words and pictures work together so that framing is as much a matter of the video as it is of the audio. There is also more of a spillover effect. Images can linger in viewers' minds, creating a stronger or more lasting impression than the story itself. Stories blur together.

Again, the pope's visit can illustrate the possibilities and the problems. Conveying the power of religion is often the easiest to do because people and their reactions have such strong visual appeal. Presenting ideas and issues is more difficult.

An off-camera reporter could tell about the pope's message while a video feed showed scenes of the Mass and close-ups of people's reactions to it or the story could be told by cutting from the pope speaking to shots showing crowd reaction to his words. In either case, video and audio would work together to convey a sense of the significance and power of religion for the faithful. Either version would lend itself to follow-up interviews with those who attended the mass, but the images could easily be so powerful that they could detract from the pope's message. With the video emphasizing the meaning of religion for the faithful, any attempt to cut to interviews with outsiders would most likely be interpreted as injecting an anti-Catholic or a-religious bias. A story with a harder edge could place the emphasis more firmly on the pope's message and make it easier to introduce outsiders' reactions to the event.

For a harder edge, the story might begin with an overview given by an on-the-scene reporter or by an anchor seated at the news desk. But in either case, the video will have a much greater effect on story framing than would photos accompanying a newspaper story. On television, a story told with the exact same words would create very different impressions depending on whether the video behind the stand-up reporter showed the pope, worshippers or protesters. For the in-studio version, a background photo of Pope John Paul II would create a very different impression than would a graphic showing his mitre and scepter. In turn, those symbols arranged with the mitre in front of the scepter would most likely convey a subtle message of papal power and authority, but the scepter lying diagonally across the mitre might convey a message of "no popes."

Efforts to create a coherent television news package often lead to placing together stories with some feature in common. Thus the telling of one story can affect understanding of the next, especially in cases where a segue creates a connection between them. A segment that packaged a religion-related story about conservative Christian influence in recent elections with one focusing on the pope's message of concern for the poor would make the papal visit seem more political than if that story were packaged with one that reported church membership data. A lead into or out of the story about the pope's message that linked it to other religious agencies ministering to the poor in New York could create an impression of beneficial religious influence. A "meanwhile in New York" transition from a story about crime statistics to the Mass or from it to one about problems of the cities might easily convey the message that religious involvement may be no more effective than whistling in the dark.

Organizing Stories

Choosing a lead is not just a matter of appropriately framing a story. "I work really, really hard on the lead," says the religion reporter Laurie Goodstein. "Sometimes, if I have 3 hours to write a story, I'll spend one and a half hours on the lead, but I don't think that's a mistake. It helps me and it helps my readers know where we're going."

The lead, then, signals and affects how information will be ordered. That organization can have profound implications for whether or not people will receive the intended message and for how they will react to the reporter's work.

Research on message design indicates that people learn most readily when information is ordered to correspond to normal thinking patterns. When there is a temporal, or time, dimension, people usually find a sequential or chronological ordering easiest to follow. Where time is a constant, a kind of coherence that promotes understanding can be achieved by arranging information topically or spatially. That is, all information about a subject—a particular religion or the religious climate in Asia—can be grouped together before tackling related subjects—another religion or the religious climate in Europe, for example.

For difficult-to-grasp or unfamiliar ideas, people learn most easily when they can reason by analogy in a way that lets them compare new ideas to things with which they are already familiar. In most cases, that would argue for putting information about Christianity or about the most widely shared issue position before information about a new religion or a less common viewpoint.

But that general principle creates something of a dilemma for reporters. People usually remember best what they hear first or last. For issue-oriented stories, people are more likely to change their minds if their position is presented first followed by a rebuttal from a credible source who presents a contrary viewpoint. At the same time, most people have come to understand that the conventions of newspaper journalism are such that reporters will place whatever they consider most important toward the beginning of the story and less important information at the end. Unless handled carefully, arrangements that violate the inverted-pyramid convention may introduce confusion.

In the third story about the pope's visit, which was excerpted in the previous section, David Briggs used a chronological order to follow the pope on his visit to various parts of the city as a way of illuminating the idea of New York as "God's playground." However, that sequential treatment of information occurred in the second half of the story. The summary lead placed the focus on the pope's message. That message and its implications were explored in conventional inverted-pyramid fashion in the first half of the story.

Where Briggs used chronology in combination with the traditional inverted pyramid convention, in the fourth version Julia I. Martin relied solely on a chronological arrangement. That order clearly showed the unfolding of events across time. At the same time, the order meant quoting President Clinton's welcoming remarks before the pope's message. That order may have signaled to some readers that the president's comments were more important than those of the pope.

Because of the nature of their remarks, that ordering probably did not cause readers to see any bias in the story for or against the president or the pope. However, such may not be the case in stories about issues, particularly where issue positions are deeply and passionately held. In those cases, journalists often find themselves in something of a catch-22 situation. No matter what order they choose, at least part of the audience will very likely see the story as being biased against their position.

Consider the stories about the religious freedom amendment. Because Rep. Istook was clearly the newsmaker, both versions began with his position. Both stories also included quotes from proponents and opponents of the amendment. The impression readers gained from the stories was almost certainly affected by leading with the comments from Rep. Istook, but the way the story ends will also have an effect.

Ending with a quote from Americans United for Separation of Church and State or from the Southern Baptist Convention, both of whom opposed the amendment, could undercut Istook's position. Ending with quotes from the Christian Coalition or from House Speaker Newt Gingrich, who supported the amendment, could re-enforce any initial impression that such an amendment is both appropriate and necessary.

By choosing a more neutral lead, Goodstein and Yang maximized the chances readers would consider both sides of the issue. They also minimized the risk that people would see their story as biased. However, because of the stronger lead in Burrell's version, readers who initially opposed the amendment might very well interpret an ending quote from an amendment supporter as an attempt to promote that position. Those who support the amendment would quite likely interpret a final quote from an opponent as the author's attempt to undercut their position.

Although no message order will satisfy everyone, in that kind of situation it is particularly important to avoid placing quotes so that they can be construed as instant rebuttals. Consider, for example, Pope John Paul II's October 1996 statement calling evolution "more than just a theory." Beginning with anything but the pope's statement about evolution would, again, have struck most people as odd if not as an outright attempt to downplay the importance of his statement. Most people would also expect there to be some attention to the position of those who do not accept evolution.

Confining the story to the pope's statement and a creationist rebuttal would produce polarization at the expense of understanding. Therefore, most stories included significant amounts of information about different Roman Catholic teachings about creation. They also included the viewpoints of creationists and of scientists who accept evolution but represent different schools of thought about it. However, regardless of how many viewpoints were presented, it would be risky to end with the widely used quote from Institute for Creation Research spokesperson Bill Hoesch, "Obviously, the pope has a lot of followers, and if he said the moon was made out of green cheese, a lot of people would believe him on that, too, but it doesn't mean it's true."

Such an ending gives the last word to those who disagree with the pope. And that, in turn, could be perceived as a not-too-subtle attempt to discredit him. Such a perception would likely occur regardless of medium, but the danger is greater on television than in newspapers because broadcast journalists commonly structure their reports to have beginnings, middles and ends. The endings, even more than the lead, point out the story's significance or provide a kind of conclusion to it.

If the danger on television is great in cases where sources speaking for themselves or their organizations provide the wrap-up, it can be even greater when reporters or anchors tell the story instead of using clips in which their sources speak for themselves. Unless they choose their words very carefully, people can easily conclude that the opinions broadcast journalists present are their own and thus are evidence of bias for or against a particular religion or religion-inspired viewpoint.

Choosing and Using Words

Pictures can provide information and create impressions, but words are the journalist's primary tools. Used carefully, they create understanding. Carelessly used, they destroy credibility. "Reporters have to be aware that, as they are writing, they are also educating," says religion writer Laurie Goodstein. "Most people don't know what a Hindu believes. Reporters have to incorporate the background and provide explanations, but they have to do it in a way that makes things understandable and that doesn't make them seem strange."

Religion is full of words and concepts that may have no meaning to outsiders. It's not just that most readers will not know what Hindus believe or what words taken from their faith may mean. Many will not understand basic Christian beliefs. Even those who do understand their own faith may not know much about another religion, its beliefs or practices.

In religion even similar beliefs may be different enough to cause problems. Failure to recognize those differences offends the faithful and misinforms others. They also make religions reporters look dumb. "Heaven help the religion reporter who writes, on the day of the Muslim Hajj, that it was Isaac whom Abraham was prepared to sacrifice to God. Every good Muslim knows it was Ishmael," says Barbara Falconer Newhall, religion writer for the *Contra Costa Times.*

If beliefs cause problems, so do words that change their meaning from one group to another and words that are different but have roughly equivalent meanings. In Roman Catholicism, brothers are members of certain religious orders; in some fundamentalist and pentecostal churches, all male members are called *brother,* while other churches reserve the term for a congregation's spiritual leader. To most Americans, *evangelical* refers to a kind of conservative Protestantism that emphasizes witnessing and proselytizing; in much of the world *evangelical,* meaning "based on the evangels or good news of the Gospel," is virtually synonymous with *Lutheran.* The Evangelical Lutheran Church in America allies itself with mainline Protestantism, not with conservative evangelicalism. The head of the Evangelical Lutheran Church in America is a bishop; the head of the Lutheran Church-Missouri Synod has the title of president; both have more authority in some areas and less in others than a Roman Catholic bishop, who is the religious leader of a geographic area but has a relatively low-level position in the church hierarchy.

Definitions taken from a dictionary are usually general ones that may not quite fit a particular situation. Conventions required by Associated Press style, or by any other stylebook, may not match preferred usage within a religion. Where they differ, it is usually better to violate the stylebook's rules than offend a religious community.

With so many differences among religions, "Religion reporters can't be afraid of asking dumb questions, and asking them repeatedly," says Gustav Niebuhr, religion writer for the *New York Times.* Even when journalists think they know what people mean, it's better to check with their sources rather than risk passing on a wrong explanation. At the same time, journalists must consider how that definition will seem to others.

Even when correctly used and carefully defined, words can label and categorize people and their religions in ways that may be offensive. Those engaged in the Right to Life movement often object to being labeled "anti-abortion." They prefer to have their position described as "pro life," but that offends others who ground their support for abortion rights in the value they place on the life of the mother. People from one branch of Christianity will often try to appropriate the Christian label for themselves; those from a "conventional" religion will often call other religions cults. At the same time, members of other Christian groups may see nothing Christian about those from other traditions that consider themselves Christian; insiders never think of themselves as belonging to a cult.

Journalists cannot entirely avoid using words that categorize, but they should avoid them as much as possible. In most cases, it is best to choose the most precise term—*Presbyterian* instead of *Christian,* for example—or the most neutral one possible—the name of a religion, *new religion* or *alternative religion* for *cult*. In other cases it may be better to omit the religious label entirely. *Muslim* and *terrorist* are not synonyms and should not be linked unless there is a very good reason for doing so.

For disputed beliefs and ideas, says Ann Rodgers-Melnick, "explain them from different points of view."

> Example: Jehovah's Witnesses regard themselves as the restoration of the one true church and believe what now passes for mainstream Christianity became apostate late in the first century.
>
> For their part, the Catholic, Protestant and Orthodox churches do not consider the Witnesses Christian, because they do not believe in the Trinity or the deity of Christ.

Sometimes those different viewpoints can be given in the same story without seeming to favor one side or the other, but in other cases it can be better to treat each one individually in separate stories.

With separate stories, each side can have its say free of what may appear to be an instant rebuttal from those who disagree. At the same time, separate accounts, whether embedded within one story or run as individual news items, can create problems if the accounts are not truly comparable. Direct or indirect comparisons across religions, issues or events can be particularly troublesome. Therefore, explanations based on an analogy should be used cautiously.

On television, those inappropriate analogies often are the result of linked stories. As Diana Butler, who writes a religion column for the *Santa Barbara (Calif.) News-Press,* noted in her critique of news coverage in the wake of the suicide of 39 members of Heavens Gate:

> [The network's] reporters covered the Heaven's Gate story. Immediately following, however, they aired a report on the Bruderhof, a Christian commune in New York.
>
> Founded in 1922, the Bruderhof is an heir of the Anabaptists, a family of Protestants originating in the 16th century. They are pacifist, communal, simple and plain. ...
>
> In the CBS report, Bruderhof emerged as a questionable cult.
>
> Like Heaven's Gate, they live together, own no personal property, dress alike and use the Internet!

Linking a religion that "exemplifies a nearly 500-year-old Christian tradition" to a new religious movement is, she points out, "historically and theologically insensitive and inaccurate." But that kind of inept comparison is common when journalists fail to look beyond superficial similarities as they grasp for ways to explain the seemingly inexplicable in religion.

Although explanations that are based on analogies can be problematic, those that describe beliefs or provide historical context are appropriate and often necessary. "The current religious climate is one of widespread theological illiteracy in which people do not understand the history or the foundational teachings behind the customs they practice or the values they or their religious bodies profess," says Ann Rodgers-Melnick, religion writer for the *Pittsburgh Post-Gazette*. It is also a period of profound historical illiteracy.

In adding explanations to stories, the goal should be to answer people's questions. For many, the underlying concerns are "Why did they do that?" "How did they get by with that?" or "Why can't they do it?" Answering those questions requires some attention to theology, history and law. For complex stories, adding that kind of background by way of explanation is often more useful than comparing one religion, issue or event to another.

Telling Stories

"Good religion reporting must reach people," says religion editor Sharon Grigsby. "At the *Dallas Morning News* we try very hard to make sure every story actually touches people's lives."

"Touching lives" does not mean the story must inspire people or touch them emotionally. "Touching lives" can also mean giving people the information they need or the tools that will help them understand complex situations. But "touching lives" first requires "reaching people."

Although most people say that religion news is very important, interest can be latent at best. Capitalizing on that rather general, free-floating interest requires capturing and holding people's attention.

Good storytelling begins with a good lead. For many journalists, that means a brightly written feature lead, but that kind of lead can be offensive. "To avoid trouble," says *Pittsburgh Post-Gazette* religion writer Ann Rodgers-Melnick, "use humor with caution. Sometimes it's OK, but people's religious beliefs should never be subject to ridicule."

Neither should the lead misrepresent a religion or a religion story. Says Laurie Goodstein, whose own reporting and writing for the *Washington Post* has made her a repeat winner of the prestigious Supple and Templeton awards for religion journalism:

> I'm seeing a problem with the easy assumption a feature or anecdotal lead is both interesting and worthwhile. It isn't always. If it doesn't get to the point and say what needs to be said, then it's a mistake.
>
> A good lead tells readers "this is what the story is about." It says, "Stick with me. This is where we are going and this is what you're going to get."
>
> The lead is a promise and you must deliver. If your story is about change, or there's a surprise to come, your lead should signal that.
>
> All your best stuff should inform your lead, but all your best stuff shouldn't be in the lead. You want your story to unfold, so you want good stuff all through it.

The "good stuff" can be facts or background information that help the audience understand by telling them things they did not know or might easily have overlooked. "Good stuff" can also be a quote or a description that helps people see and understand for themselves.

Goodstein's technique can be seen in the June 16, 1995, story that captivated judges, making her a repeat winner of the Templeton Award. Instead of producing what could have been just another deadly dull story about fiscal impropriety, Goodstein framed her story of Ellen Cooke, the chief financial officer for the Episcopal Church who used her position to embezzle $2.2 million, as a paradox.

The lead set the tone, but in it Goodstein also promised to unravel the mystery of Cooke's "lifetime built on illusion:"

> Ellen Cooke left no doubt that she came from a monied family—a background befitting the chief financial officer for the Episcopal Church's national headquarters in Manhattan.
>
> Friends had heard her "Gone With the Wind" accounts of relatives hiding their jewelry in the draperies during the Civil War. ... Churchgoers knew that when the New Jersey church her husband pastored lacked a coat rack or a new altar, the Cookes' largess could cover it.
>
> So last month, people who thought they knew her were stunned to learn that the money Cooke had spent so freely was neither hers nor her family's. ...
>
> Church and bank officials have slowly reconstructed exactly how Ellen

Cooke duped them. She manipulated trust funds and trust. She exuded absolute confidence and control.

Goodstein then led her readers through multiple paradoxes before ending her story with the ultimate irony:

> Faced with the hard example of betrayal by a trusted insider, many dioceses and parishes are reviewing their own accounting procedures. In January, the church published a revised 185-page *Manual of Business Methods in Church Affairs*. ...
>
> "Dear Friends," says the introductory letter in the manual. "The church has entrusted us with funds placed in its hands for mission and ministry. This trust is deserving of our nurturing and careful attention to detail, and demanding of our accountability."
>
> The letter is signed, "Mrs. Nicholas T. Cooke III."

By piling up contradictions, fleshing out the details with "good stuff" as she proceeded, Goodstein enticed readers to stick with her through a story that ran just over 3500 words and incorporated information from at least 40 different sources. Besides serving as hooks and transitional devices, using a series of paradoxes to tell the story let Goodstein tuck in information to help readers understand how Cooke operated and why her duplicity took so long to detect:

> She won respect for narrowing the gap between the salaries and benefits of the mostly female lay employees and the predominantly male clergy who worked at headquarters. She computerized the accounting procedures.
>
> Meanwhile, Cooke undermined the church's own version of separation of powers. ... Cooke persuaded the church's corporate legal counsel to combine two positions that, traditionally, had kept each other accountable.

Word pictures let readers create their own mental image of Ellen Cooke:

> She dressed primly in flowered Laura Ashley dresses and matching headbands, white stockings and a Dutch-boy bob. She ran the treasurer's office, say co-workers, like Marie Antoinette.

> ... Contradicting stereotypes of stuffy Episcopalians, [church headquarters] is an informal place where laypersons call priests by their first names

and even the church's leading cleric—Presiding Bishop Edmund L. Browning—is referred to by many as "the PB" or just "Ed."

Ellen Cooke, however, insisted that she be addressed as "Mrs. Cooke" and signed her correspondence "Mrs. Nicholas T. Cooke III."

Instead of pointing a finger at Cooke or at her church, Goodstein added details and imagery to a story presented as a series of paradoxes in a way that freed her readers to draw their own conclusions.

Most stories, of course, do not lend themselves to the framing Goodstein chose for her story of Ellen Cooke, but reaching readers always requires selecting an inviting approach and then leading readers through the story. That means selecting an appropriate framework and then adding to that frame the facts, background information, context, quotes and physical details that let people see for themselves and draw their own conclusions.

For Further Reading

Althiede, David L., and John M. Johnson. *Bureaucratic Propaganda.* Boston: Allyn and Bacon, 1980.

    This book examines the way institutions gather and edit information to produce reports that appear neutral but really serve the organization's interests. Chapters dealing with reports from evangelistic crusades and with the production of television news stand as cautionary tales against too readily accepting angles and evidence for stories.

Bromley, David G., Anson D. Shupe Jr., and J.C. Ventimiglia. "Atrocity Tales, the Unification Church, and the Social Construction of Evil," *Journal of Communication* 29, no.1 (1979):42-53.

    This study of media coverage of an alternative religion examines media practices and their implications for the religion and for public understanding.

Entman, Robert M., and David L. Paletz, "Media and the Conservative Myth," *Journal of Communication* 30, no. 4 (1980):154-165.

    This article explores the potential impact of the way the media choose to frame a situation and of reliance on certain sources to confirm that frame.

"Language of News." *Journalism Quarterly* 73, no. 4 (Winter 1996):784-856.

    Five research articles in this special section explore storytelling conventions and their effects in print and broadcast journalism.

Lewis, James R. (ed.) *From the Ashes: Making Sense of Waco.* Lanham, Md.: Rowman & Littlefield, 1994.

The chapters in this edited collection are of uneven quality, but several provide thoughtful comments about story framing, media performance and media responsibility.

McDannell, Colleen. *Material Christianity.* New Haven, Conn: Yale University Press, 1995.

This nicely illustrated book provides useful background for reporters who must describe and explain the religious artifacts many people have in their homes and offices.

Nimmo, Dan, and James E. Combs. *Nightly Horrors: Crisis Coverage by Television Network News.* Knoxville: University of Tennessee Press, 1985.

This book explores the potential effect of storytelling conventions on people's perceptions. Case studies of crisis news include the religion-related People's Temple massacre and the Iranian hostage crisis.

Ross, Raymond S., and Mark G. Ross. *Understanding Persuasion.* Englewood Cliffs, N.J.: Prentice Hall, 1981.

This basic text has an excellent chapter on strategies for organizing information and the implications of those strategies.

CHAPTER 12

IMPROVING RELIGION REPORTING

To hear critics tell it, religion news coverage is abysmal. Journalists who cover religion are ignorant and incompetent, if not downright biased. Those allegations, however, are more myth than fact.

The best religion reporters are highly educated and experienced. They know as much about the subject matter they deal with as other specialty reporters know about their subjects. Neither are they biased against religion. Most, in fact, are highly religious and active in their faith. But neither are they shills for any religion, including their own. They report accurately and fairly regardless of the religion or the topic they are covering. Although those from other beats may, on average, be less religious than the typical religion journalist, the best general assignment reporters and reporters from other beats who sometimes cover religion are also well qualified.

Many newspapers and television stations cover religion very well. Whether produced by religion specialists or nonspecialists, the best stories about religion are as good as, and sometimes better than, the best stories from other beats. In general, the quality of religion reporting at most media pretty closely matches the quality of reporting from other beats.

The problems with religion news coverage are not much different than the problems with other kinds of news. Those who are interested in a particular subject complain there isn't enough news about it; everyone else complains there is too much.

People criticize political reporters for missing stories, for failing to provide necessary background and for being biased for or against a political party, a candidate or an issue position. Whenever there is an election, both media critics and the public complain vociferously about the media's emphasis on strategy and tactics, who's winning or losing. The media, they say, gives them too little meaningful information about candidates' positions on issues and on their priorities.

Science reporters constantly deal with charges that they know nothing about science, misrepresent science and scientists and sensationalize the news. Business reporters and education reporters hear similar complaints. So do sports reporters. Even though the public says it is most satisfied with sports reporting, people complain constantly: reporters are "homers" or else they are too critical of the home team, they gave one school more coverage than another, they make heroes of jerks and unfairly pry into the private lives and the misdeeds of stars.

Specialists and nonspecialists who report on religion hear the same kinds of complaints, but the complaints about religion news coverage carry a weight equal only to the equally severe charges levied against political reporters. Like government and politics, religion affects everyone—both those who are directly involved and those who are not. But many more people have a personal stake in religion and religion affects them much more personally than is true for government and politics. Because so many people care deeply about religion and because religions have such enormous potential effects on members and nonmembers, people want and deserve good religion reporting.

If religion reporting isn't as bad as the critics contend, neither is it as good as it could be and should be. Sometimes reporters and the media they work for are guilty as charged. They miss stories or overreport and sensationalize them. They get their facts wrong or pass off opinions as if they are facts. But the culprit is rarely a bias against religion. The major problem is one of resources. Too many media do not have a religion beat, or if they have one, assign a person to it only part time. Frequently they don't even demand any expertise beyond basic reporting skills when they do assign someone to the religion beat. Media that expect all of their reporters to know something about government rarely inquire whether reporters have even minimal knowledge about religion.

Even media managers who hire for expertise may skimp on support for the religion reporter. Sometimes they give the reporters too little time to do a thorough reporting job or too little space in which to tell their stories. On other occasions, they may fail to provide the photographers or graphic artists necessary to make the stories truly informative and appealing.

Without commitment from management, real improvement in religion reporting will be slow and intermittent at best. But even where commitment isn't forthcoming, improvement can happen. All it takes is for reporters to decide that religion is important and then vow to find stories about religion, make a strong case for their importance, and then cover them well. To do that, both religion journalists and journalists from other beats need to:

1. **Prepare.** Nobody becomes an instant expert on religion, but without some background knowledge neither can anybody cover religion well.

   Developing expertise begins by taking little steps. Read about religion, but also read widely and deeply in the fields of history, politics, sociology. Check out literature, music and the arts. Check out religious media and the work of other reporters who cover religion for the mass media. Talk to people about what is important to them, about their values and their beliefs. Visit places of worship, religious shrines and memorials.

   In the short term, the process should reveal some information about religion that belongs in stories reporters were expected to cover and some stories about religion that otherwise would have been missed. The goal, however, is to acquire the background necessary to see connections between religion and what is going on in the world today and to develop the reservoir of ideas, information, sources and contacts necessary to sustain thorough reporting about religion.

2. **Keep the audiences in mind**. Religion potentially affects everyone. Most people are interested in religion. But not everyone has the same needs or tastes when it comes to news about religion. People may also have very different levels of background knowledge and different learning styles.

   Matching audience characteristics with news preferences is a first step, but it's also important to remember and reach those with different preferences. Reaching the multiple audiences for religion news requires understanding them, but it doesn't mean reporters need be overly sensitive or shy away from sensitive topics or be afraid to engage in investigative reporting.

3. **Think broadly.** Religion news is more than just news about religious institutions, people and events. It's also more than just stories about Judeo-Christian religions or other widely recognized and accepted faiths.

People and event stories are important because they help create a picture of the religious community, but almost anything can affect religious people and their organizations. Issues are important. Religious people and institutions get involved and their involvement produces ripple effects throughout society. Therefore, religion news also means stories about ideas, trends and values.

Not all religions have a transcendent god; not all have well-defined organizational structures. Some religions are more akin to personal philosophies; some religious institutions are loose affiliations of people with similar interests or lifestyles. Not everyone will accept them as "real religion," but if they help people find or express meaning and purpose, they should be included.

In order to provide the kind of comprehensive coverage that addresses the needs of multiple audiences, it's important to define religion news as broadly as possible so that it includes all manner of beliefs and practices and recognizes diverse values and concepts of morality.

4. **Honor the First Amendment.** Although people frequently complain when the media cover stories on sensitive topics or about people or groups they find offensive, in the long run a marketplace of ideas best serves a democratic and pluralistic society. Reporters must constantly remind themselves that the First Amendment protects all religions. They must also be prepared to remind their audience that their freedom to believe and worship as they choose is intimately connected to the right of others to make different choices.

With so many religions and attitudes toward religion, the only way to serve the public is by providing diverse coverage. In religion reporting, diverse coverage includes coverage of all religions and all kinds of religiosity. It also recognizes differences in audience interests by including different kinds of news about religions and by employing different reporting styles and storytelling techniques in an effort to reach people with different religious sensitivities, levels of knowledge and learning styles.

5. **Practice religion journalism.** Good religion reporting requires resisting all temptations to practice religious journalism. Religious journalism promotes or defends religion or a particular religion. It is an honorable profession, but it belongs in religious media or in

opinion columns. The goal for mass media should be religion journalism—an accurate, fair account of what is going on in the world of religion.

6. **Put religion in the religion news.** Reporters who work for mass media should avoid religious journalism, but they can't avoid religion.

Reporting beliefs, religiously inspired opinions and allegations is part of showing the meaning, purpose and influence of religion in people's lives and the implications of a religion for others. Explaining theology or quoting from religious texts is a necessary part of providing the background that helps people understand the source of people's beliefs and judge those beliefs for themselves.

Reporting what others believe and the religious sources for those beliefs isn't practicing religious journalism. It's simply using evidence the same way reporters from other beats quote the opinions of their sources or use quotes from court decisions, a budget or an annual report. The practice becomes religious journalism only when journalists substitute their own beliefs or choice of proof texts for those of their subjects.

7. **Show. Don't tell.** Religious journalism can appropriately tell people how things are, why they are that way, how they should be and how to make them that way. Religion journalism gives people the information they need in order to understand and reach their own conclusions.

Showing requires providing facts, background information and context, details and descriptions. The goal is to reach people by helping them find answers to their questions without providing the answers for them.

Showing also means letting people speak for themselves, so others can draw their own conclusions about them and their causes. Sometimes that may mean avoiding the balanced story with its penchant for instant rebuttals in favor of separate stories devoted to different religious institutions or perspectives.

Personality profiles and personal experience stories can also show without telling by putting a human face on complex issues or demystifying beliefs or practices that may strike many people as strange.

8. **Watch the language.** Good religion reporting requires using words carefully. Words inform, but they can also mislead, anger and ostracize.

Like everything else, religion has its own jargon. But in religion, the same word often has several meanings. Journalists must be sensitive to those different meanings in order to understand their sources. Because of those different meanings, good reporting requires defining words carefully, but even with careful definition, words that categorize people and their religions can cause problems.

Words such as *liberal, fundamentalist, charismatic, cult, sect,* even *catholic* or maybe *Catholic, Jew* or *Protestant* are all perfectly good labels, but carelessly used they can introduce confusion or invite misunderstanding. Good reporters avoid imposing labels as much as possible; they also take steps to make sure they don't let their sources appropriate favorable labels for themselves while imposing unfavorable stereotypes on others.

9. **Check carefully.** Even the best reporters sometimes make mistakes, but because of the variety of religions and the complexity of the subject matter, religion reporting has long suffered from more than its share of sloppy, inaccurate stories. Improving religion reporting requires reducing sins of commission and sins of omission to an absolute minimum.

Sins of commission are largely a matter of factual errors, but they also occur when reporters inject their own biases, pass on questionable allegations as if they are facts, or overplay stories. Sins of omission stem primarily from missing stories that properly have a religious dimension or from failing to find sufficient, appropriate and equivalent sources to reflect the multiplicity of religions and religious viewpoints. Sins of commission mislead by misinforming. Sins of omission leave people's questions unanswered. They hide important information and ideas from public scrutiny.

Avoiding the problems requires checking and double-checking each story at multiple levels: for factual accuracy, and also for detecting and fixing problems with terminology and language use. It also requires checking for fairness to all religions and religious perspectives, for balance in selection and use of sources, and for completeness.

Fairness and completeness, however, also require checking across stories over time to make sure coverage is equitably allocated among religions, topics and viewpoints and that no relevant ones are missing. Keeping track of reporting and writing styles provides a further check on whether the coverage addresses the needs of different audiences.

10. **Fight for resources.** As an enduring part of culture and a subject with wide appeal, religion news deserves space. Stories should get space according to their importance and subject matter. Although dedicated space should never be the sole repository for stories about religion, having space set aside for religion is valuable because it gives public recognition to religion's importance, provides a place for little stories that otherwise might get lost, and allows for more flexible and creative display.

Journalists who understand the potential demand for good religion reporting and have prepared themselves to provide it can usually get the space they need for their stories by making a strong case for their importance. However, individual efforts can do only so much.

Complete, thorough coverage requires the time to develop story ideas, do the reporting and then produce a finished product. Time can come from fighting for full-time assignment to the religion beat, but it can also come from figuring out ways to collaborate with other reporters on stories that transcend beats. In cases where neither approach is possible, much the same effect can be achieved by looking for stories from the wires, syndicates or other sources that can be used along with more quickly produced local sidebars.

Resources are not an end in themselves. They are a means to achieving the end of providing thorough, thoughtful coverage that reaches people and serves them well. Using well whatever resources are available will improve religion reporting. With good work and support from the public, more resources will follow. Those additional resources can then be used to further improve religion reporting.

For Further Reading

"Covering the Culture War." *Columbia Journalism Review* July/August 1993:29-33.

Articles by James Davison Hunter, a sociologist, and Laurence I. Barrett, who covers politics for *Time* magazine, offer good advice for covering religio-political issues and organizations.

Willey, Susan. *A Critical Analysis of Religion News in Culture, the Newsroom and the Academy.* St. Petersburg, Fla.: Poynter Center for Media Studies, 1995.

In this monograph based on her master's thesis, a veteran religion reporter offers insight into the importance of religion and religion reporting and offers her suggestions for improving coverage of religion news.

REFERENCE MATERIALS

Every reporter needs ready access to information. The items marked with an asterisk are those that many religion reporters surveyed in 1995 said are most useful to them. Other items come highly recommended.

Scriptures

Reporters need ready access to the scriptures for the major religions they cover regularly. For most, this means having a copy of the *Bible, including the *Apocrypha, the *Qu'ran, and perhaps the Book of Mormon. They are available in print and on CD-ROM from many publishers. Most CD-ROM versions have search or other functions that make it easy to find particular passages and compare them, but they are difficult to access while using a computer for other purposes such as writing stories. Print versions with a concordance are easiest for finding passages; annotated versions provide help understanding passages and matching them to other Bible texts. While they are not as easy to use as most CD-ROM versions, they can be accessed when a computer is unavailable or is tied up with other tasks.

Most reporters consider the Bible with Apocrypha a "must have." It is the authoritative Word of God for Christians; its Old Testament is the Jewish or Hebrew scripture and is also considered instructive by Muslims. The Apocrypha is a series of books found between the Old and New Testaments that Catholics consider canonical, or part of scripture. Other Christians may consider those books instructive or think of them simply as related documents. For everyday use, the most useful translations are the New Revised Standard Version (NRSV) and the New International Version (NIV). Other translations, such as the old King James Version, can be useful for special purposes, as can various paraphrases such as The Living Bible or Good News for Modern Man.

Many religion writers like to have a parallel version that provides several translations in adjacent columns. Similarly useful are books that include scripture from several different religions with helps for finding related passages. Good works of this type include:

Batlou, Robert O. (ed.) *The Portable World Bible.* New York: Penguin, 1994.
> This inexpensive book contains portions of Jewish, Christian, Buddhist, Confucian, Muslim and Zoroastrian sacred writings.

Holm, Jean, and John Bowles. (eds.). *Sacred Writings.* London, UK: Pinter Publishers, 1994.
> In addition to providing sacred texts from Judaism, Christianity, Buddhism, Hinduism, Islam, Sikhism, and Chinese and Japanese religions, this comprehensive book includes information about the religions.

Peters, F. E. (ed.) *Judaism, Christianity and Islam: The Classical Texts and their Interpretation.* Princeton, N.J.: Princeton University Press, 1990.
> This is a useful work for understanding how the same or similar scriptural passages are understood in the different Western religious traditions.

Wilson, Andrew. (ed.) *World Scripture: A Comparative Anthology of Sacred Texts.* New York: Paragon House, 1995.
> This is another good compendium of sacred texts from world religions that also contains information about them.

General Reference Works

These works are useful for finding answers to common questions.

Catholic News Service. *Stylebook on Religion.* Washington, D.C.: Catholic News Service, 1990.
> This handy glossary is the best guide to proper usage of Roman Catholic clerical titles, nomenclation and theological terms.

Dart, John. *Deadlines and Deities.* Nashville, Tenn: The Freedom Forum, 1995.
> This very readable booklet provides useful advice from the veteran religion reporter for the *Los Angeles Times.* Useful features include a list of commonly misused and misspelled words and a listing of major holy days in world religions.

*Hexhorn, Irving. (ed.). *Concise Dictionary of Religion.* Downers Grove, Ill.: InterVarsity Press, 1993.

This is one of the best of the many references that provide brief explanations of Christian and non-Christian religions and definitions of religious terminology.

*Magida, Arthur J. *How To Be a Perfect Stranger: A Guide to Etiquette in Other People's Religious Ceremonies.* Woodstock, Vt.: Jewish Lights, 1996.

This handy book provides guidance for proper behavior when visiting Jewish synagogues, Catholic churches, and churches from the major Protestant denominations. A companion volume, published in 1997, provides information on smaller Protestant denominations and other religions.

*Mather, George A., and Larry A. Nichols. (eds.). *Dictionary of Cults, Sects, Religions and the Occult.* Grand Rapids, Mich.: Zondervan, 1993.

Entries provide brief explanations of almost 100 religions and thousands of religious terms. Because the editors define *cult* as a religion outside the societal mainstream, entries include some world religions and some common variants of Christianity such as Christian Science. Appendix 2 summarizes beliefs about Jesus for many variants of Christianity. Appendix 4 diagrams root religious influences on alternative religions.

*Melton, J. Gordon. (ed.). *Encyclopedia of American Religion.* Detroit: Gale Research, 1993.

Part 1 of this standard reference work provides an overview of the history of religion in the United States and Canada. Part 2 contains brief historical essays on 22 Christian and non-Christian faith families plus some religions that are not easily classifiable. Part 3 gives directory listings by religious family. Indexes are by master name, key word, subject and geography.

*The National Conference. *Calendar.* 71 Fifth Ave., New York, N.Y. 10003.

This interfaith organization dedicated to fighting religious bigotry publishes a very good calendar of holidays and holy days for major religions.

*Smith, Jonathan Z. (ed.). *The HarperCollins Dictionary of Religions.* San Francisco: Harper, 1995.

This dictionary covers Christian and non-Christian religions. There are entries for religions, religious people, beliefs and religious terminology. There are also some entries for nations or geographic regions. Eleven feature articles provide information on each of the major faiths as well as religion in antiquity, religion in major nations, and religion among traditional peoples.

Stein, Gordon. (ed.). *The Encyclopedia of Unbelief.* Buffalo, N.Y.: Prometheus Books, 1985.

This two-volume work has entries for most historical and modern movements and for people associated with agnosticism, atheism and skepticism and other rejections of or doubts about god and the supernatural.

Directories

Most reporters find it useful to have the directories that provide information about individual Protestant denominations they cover regularly. Many also find the directories or lists of members published by congregations useful for tracking down sources. However, almost all find they need a Catholic directory and some of the more general national directories at least occasionally. Recommended ones include:

Bagby, Ihsan (ed.). *Muslim Resource Guide.* Fountain Valley, Calif.: Islamic Resource Institute/International Islamic Educational Institute, 1994.
    This is the best available source for tracking down people and organizations affiliated with Islam.
*Bedell, Kenneth B. *Yearbook of American and Canadian Churches.* Nashville, Tenn.: Abingdon Press, annual.
    This book, published annually, is the best single directory of names, addresses and phone numbers of religious leaders from Christian churches in the United States and Canada. It also includes some listings for Judaism and Islam.
Fieg, Eugene C., Jr. (ed.) *Religion Journals and Serials: An Analytic Guide.* New York: Greenwood Press, 1988.
    This directory provides information about content, target audience and availability for approximately 300 magazines and journals devoted to religion. Sections are devoted to Christianity, Judaism, Islam, neareastern, eastern and modern religions.
*Foy, Felician A. (ed.). Catholic Almanac. Huntington, Ind.: Our Sunday Visitor, annual.
    This is the authoritative source for background information about the Roman Catholic Church and for contact information for Catholic institutions and leaders.
Holm, Jean (ed.). *Keyguide to Information Sources on World Religions.* London: Mansell Publishing, 1991.
    This book has 1074 entries for periodicals, theses, series and surveys indexed by religion and by geographic region.
*Kellner, Mark A. *God on the Internet.* Foster City, Calif.: IDG Books Worldwide, 1996.

This is the best compendium of information and Internet addresses for websites, bulletin boards, newsgroups and chatrooms devoted to major religions including Christianity, Islam, Judaism, Hinduism, Buddhism and New Age.

*National Association of Evangelicals. *National Evangelical Directory*. Carol Stream, Ill.: National Association of Evangelicals, annual.

This is the source for tracking down organizations and people affiliated with conservative Protestantism.

*Payne, Wardell. (ed.). *Directory of African American Religious Bodies*. Baltimore: Howard University Press, 1995.

This is a comprehensive reference work that includes essays about African American religious traditions and listings for denominations, religious educational institutions, professional religious organizations and African American scholars of religion.

Singer, David. (ed.). *American Jewish Year Book*. New York: American Jewish Committee, annual.

This annual publication provides information on Judaism, Jewish organizations and their leaders.

*Weber, Paul J., and W. Landes Jones. (eds.). *U.S. Religious Interest Groups: Institutional Profiles*. Westport, Conn.: Greenwood Press, 1994.

This reference provides information on the history, leadership, religious orientation, goals and strategies for most lobbying and special-purpose groups in the United States.

Religious Publications

Religious newspapers and magazines can be useful for finding out what people from different religious traditions think is important and for tracking down sources to use in stories. For religions with associational polity and for those congregations that are truly independent, the religious media their members read can sometimes be the only window into their world.

In addition to the denominational publications for the religions that are strong in their area and regional ones such as the newspapers published by each Roman Catholic diocese, most religion journalists find it important to have regular access to some national publications. Among the most useful are:

America. 106 W. 56th St., New York, N.Y. 10019.

This Roman Catholic magazine, known for its thoughtful commentary, is edited by Jesuits and reflects the concerns of that religious order.

The Christian Century. 407 S. Dearborn St., Chicago, Ill. 60605.
With its ecumenical perspective, this magazine is the pre-eminent voice of moderate to liberal Protestantism.

Christianity Today. 465 Gunderson Dr., Carol Stream, Ill. 60188.
This nondenominational magazine presents the conservative, evangelical Protestant perspective.

Commonweal. 15 Dutch St., Room 502, New York, N.Y. 10027.
This lay-edited magazine is another influential voice within Roman Catholicism.

Focus on the Family. 8605 Explorer Dr., Colorado Springs, Colo. 80920-1051.
This highly influential magazine presenting the conservative Protestant perspective on child rearing, family values and related concerns circulates widely among people of all faiths, as does a sister publication, *Citizen,* which addresses other issues and political concerns.

Hinduism Today. 107 Kaholaiele Rd., Kapaa, Hawaii 96746.
This publication reports news about Hindus worldwide. It represents the Sanathana Dharma perspective.

Islamic Horizons. P.O. Box 38, Plainfield, Ind. 46168.
This publication from the Islamic Society of America/Muslim Students Association of the United States and Canada circulates among immigrants and students.

The Minaret. 434 S. Vermont Ave, Los Angeles, Calif.
This is the publication of the Islamic Information Center in Los Angeles.

Moment. 3000 Connecticut Ave., N.W., Suite 300, Washington, D.C. 20008.
This magazine is useful for a Jewish perspective.

The National Catholic Register. 15760 Ventura Blvd., Suite 1201, Encino, Calif. 91436.
This newspaper covers national and world news from a fairly conservative Roman Catholic perspective.

The National Catholic Reporter. P.O. Box 419281, Kansas City, Mo. 64141.
This independent newspaper covers national and world news from a more liberal Roman Catholic perspective.

The Reconstructionist. Church Rd. and Greenwood Ave., Wyncotte, Pa. 19095.
This Jewish publication is most similar to the influential nondenominational and ecumenical Protestant Christian magazines such as *Christian Century* and *Christianity Today.*

Sojourners. 2401 15th St. NW, Washington, D.C. 20009.
This is the magazine for the socially active wing of evangelical Protestantism.

Tricycle. 163 W. 22nd Ave., New York, N.Y. 10011.
>This is the largest independent Buddhist publication in the United States.

Wheel of Dharma. 1710 Octavio St., San Francisco, Calif. 94109.
>This is the official publication of the Buddhist Churches of America.

Other Publications

To keep abreast of the latest developments in scholarly thinking about religion and the latest research about religion, religion journalists recommend keeping abreast of the academic research literature. Although useful work may be published almost anywhere, a few publications are most helpful:

*Journal of Church and State. J.M. Dawson Institute, Baylor University, Waco, Texas 76798.
>This journal contains articles and commentary written from a historical or legal perspective, book reviews and a list of recent doctoral dissertations on the relationship between religion and government over time and around the world.

*Journal for the Scientific Study of Religion. Society for the Scientific Study of Religion, Sociology Department, 1365 Stone Hall, Purdue University, West Lafayette, Ind. 47907-1365.
>This journal publishes original, empirical research. Its emphasis is on trends and effects of religion and effects on religion.

*Review of Religious Research. Religious Research Association, 108 Marist Hall, Catholic University of America, Washington, D.C. 20064.
>This journal publishes original, empirical research on all religions. Emphasis is on trends, developments and effects within religions, but many articles have a broader, societal focus.

*Religion Watch. P.O. Box 652, North Bellmore, N.Y. 11710.
>This inexpensive, independently published newsletter provides a valuable abstracting service by publishing brief summaries of recent religion-related research and of articles from secular and religious media. It also contains occasional brief book reviews.

Sociology of Religion. Association for the Sociology of Religion, 108 Marist Hall, Catholic University of America, Washington, D.C. 10064.
>This sociology journal publishes original, empirical research on subjects related to religion. Articles tend to be somewhat more theoretical than those published by the other social science journals.

History and Law

These books are good sources for the facts and for the historical documents and court decisions journalists may need to provide background and context for their stories.

*Ahlstrom, Sydney. *A Religious History of the American People.* New Haven, Conn.: Yale University Press, 1972

This is one of the standard histories. Although it is most useful for tracing the history of various Christian groups in the United States, it also provides information on Judaism and some other minority religions.

*Eastland, Terry. (ed.). *Religious Liberty in the Supreme Court: The Cases that Define the Debate over Church and State.* Grand Rapids, Mich.: William B. Eerdmans, 1993.

Section 1 gives key excerpts from majority and minority opinions and some public reaction to court rulings for 25 landmark cases decided by the Supreme Court between 1940 and 1992. Section 2 provides three commentaries on the meaning and scope of religious freedom.

Gaustad, Edwin S. *A Documentory History of Religion in America.* Grand Rapids, Mich.: William B. Eerdmans. Vol. 1, 1982; Vol. 2, 1983.

These volumes contain the full text of important documents relating to religion in the United States. Volume 1 covers the period from the Mayflower Compact to the Civil War. Volume 2 covers the period since the Civil War.

*Lynn, Barry, Marc D. Stern and Oliver S. Thompson. *The Right to Religious Liberty: The Basic ACLU Guide to Religious Rights.* Carbondale, Ill.: Southern Illinois University Press, 1995.

This handbook answers most common questions about people's rights under the free exercise and establishment clauses. Appendices cover the Religious Freedom Restoration Act and the Equal Access Act for public schools.

Maclear, J.W. (ed.). *Church and State in the Modern Age: A Documentary History.* New York: Oxford University Press, 1995.

This book, covering the years from 1682 through 1992, contains the full text or key excerpts from documents and court cases from the United States and from Europe.

IMPORTANT MEETINGS

Attending meetings of religious, academic and professional organizations is a good way to size them up, make contacts, be on the scene when news is made and find story ideas and sources for them, meet other religion journalists and build a professional support network.

For covering news at the local level, it's a good idea to contact local ministerial alliances and ecumenical organizations, meet their members and attend their meetings as often as possible. Of course, journalists will also want to attend some national meetings of religions that are strong in their area in order to be on the scene as they discuss issues and hammer out policies. The meeting times and places for these important meetings vary from organization to organization and often from year to year for each organization. Therefore, the only way to find them is to look for news releases about them or announcements in religious publications.

Circumstances and events can make any religion's meetings important, but the national meetings of individual religions that are most often newsworthy are those of the U.S. Catholic Conference, the Evangelical Lutheran Church of America, National Baptist Convention USA, Presbyterian Church-USA, Southern Baptist Convention, and the United Methodist Church. Among the most useful general meetings are the annual conventions held by the National Religious Broadcasters and by the Christian Booksellers Association.

To meet academic experts and get information on the latest research before it is published, annual meetings of the American Academy of Religion, Association for the Sociology of Religion, Society of Biblical Literature, and the joint meeting of the Religious Research Association and the Society for the Scientific Study of Religion are most useful. Although it's a good idea to attend these meetings whenever possible, journalists can usually get a copy of the program and then contact speakers directly to find out about research that looks interesting.

For networking with other religion reporters, gathering tips on the latest issues and trends in religion and how to cover religion news, nothing beats the annual meeting of the Religion Newswriters Association. Dates and locations change from year to year, but meetings are usually held in the summer or early fall. In some years the meeting is held in the same city and at the same time as an important meeting of a religious organization. In other years it may be held in a city with sites of particular interest to religion reporters.

APPENDIX C

PROFESSIONAL SUPPORT GROUPS

Because few media have more than one religion journalist, religion reporters maintain contact with others who share their professional interests by joining national organizations and by turning to the Internet. For those who cover religion regularly the most important groups are:

Religion Newswriters Association. Debra L. Mason, executive director. 88 W. Plum Street, Westerville, Ohio 43081-2019.

This organization, founded in 1949 to improve religion reporting, is the major professional organization for journalists who cover religion news on a full- or part-time basis for print and broadcast media. Membership is not open to those who work for religious media. RNA's bimonthly newsletter provides a forum through which religion reporters can exchange ideas and keep abreast of trends and changes in religion and in religion reporting. At an annual convention held in the summer or early fall, reporters can network with each other and meet with religious scholars or other experts in the field of religion and religion reporting.

Religion and Mass Media Interest Group. Association for Education in Journalism and Mass Communication, University of South Carolina, Columbia, S.C. 29208-0251.

This group is a part of the major professional organization for journalism educators. At the annual AEJMC convention, which is usually held in August, members present original research, hold panel discussions or sponsor symposia and workshops. Most members are professors or graduate students who conduct research on various aspects of religion and the media; many are former religion reporters. Although membership is open to journalists, most reporters will find the group useful primarily as a source of expertise and advice.

Majordomo@iclnet93.iclnet.org

By sending the message "subscribe JREL-L" to this e-mail address, those with a professional or academic interest in religion reporting get e-mail access to a network of reporters, professors, graduate students, and others who share an interest in religion news. Most postings are requests for information or for help finding sources. Tim Morgan, associate editor of *Christianity Today*, manages this service.

APPENDIX D

CONTESTS

In an effort to encourage and improve religion reporting, Religion Newswriters Association sponsors five annual contests:

*Templeton Award for Religion Reporter of the Year.
> This $3500 award for excellence in enterprise reporting in the field of religion in the secular press is open to all religion journalists at secular media.

*Supple Award for Religion Writer of the Year.
> This is a $1000 award for writing skills. The contest is open to all religion journalists at secular media.

*Cornell Award for Mid-Sized Papers.
> This $400 award is for religion reporting and writing by journalists at secular newspapers and news magazines with circulations between 50,001 and 150,000.

*Cassels Award for Smaller Papers.
> This $400 award is for religion reporting and writing by journalists at secular daily, weekly or semiweekly newspapers without national circulation and with a weekday circulation of 50,000 or less.

*Schachern Award for Religion Pages or Sections.
> This $1000 award is for best coverage in space set aside for religion in secular newspapers and news magazines.

In addition to the first place prize in each of these contests, there are awards for second and third places and for honorable mention. Details for entry are available from Religion Newswriters Association. Deadlines are usually February 1. Entries are articles or sections published the previous year.

Entering other contests can also be a good way for journalists to measure their own work against that of other professionals and to showcase themselves and their employers. Contests sponsored by local and national press associations and professional organizations are open to all journalists. Stories about religion can and do win.

Although entering contests sponsored by Religion Newswriters Association or by other journalism organizations presents few ethical dilemmas, more problematic are those contests open to journalists from mass media but that reward those that promote a particular viewpoint or perspective. Among these are the contests sponsored by the Amy Foundation, the Associated Church Press, Catholic Press Association, Merrell Enterprises, Religious Heritage of America and the Religious Public Relations Council.

Before entering any contests, journalists should always check company policy.

EDUCATIONAL OPPORTUNITIES

Journalism students who know they want to be religion reporters should seriously consider combining a minor in religion or religious studies with their course work in journalism. Because all journalists are very likely to find themselves covering religion stories at least occasionally, all journalism students could profit from taking courses in Eastern and Western religion and the sociology of religion. Many colleges also offer courses on Islam, Native American religions, the Reformation and the Bible as literature which provide useful background information about religion and can, in many cases, also be used to fulfill degree requirements.

Working journalists who feel they lack appropriate background in religion have two options. They can embark on a course of on-the-job training or they can return to school. Many excellent religion reporters are essentially self-taught; others pursued an advanced degree.

Those who choose the "do-it-yourself" route might begin by reading books about religion and by talking to local religious leaders. Those who want more direction might also take or audit religion-related courses at a local college or buy and study the books for those courses. They can also attend professional workshops, symposiums and short courses on religion reporting. Although there is no way to predict when or where these will be held, they are becoming increasingly common. Many are excellent. Most are sponsored by professional organizations, foundations or colleges and advertised through announcements in trade magazines such as *Editor & Publisher* and

Quill or through news releases and registration materials sent directly to the media or to individual reporters.

For others, pursuing a graduate degree may make more sense. Many master's programs and some doctoral programs allow people to take one or two courses a semester while continuing to work full time. Others do not allow part-time study. Although returning to school on a full-time basis may require some sacrifices, it need not be expensive. Many schools award teaching or research assistantships to students who have some professional experience. Assistantships pay for tuition and provide a monthly stipend which can be supplemented with other part-time work.

Northwestern University's Medill School of Journalism offers a master's degree program in religion reporting in conjunction with Garrett Theological Seminary. Temple University's departments of journalism and religious studies offer a joint master's program for religion journalists. Although it does not have a formal master's degree in religion reporting, Columbia University's Graduate School of Journalism offers courses in religion reporting as part of its professional master's degree program.

Although only a handful of schools offer formal course work in religion reporting, others have faculty with expertise in the area. Still others have strong reporting programs that are quite flexible, allowing students to take courses outside the department to develop areas of substantive expertise.

A journalism degree program, especially at a school that has good supporting courses in religious studies or the sociology of religion, has the advantage of courses that help journalists think critically about their work as they improve their professional skills. However, there are also advantages to pursuing a degree in religion, religious studies or the sociology of religion. Such programs can provide broader and deeper information about religions as well as the analytical tools for studying them. If the programs are flexible enough to allow students to take a few journalism courses as part of the degree department, they can be ideal. However, some programs, such as those at seminaries or church-related colleges may approach the subject from a particular religious viewpoint that may not be well suited to the needs of journalists who must deal with all religions. Programs at state universities tend to be more neutral, but some take an outsider's approach that can also be problematic.

The American Sociology Association and the Association for Education in Journalism and Mass Communication publish directories that can be used to locate schools. There is also a *Guide to Schools and Departments of Religion and Seminaries in the United States and Canada* compiled by Modoc Press and published by Macmillan. Before enrolling in any graduate program, prospective students should contact the schools, examine course offerings and talk to faculty to make sure the programs they are considering offer what they want and need.

GLOSSARY

Aaronic Priesthood. In the Church of Jesus Christ of Latter-day Saints, the lower priesthood to which all male members can aspire.

agnostic. One who claims not to know whether there is a god.

Allah. Arab word meaning god. Name for the Islamic deity.

alternative religion. Any religion outside the mainstream.

angel. A messenger of god; in Christianity, also a guardian spirit.

animism. Belief that the world and all its elements such as rocks and trees are alive and filled with unseen spirits to be worshipped or placated.

apocalypse. Writings prophesying or telling of cataclysmic events through which forces of evil will be destroyed. In Christianity, cataclysmic events leading to the end of the world.

Apocrypha. Books included in the Catholic Bible but not considered a part of scripture by most Protestants; also other early Christian writings that are not part of the Bible.

apostate. One who no longer accepts a religion's teachings and leaves the faith.

apostle. In Christianity, one of the 12 original disciples of Jesus. Although not one of the original 12, most Christians also consider Paul one of the apostles.

apostolic succession. In Christianity, the tracing back of religious leadership through a continuous chain of authority to one of the original apostles, especially the disciple Peter.

archdiocese. In Roman Catholicism, a geographic and administrative unit consisting of several diocese and presided over by an archbishop.

Armageddon. In Christianity, final battle between the forces of good and evil.

Ash Wednesday. In Christianity, first day of Lent. Commemorates the triumphal entry of Jesus into Jerusalem.

atheist. One who believes there is no god.

Avatar. Incarnation of a god in Hinduism.

Bab. "The Gate"; prophet, founder of Baha'i faith.

Baha'u'llah. The "Glory of God"; prophet or messenger of the Baha'i faith; successor to the Bab.

baptism. Christian initiation rite or sacrament, consisting of being immersed in water or anointed with water.

bar mitzvah, bat mitzvah. Jewish rituals through which young men and women respectively become adult members of the religious community.

Bhagavad Gita. "The Song of the Blessed Lord." Epic poem of Hinduism.

bhakti. Devotion to Hindu gods.

Bible. Christian scripture; consists of Old and New Testaments.

bishop. Christian religious leader; exact rank and responsibilities vary by tradition.

Bodhisattava. In Buddhism, an enlightened one who forgoes entry into Nirvana in order to work for the liberation of others.

Book of Mormon. Scripture for Latter-day Saints, telling of God's covenant with people of the New World.

born again. Term for one who has acquired a "new life" through acceptance of the Christian god; in conservative Protestantism, this acceptance occurs in later childhood or as an adult and precedes baptism into the faith; in Catholicism and mainline Protestantism, one is "born again" when one is baptized, usually as an infant.

Brahma. One of the three major gods in Hindu worship; usually regarded as the creator God.

Brahman (or Brahmin). Upper or priestly caste in Hinduism.

brother. Term for male members of some conservative Protestant churches and for members of some Roman Catholic religious orders.

caliph. "Deputies of the Prophet"; an Islamic religious leader.

canon. The set of writings considered authoritative by a religion.

cardinal. A high official within the Roman Catholic Church. Upon the death of a pope, the College of Cardinals selects a new pope.

catholic. "Universal." Usually refers to one of the main branches of Christianity, especially the Roman Catholic Church. Protestants may also use the term to underscore the universal nature of their teachings or of their church.

channeling. In New Age religion, the belief that people who lived in the past speak through or "channel" through people living today (channelers), usually those who are their present incarnation.

chant. Reciting of religious phrases, passages or other sounds or phrases as part of a spiritual or religious exercise or worship; a form of Christian music with a repetitive melody, usually with few notes.

charisma. In Christianity, "gift of the Spirit," such as faith healing or speaking in tongues.

Christ. In Christianity, name or title for Jesus, especially in his role as savior or messiah.

Christmas. In Christianity, holy day celebrated December 25 to mark the birth of Jesus.

church. A religion with a hierarchical, bureaucratic organizational structure and claiming to be the true religion; a Christian denomination; a place of Christian worship.

communion. Christian sacrament or rite involving partaking of bread and wine or grape juice; commemorates the Last Supper Jesus had with his disciples. Also called the "eucharist."

confirmation. Sacrament in Catholicism or rite in mainline Protestantism by which young people accept and profess their faith and become a part of the church.

convent. Home for female members of a Roman Catholic religious order, especially a cloistered one.

cult. A new or alternative religion centered around a living, charismatic leader who claims a new revelation or teaching about a god or the gods; also any religion outside the mainstream in a particular area.

deacon. "Servant." A position within a congregation or church; responsibilities and authority vary among Christian traditions.

deism. Belief in a detached, impersonal creator god.

deity. A god.

denomination. A specific faith family or group within a larger religious tradition, most often used within Protestantism.

devil. An evil spirit or god; alternate name for Satan, the supreme evil personage in Christianity.

dharma. Hindu and Buddhist concept of the law of the cosmos; duties imposed or required by a situation; Buddha's teachings.

diocese. In Roman Catholicism, the geographic and administrative unit presided over by a bishop.

Easter. In Christianity, holy day celebrated on a spring Sunday to mark Jesus' resurrection following his crucifixion.

ecumenical. Promoting unity among Christian faiths.

elder. A sage or wise person, especially an older person; a leadership position, with authority and responsibility varying among Christian traditions; among Mormons, a member of the Melchizedek priesthood.

eschatology. Teachings concerning the end of the world.

eucharist. See communion.

evangelical. Pertains to the "good news" about Jesus, the Savior; in the United States, that branch of conservative Protestantism that puts greatest emphasis on evangelism, or efforts to convert others to Christianity by telling them about Jesus; elsewhere, refers to Lutheranism.

Five Pillars. The basic teachings of Islam.

Four Noble Truths. The major teachings of classic Buddhism.

fundamentalism. Most conservative branch of a religion; in Christianity, refers to those who believe every word of the Bible is literally true.

Gautama Buddha. Religious leader whose teachings form the foundation of Buddhism.

glossolalia. Speaking in tongues, or unknown languages; in pentecostalism, the practice is considered evidence of the presence of the Holy Spirit.

Good Friday. Christian holy day commemorating the crucifixion of Jesus.

Gospel. In Christianity, that part of the New Testament that tells about Jesus as Savior; the first four books (Matthew, Mark, Luke and John) of the New Testament.

guru. A religious or spiritual teacher. The term is most appropriately used in the Hindu and Sikh religions.

hajj. Pilgrimage to Mecca that Muslims are expected to make once during their lifetime.

Hannukah (Chanukah). In Judaism festival celebrating the rededication of the temple by Judas Maccabaeus.

heaven. In Christianity, dwelling place of God; place where Christians will live with God after death.

Hebrew Bible. Authoritative scripture of Judaism.

hell. In Christianity, dwelling place of the devil; place of eternal torment where those who are not saved will dwell after death.

heresy. Beliefs deviating from the approved orthodoxy of a religion. Primarily a Christian concept.

Holy Spirit (Holy Ghost). One of the three persons in the Christian triune God, involved with creating and sustaining faith.

I Ching. Ancient Chinese book of divination (predictions of the future through magical means).

iman. Muslim religious leader; for Sunnis, the one who leads the community in prayers; for Shi'ites, the legitimate successors of Ali, the cousin, son-in-law and successor to Muhammed.

incarnation. The appearance of a divinity in material form. In most Christian traditions, Jesus is God Incarnate.

Jesus. In Christianity, the name for the Son of God in his human form.

jihad. In Islam, a holy war or struggle between forces of good and forces of evil.

karma. In Eastern religion, especially Hinduism, that which binds one to the endless cycles of life, death and rebirth; the law of cause and effect, action-reaction, that governs the cosmos.

Koran. See Qur'an.

kosher. In Judaism, items, especially food, that have been handled according to Jewish law and are ritually fit for consumption or use.

Krishna. In Hinduism, incarnation of the God, Vishnu, who appears as a main character in the Bhagavad Gita.

Lent. In Christianity, 40 days between Ash Wednesday and Easter marking the end of the earthly ministry of Jesus.

magic. Attempt to influence nature through special practices or rituals.

mainline. Conventional and historical term for moderate to liberal Protestant denominations that were the dominant churches in the United States through much of the 19th and 20th centuries. "Oldline" is sometimes used as a synonym.

mantra. Ritual sound, word or phrase used to invoke a religious effect.

Mass. Catholic worship service, high point of which is the celebration of the eucharist.

meditation. Practice of contemplating sacred or spiritual things; especially in Eastern religions may involve chanting or reciting of mantras.

Melchizedek priesthood. The higher priesthood in the Church of Jesus Christ of Latter-day Saints. Members are called "elders."

metropolitan. A high religious leader in Eastern Orthodoxy.

millennium. Thousand year period of peace and holiness at the end of time during which Christ will reign on earth.

minister. Generally applicable title for religious leader of a Protestant congregation.

Mishnah. Collection of Jewish oral laws.

monastery. Home for male members of certain Roman Catholic religious orders, especially those that are cloistered.

monk. In Roman Catholicism, male member of certain religious orders whose home is a monastery; in Buddhism, certain religious leaders or teachers.

monotheism. Belief in one god.

Moroni. Angel who revealed Book of Mormon to Joseph Smith.

mosque. Muslim house of prayer.

muezzin. In Islam, the one who calls the faithful to prayer five times a day.

Muhammed. In Islam, the last and most important in a series of prophets and messengers through whom God revealed his will.

New Age Religion. An alternative religion incorporating pantheistic and Eastern beliefs such as the healing power of crystals and reincarnation.

new religious movement. Generally preferred term for cult or other modern religion outside the cultural mainstream.

New Testament. Part of Christian Bible that tells of salvation through birth, ministry, death and resurrection of Jesus and that recounts the early days of the Christian Church.

Nirvana. In Hinduism, final cessation of human individuality and desires; final freeing of person from all that enslaves; the final dwelling for those who have been freed.

nun. In Roman Catholicism, a female member of a cloistered order; also any female member of a religious order.

occult. Hidden, or magical powers; a religion based on beliefs in magic or other forms of divination.

Old Testament. Part of the Christian Bible that tells of God and God's dealings with his people before the birth of Jesus.

order. In Roman Catholicism, a special purpose organization of men or of women who have taken religious vows and engage in spiritual and religious works; some orders are cloistered with members living apart from the world, but others are not.

pagan. In Christianity, one who does not accept the Christian God, especially one who practices a pantheistic or animistic religion. Neo-pagans attempt consciously to revive older, earth-oriented and female forms of spirituality including goddess worship.

pantheism. Belief that all things contain or are infused with something of the divine or sacred.

parish. Geographic area, especially in Roman Catholicism, served by one priest and with one place of worship.

Passover. Jewish holy day celebrated in the spring to commemorate the deliverance of the Israelites from captivity in Egypt.

pastor. Title given to spiritual leader of a congregation. Most often used for Roman Catholic priests and Lutheran clergy.

patriarch. A high religious leader within Eastern Orthodoxy. The head of the Eastern Orthodox Church is the Patriarch of Constantinople.

penance. Sacrament in Catholic and Anglican churches involving confessing of sins and receiving forgiveness; also an act done to show remorse for sin.

Pentateuch. First five books in the Hebrew Bible or the Christian Old Testament.

Pentecost. Christian holy day commemorating the descent of the Holy Spirit on early Christians.

pentecostalism. Branch of conservative Christianity that emphasizes receiving gifts of the spirit including faith healing and especially speaking in tongues.

polytheism. Belief there is more than one god.

pope. Spiritual head of the Roman Catholic Church.

prayer. Devotional act of addressing or talking to a god, especially with words of confession or supplication. The term is most commonly used with Christianity.

priest. Religious leader of an Anglican, Episcopal or Catholic congregation; religious leader empowered to perform rituals, especially ritual sacrifices.

profane. The realm of routine, everyday life; also anything that is not holy or consecrated; holy or consecrated things that have been defiled.

Purim. Jewish holy day celebrating deliverance of Jews from destruction at hands of Persians.

Quorum of Twelve Apostles. Governing body of Church of Jesus Christ of Latter-day Saints.

Qur'an (Koran). Muslim scripture.

rabbi. Teacher or master; term used in Judaism for spiritual leader at a synagogue.

Ramadan. Month in spring during which devout Muslims fast from sunrise to sunset to commemorate the month in which the Prophet Muhammed received the Qur'an.

reincarnation. Belief, especially in Hinduism and some New Age religions, that after death one lives again in another earthly form.

religion. A unified system of beliefs and practices regarding the sacred or that which is held ultimate.

rite of passage. A ritual marking transition from one phase in a person's life to another, such as baptism, bar or bat mitzvah, marriage, death.

ritual. A regularly repeated, traditional and carefully prescribed behavior intended to symbolize or transmit a belief.

Rosh Hashanah. Jewish New Year.

sabbath. The seventh day (Saturday) on which the god of Judaism and Christianity rested after having created heaven and earth; day set aside for worship in Judaism and in some forms of Christianity.

sacrament. In Christianity, a ritual instituted by Christ. Most Protestants recognize two (baptism and communion); Roman Catholics recognize seven (baptism, communion, confirmation, holy orders or ordination into the priesthood, matrimony, penance and extreme unction or last rites).

sacred. That which is holy or apart from everyday life; the realm of religion or of the deity.

saint. In Christianity, a holy person or a Christian who has died; in Catholicism, one officially recognized after death as having lived an exemplary life and having performed miracles.

Satan. The devil of Christianity.

sect. Any group that breaks away from an existing religion, believing it is the remnant of the faithful and the preserver of the true faith.

secular. That which is part of the profane or everyday world; indifferent to or not bound by religious teachings; also refers to a transference of authority away from the deity, as for example, to human reason.

Shari'a. Body of Islamic teachings, formalized as the law and code of conduct.

sin. Any transgression of a god's commands. Usually associated with Christianity.

sister. Term sometimes used in conservative Protestantism to refer to any female member of the faith; in Roman Catholicism, a female member of a religious order, especially an uncloistered order.

speaking in tongues. See glossolalia.

stake. A geographic, administrative unit within the Church of Jesus Christ of Latter-day Saints, comprised of several wards.

Sunday. First day of the week; day set aside for worship in most Christian faiths to commemorate the resurrection of Jesus following his crucifixion.

Surah. Chapter division within the Qur'an.

synagogue. In Judaism, the place for corporate worship, study and prayer.

Talmud. Collection of Jewish writings including the Mishnah and rabbinical writings that are the religious literature of postbiblical Judaism.

temple. Place of worship or dwelling place of god or gods, especially in Hinduism and Buddhism; in Judaism, the house of God, or Yahweh, in Jerusalem.

Torah. General term for the Hebrew Bible or Jewish scripture; more narrowly, divine law or the Pentateuch.

Trinity. Collective term for the three personages (Father, Son and Holy Spirit) of the Christian God. Although a monotheistic religion, most Christians believe their one God has three distinct natures.

triune. In Christianity, relating to the tripartite nature of God.

Upanishads. Hindu texts; part of the Vedic literature.

Veda. Term applied to entire collection of Indian or Hindu sacred literature; also a collection of hymns to the gods.

Vishnu. Creator God of Hinduism.

ward. Smallest geographic, administrative unit within Church of Jesus Christ of Latter-day Saints; a Latter-day Saint congregation.

witch. A female member of wicca or a related neo-pagan religion; also a term historically used for women who were believed to have received malevolent powers by consorting with the devil.

worship. Any ritual act of devotion to or adoration of a god or gods; in Christianity, especially a gathering together of the faithful as a congregation to participate collectively in acts of devotion.

Yahweh. Hebrew name for God. Used in Judaism and some Christian or Judeo-Christian sects.

yang. In Chinese religion, the positive force in nature.

yarmulke. Skull cap worn for worship by male Jews.

yin. In Chinese religion, the negative force in nature.

Yom Kippur. Jewish Day of Atonement, a fall holy day.

Index

Abortion, 68, 121
Academic journals, 141
Academic research literature, 203
Adventists, 46
African American Protestant churches, 55
African Americans, 12, 55
African Methodist Episcopal Church, 55
African Methodist Episcopal Church Zion, 55
Africa v. *Commonwealth of Pennsylvania,* 28
Agate stories, 145
Alcohol laws, 29–30
Alien and Sedition Act (1798), 24
Allen, Jimmy, xvii
Allocation of space, 123–24
Alternative bookstores, 143
Alternative religions, 53, 54, 77
Amana, 10
American Academy of Religion, 205
American Agenda, 99
American Council of Christian Churches, 85
American Jewish Committee, 85
American Jewish Congress, 85
American Sociology Association, 212
Americans United for Separation of Church and State, 180
Amicus curiae briefs, 149, 168
Amy Foundation, 210
Anecdotal lead, 176
Anglicans, 7
Anti-Defamation League of B'nai

B'rith, 85
Anti-pornography legislation, 121
Antiwar demonstrations, religious involvement in, 120
Apocrypha, 197
Ashkenazim, 51
Ashland (Ky.) *Daily Independent,* 124
Ashrams, 13
Associated Church Press, 85, 210
Associated Press, 94
Associational polity, 80
Association for Education in Journalism and Mass Communication, 213
Association for the Sociology of Religion, 205
Atkins, Gary, 121
Atlantic Monthly (magazine), 97
Audiences for religious news, 105–15, 191

Baha'i faith, 13, 40, 53
Baptism, 62
Baptists, 9, 10, 46
Barker, Don, 111
Base communities, 13
Bearden, Michelle, 100, 126–27
Behaviors, beliefs and, 59–71
Beliefs, 59–71, 158–59
Bennett, James Gordon, 92–93, 101, 109
Berger, Peter, 59
Bible, 41, 46, 47, 197–198
Black theology, 12

Blue laws, 121
Book of Mormon, 197
Bradley, Dan, 126–27
Brigg, Donna, 96
Briggs, David, 174, 175, 179
Broadway, Bill, 121
Brook Farm, 10
Buckley, William F., 96
Buddhism, 12, 40, 42, 52, 54, 63
Burrell, Cassandra, 176
Butler, Diana, 183

Calvin, John, 4, 5
Calvinists, 5
Capitol Square and Advisory Board v. Pinette, 32
Carter, Jimmy, 95
    Playboy interview, xiv
Cassels Award for Smaller Papers, 209
Cassels, Louis, 94, 145
Catholic Press Association, 85, 210
Catholics, 10, 44–45, 54, 55
    faith families of, 45
    forms of worship, 62
    structure of, 82–83
Centralized religions, 84
Chambers, Steve, 128, 142
Christian Booksellers Association, 205
Christian bookstores, 143
Christian Coalition, 85, 141, 148, 180
Christianity, 40, 42
Christian Episcopal Church, 55
Christian radio stations, 112
Christian Right, 148
Christian religions, classification of, 43–51
Christian Science, 10, 46
Chronological order, 179
Church, definition of, 75–77
Churches of Christ/Disciples of Christ, 46
Churches of God, 46
Church of England, 4–5
Church of God in Christ, 55
Church of Jesus Christ of Latter-day Saints. *See* Mormons
Church of Leucoma v. *Hialeah,* 29

Church of Scientology, 53, 167
Church-pages as approach to religion news, 94–95, 120–21
Church polity, 77–81
Church-sect typology, 74–77
Citizen (magazine), 85
Civic journalism, 102
Civil rights, religious involvement in, 120
Clergy, 160
Clinton, William, 24, 30, 179
Columbia University, 212
Communion, 62–63
Comstock laws, 11
Concerned Women for America, 85
Confirmation, 62
Confucianism, 12, 42, 53
Congregational Church, 6, 7, 9, 23
Congregational polity, 79
Conservatives, 48–51
Constitutional religion clauses
    applying, 26–27
    court interpretations of, 27–29
    recurring problems with, 29–32
Contests, 209–10
Cooke, Ellen, 185–87
Cornell, George, 3, 94
Cornell Award for Mid-Sized Papers, 209
Corporate worship, 61, 63
Cosmopolites, 108, 113, 151
Covens, 13
Credal churches, 46–47
Cult, definition of, 75–76
Culver, Virginia, 123

Dallas Morning News, 123–24, 125, 145–46
Danbury Baptist Association, 24
Dart, John, xvii
Dedicated space, religion stories for, 144–48
De facto established religion, 22, 27
Deism, 7
Democratic Party, 70
Denomination, definition of, 75–76
Denver Post, 123

Directories, 200–201
Disciples of Christ, 10
Dobson, James, 85, 148
Documentary sources, 165–68
Douglas, William, 27–28
Dress codes, 66
Druidism, 64
Duggan, Joseph, 119

Early American journalism, 91–92
Eastern mysticism, 13
Eastern Orthodox Church, 45
Eastern religions, 40–42, 77
Educational opportunities, 211–13
Edwards, Jonathan, 7
Emerson, Ralph Waldo, 52
Employment Division v. *Smith,* 30
Episcopal Church, 9, 23
Eucharist, 62
Euthanasia, 121
Evangelical Lutheran Church of
    America, 83, 182, 205
Evangelical Press Association, 85
Event coverage, 121
Ex cathedra, 45
"Eye on America," 99

Faith families, 44–47, 50
Facts, 158
Family Circle (magazine), 97
Family Research Council, 85, 141
Featured stories, 146–47, 175
Federated organizational structure, 79
Feminist theology, 12
Finke, Roger, 4
First Amendment, xiii, 19–33, 192
Five Pillars of Faith, 65
Focus on the Family (magazine), 85
14th Amendment, 25–26
Freedom from Religion Foundations,
    111
Free exercise clause, 31

Garrett Theological Seminary, 212
Geographic schemes, 40–42

German Lutheran churches, 55
Gibson, David, 174–75
Gingrich, Newt, 180
Good News for Modern Man, 198
Goodstein, Laurie, xvii, 16, 144, 157,
    175, 176, 178, 180, 181, 185–87
Great Awakening, 7
    first, 10
    second, 8, 10–11
Greek Orthodox Church, 45
Grigsby, Sharon, 125, 140, 145, 184

Harper's (magazine), 97
Hasidic Judaism, 51
Healy, Brian, xvii
Hearst newspapers, 91
Henry, Patrick, 25
Hierarchical structure, 78
Hinduism, 13, 40, 42, 52, 54, 63
Home-based observances, 65
House of God, 155–56
Hubbard, L. Ron, 53
Hunter, James Davison, 14, 22
Hutchinson Commission on Freedom
    of the Press, ix, x, 101, 122

IMPACT, 85
Imported religions, 53
Indigenous religions, 42, 53
Institutionalized religion, 74
Institutional stories, 144
International reporting, religion in,
    149
International Society for Krishna
    Consciousness, 52
Internet, 141, 169
Inverted pyramid convention, 179
Islam, 13, 40, 42, 51–52, 54, 63, 81
Issue-oriented reporting, 97
Istook, Ernest, 175, 176, 179–80

Jackson, Jesse, 22
Jainism, 40
Jargon, 194
Jefferson, Thomas, 24, 25, 28

Jehovah's Witnesses, 32, 46, 77
Jodu Shinshu Buddhism, 52
John Paul II, 98, 173, 174, 177, 180
Johnson, Lyndon, 70
Johnson, Stephen D., 141
Journalism
    civic, 102
    religious, 91–92, 100–101, 128–31,
        192–93
    stenographic, ix
Judaism, 40, 42, 51, 54, 61, 80–81

Keeler, Bob, xvii
Kennedy, John F., 70
Khomeini, Ayatolleh Ruhollah, 95
Kim, Gertrud (Sister), 82–83
Know Nothing Party, 14
Korean Presbyterian Church, 54
Krishna Consciousness, 13
Ku Klux Klan (KKK), 32

Lead, 172–73
    anecdotal, 176
Lemon Test, 28, 32
Lemon v. Kurtzman, 28
Liberals, 48–51
Liberation theology, 12
Licht, Howard, 100
Living Bible, 198
Localites, 108, 113, 114, 150–52
    localite-cosmopolite distinction,
        115n
Local religions, 40, 42
Locke, John, 7, 19–20
Luther, Martin, 44
Lutherans, 46, 54, 79, 182

MacNeil-Lehrer News Hour, 99
Madison, James, 24–25
Magazines, coverage of religion in,
    96–97
Mahayana Buddhism, 52
Majordomo@iclnet93.iclnet.org, 208
Martin, Julia I., 174, 175, 179
Marty, Martin, 10, 59–60

Mather, Cotton, 7, 20
Mattingly, Terry, 123
Mayflower Compact, 5
Mead, Sydney, 14
Mecca, visiting, 65
Media General, 126
Media managers, 190–91
Media-related organizations, 85
Meetings, attending, 205–6
Melton, J. Gordon, 37
Mennonites, 46
Merrell Enterprises, 210
Mesmerism, 10
Message design, research on, 178
Methodists, 8–9, 10, 46, 76
Millerism, 10
Million Man March, 32
Milton, John, 19–20
Missionary societies, 140
Mong, Bob, 125
Monotheistic religions, 38–39, 40, 42
Moody, Dwight, 9
Moral Majority, 85, 148
Mormons, 10, 46, 77, 78–79, 82
Moyers, Bill, 100
Muslims. See Islam

National Association of Evangelicals,
    85
National Association of Religious
    Broadcasters, 85
National Baptist Convention, USA, 55,
    205
National Baptist Convention of
    America, 55
National Conference, 85, 102n
National Conference of Christians and
    Jews, 94, 102n
National Council of Churches, 140
National Council of Churches of
    Christ, 85
National Public Radio, 98, 126–27
National religions, 40, 42
National Religious Broadcasters, 205
Nation of Islam, 42, 53
Native American religions, 12, 30, 53,
    64

Neary, Lynn, 98
Nelson, Marcia Z., 33, 82, 120
Neo-Nazi parade, 32
New Age religions, 53
New Christian Right, 95
Newhall, Barbara Falconer, xviii, 181
New Harmony, 10
Newhouse Publications, 102n
New religious movements, 53
Newsletters, 140–41
Newspaper coverage of religion, 94–96
News releases, 140–41
News values, 138–40
Newsweek (magazine), 97
New Yorker, The (magazine), 97
New York Herald, 92–93
Niebuhr, Gustav, xviii, 14, 160, 182
Noncredal churches, 46
Nonpreferentialists, 26, 27
Northwestern University's Medill
    School of Journalism, 212
Novak, Michael, 96

Off-camera reporter, 177
Onassis, Jacqueline Kennedy, 120
"One chance" religions, 39
Oneida, 10
On-the-scene reporter, 177
Opinion, 158
Original intent, understanding, 22–26
Orthodox churches, 51, 54
Ostling, Richard, 99

Pantheistic religions, 38, 39–40, 42
Parachurch organizations, 140
Park, Robert, 91
Patriarch of Constantinople, 45
Penn, William, 6
Pentecostal faith, 46, 62
People, dealing with, as news source,
    163–65
Personal expressions of religiosity,
    64–66, 93
Phrenology, 10
Pilgrims, 4–5
Political concerns, 148–50

Political party preference, influence of
    religion on, 69–70
Polytheistic religions, 38, 42
Prayers, 32, 65
    call of the faithful to, 63
Predestination, 7
Preferentialists, 26–27
Presbyterians, 9, 46, 79, 205
Primary evidence, 159–60
Princeton Religion Research
    Center, 4
Professional support groups, 207–8
Prohibition, 29–30
Promise Keepers, 32
Protestant Radio and Television Center,
    85
Protestant religions, faith families,
    44–47
PTL scandals, 112
Public religion, 66–69
Pulitzer newspapers, 91
Pure Land Buddhism, 52
Puritans, 4–6

Quakers, 10, 46, 63, 77
Qur'an, 197

Radio coverage of religion, 97–98
Ramadan, 65
Rastafarian, 53
Rauschenbusch, Walter, 9
Reading (Pa.) *Eagle-Times,* 125–
    26
Reference works, 198–200
    academic, 203
    directories, 200–201
    history, 204
    legal, 204
    religious, 201–3
Reform, spirit of, 7–9
Reformation, 45
Regional religions, 40, 42
Reincarnation, 13
Religion, in the United States, 3–16
Religion and Mass Media Interest
    Group, 207–8

Religion news
  audiences for, 105–15
  birth of modern reporting, 92–94
  definition of, 137–38
  importance of, xiii, 106
  recognizing and reporting, 137–53
  reporting with understanding, 33
  trends in, 91–102
Religion News Service, 102*n*
Religion Newswriters Association, 125,
  207, 210
Religion reporter, 127
Religions
  alternative, 53, 54, 77
  classification of
    Christian, 43–51
    general schmes, 38
    geographic schemes, 40–42
    structural schemes, 74–81
    theological schemes, 38–40
    using schemes, 43
  Eastern, 40–42, 77
  imported, 53
  indigenous, 42, 53
  local, 40, 42
  monotheistic, 38–39, 40, 42
  national, 40, 42
  Native American, 12, 30, 53, 64
  pantheistic, 38, 39–40, 42
  polytheistic, 38, 42
  regional, 40, 42
  in United States, 37–57
  Western, 40, 41, 42
  world, 40–42, 51–53
Religion specialists, 125
Religiosity
  in the United States, 3–18
  personal expressions of, 64–66
Religious coverage
  complaints about, xiii–xv
  improving, 189–95
  magazine, 96–97
  media grade for, xiii
  newspaper, 94–96
  problems with, x–xi, 189
  radio, 97–98
  religious criticisms of, 109–11
  studies of, 138

  television, 98–100
Religious criticisms of religion news
  coverage, 109–11
Religious freedom amendment,
  175–76, 179–80
Religious Freedom Restoration Act, 30
Religious Heritage of America, 210
Religious journalism, 91–92, 100–101,
  128–31, 192–93
Religious News Service, 94
Religious organizations, structure of,
  77–81
Religious publications, 201–3
Religious Public Relations Council, 85,
  94, 210
Religious Research Association, 205–6
Religious stories
  dedicated space for, 144–48
  framing, 172–78
  organizing, 178–81
  telling, 184
  writing, 171–87
Religious toleration statutes, 23
Renner, Gerald, 137, 142
Republican Party, 70
Reputation, developing, for accurate
  and sensitive reporting, 163–64
Revivalism, 7–9, 10
Revivals, 8
Reynolds v. *United States,* 29
Rivers, William, 121
Rocky Mountain News, 123
Rodgers-Melnick, Ann, xvi, 22, 82,
  138, 183, 184
Rohde, David, xvii
Roman Catholics. *See* Catholics
Roosevelt, Franklin, 70
Rousseau, Jean-Jacques, 7, 19–20
Ruggles v. *Williams,* 27–28
Rutherford Institute, 141

Sacraments, 62
Santeria, 53
Scalia, Antonin, 33
Schachern Award for Religion Pages or
  Sections, 125, 209
School vouchers, 32

Scott, Rebekah, 14, 22, 138
Scriptures, 197–98
Secondary evidence, 159
Sect, definition of, 75
Self-Realization Fellowship of Los
    Angeles, 52
Sephardim, 51
"700 Club," 112
Seventh-Day Adventists, 10, 61–62,
    109
Shi'ism branch of Islam, 51–52
Shintoism, 42
Siddha Yoga Movement, 52
Sidebar story, 151
Simpson, O. J., 141
Smith, John W., 125, 156
Society for Scientific Study of
    Religion, 206
Society of Biblical Literature, 205
Sources, choosing and using, 155–69
Southern Baptist Convention, 80, 83,
    205
Special purpose organizations, 84–86
Spiritual Regeneration Movement
    (Transcendental Meditation), 52
Staffing arrangements, 124–28
Stark, Rodney, 4
Stenographic journalism, ix
Stiles, Ezra, 7
Story ideas, finding, 140–44
Story length, 124
Sufi, 53
Sunday, Billy, 9
Sunday Cover, 99
Sunni branch of Islam, 51–52
Supple Award for Religion Writer of
    the Year, 185, 209

Taoism, 13, 42, 53
Television
    coverage of religion on, 98–100
    efforts to create coherent news
        packages, 178
    local station coverage, 147–48
    ministries on, 140
Templeton Award for Religion Reporter
    of the Year, 185, 209

Temple University, 212
Temple worship, 63
Ten Commandments, 67
Theological schemes, 38–40
Therada Buddhism, 52
Thomas, Cal, 96
Thoreau, Henry David, 52
Time (magazine), 96, 97
Tocqueville, Alexis de, 20, 21, 73
Torkelson, Jean, 123
Touching lives, 184
Traditional religious institutions, 74
Transcendentalism, 10, 13
Truman, Harry S, 70

Unification Church, xiv, 42, 53
Unitarian-Universalists, 10, 46
United Methodist Church, 205
United Press International, 94
United States
    religion in, 3–16
    religions in, 37–55
United States Catholic Conference,
    205
UPI Radio Network, 97–98
Utopian communities, 10

Values, debates about, ix–x
Virginia Declaration of Rights, 25
Voluntary organizations, leadership in,
    81–84
Voodoo, 53

Ward, Hiley, xvi
Washington, George, 24, 25
Wehmeyer, Peggy, 99
Whitefield, George, 7
Wicker, Christine, 125
Wildmon, Donald, 110
Wilgoren, Debbi, 174–75
Will, George, 96
Williams, Roger, 25, 28
Wills, Garry, xvi
Woman's Day (magazine), 97
Woodward, Kenneth, 120

Word pictures, 186–87
Words, choosing and using, 181–84
World Council of Churches, 85
World religions, 40–42, 51–53
Worship practices and rituals,
    61–64

Yang, John E., 176, 180
Yellow press, 91

Zen Buddhism, 13, 52
Zoroastrianism, 40, 42

RELIGION. It's the greatest story never told—or, at least, the greatest story that's rarely told very well.

According to conventional wisdom, a good reporter can handle any story. But that may not be true when the story is about religion. Although the public now ranks religion news second only to education news in importance, religion news is last in terms of audience satisfaction.

Reporting News about Religion is the only "how to" book dedicated to this complex specialty. Firmly grounded in the social sciences and in the First Amendment, this book describes how to avoid the pitfalls and biases often found in religion news.

Both students and working journalists who find themselves covering religion news will discover the substantive information about religion and the religion beat as well as the practical advice they need to be able to cover stories thoroughly and sensitively. Appendixes provide a wealth of references and resources.

JUDITH M. BUDDENBAUM is Professor, Department of Journalism and Technical Communication, Colorado State University, Fort Collins. She has worked as a newspaper and magazine religion reporter and a communication researcher for the Lutheran World Federation. Her research on religion and mass media has been published in journals and books, including *Religion and Mass Media: Audiences and Adaptations,* which she co-edited with Daniel Stout.

IOWA STATE UNIVERSITY PRESS
2121 South State Avenue
Ames, Iowa 50014

Orders: 1-800-862-6657
Office: 1-515-292-0140
Fax: 1-515-292-3348
Web site: www.isupress.edu

ISBN 0-8138-2977-1

90000

9 780813 829777